I opened your book and read what is virtually your opening sentence: *This book uncovers information never published before – if it was even known.* I was sceptical when I read those words. But you proved me wrong. Your approach to the theme is indeed unique. I have never read anything like it, and I found it fascinating.

    Dr KD Chant (OAM, MRE, PhD)
    Australian Director, Vision Christian College

Really enjoyed the read—the clearly laid out manner in which it is presented, the mix of analysis, personal experience, and historical evidence. Our Leadership group focuses on moving people from belief to experience based on a firm biblical foundation through practical application. *The Holy Spirit Factor* has been slotted in as a 'must read' for our group.

    Phil Tong
    Senior Minister, Hilltop Church, Ballarat, Victoria, Australia

What a fresh approach to the Holy Spirit! What Dennis does is challenge preconceived mindsets and open us up to experiencing Holy Spirit anew. To me the key to what he writes lies in the title... It's the Holy Spirit 'FACTOR'! 'Factorization' in Mathematics means to 'reduce to simpler elements'. And life amidst its complexities, is reduced to a much more fundamental form when Holy Spirit is 'factored' into our lives! Let this book take you on a renewed journey of discovery of Holy Spirit. It did that for me!

    Hans Voortman
    State Pastor
    South Australia, Western Australia, Northern Territory CRC Churches International, Australia

Dennis Prince takes a fresh approach to the debates about Pentecostalism in this intriguing book. Starting with some incontrovertible facts about church growth and church life, he shows why Christians should take the Pentecostal and charismatic stream seriously. This is then backed up with biblical, theological and historical discussion. A challenging and life- expanding read. Warning: you might even become a Pentecostal after reading it.

    Associate Professor Jon Newton, Alphacrucis College, Australia

In *The Holy Spirit Factor*, Dennis Prince offers a refreshing collection of practical observations and anecdotes which argue in favour of a prominent role for the Holy Spirit in shaping faith in any era. This unique overview of an increasingly neglected facet of contemporary ministry impact takes the reader on a confronting journey through history, one which showcases many inspiring stories of Spirit empowerment that remain just as relevant today as ever. With the experience he and his wife, Nolene, have had in shaping the musical profile of contemporary Australian churches over many years of successful ministry, Dennis is well placed to highlight the important contribution that Pentecostal worship and theology have made, and continue to make, to the health of Christian churches across this nation.

    Dr. Rob Nyhuis
    State Executive Officer and National Chair
    Churches of Christ, Victoria, Australia

THE
HOLY SPIRIT FACTOR

The untold FACTS, THEOLOGY and
HISTORY of the Spirit baptism
and speaking in tongues

Dennis C Prince
Author of bestseller Nine Days in Heaven

"Your approach to the theme is indeed unique.
I have never read anything like it, and I found it fascinating."

—Dr KD CHANT OAM, MRE, PhD

THE HOLY SPIRIT FACTOR

The untold FACTS, THEOLOGY and HISTORY of
the Spirit baptism and speaking in tongues

First released in 2022
Revised 2023

Copyright © 2022, 2023 by Dennis C Prince
All rights reserved

Cover design and layout: Jose Pepito
Photography: Alexei Domorev: Greenlamp Marketing

No part of this publication may be reproduced, stored in a retrieval system, or transmitted in any form or by any means without the written permission of the publisher.

Published by RCM Publications, Australia.
www.resource.com.au
info@resource.com.au

In this book, unless otherwise noted, direct Bible quotations are taken from the HOLY BIBLE, NEW INTERNATIONAL VERSION (NIV). Copyright 1973, 1978, 1984 by International Bible Society. Used by permission of Zondervan House. All rights reserved.

ISBN: 978-0-6454884-3-2

When asked to suggest a book both agreeable and useful, Martin Luther replied: "Such a question is beyond my ability. The better things are, the less they please".

...the doctrine of the Holy Spirit...may well be the work of our age.
Augustus H Strong

...you will receive power when the Holy Spirit comes on you...
Jesus

My message and my preaching were not with wise and persuasive words, but with a demonstration of the Spirit's power, so that your faith might not rest on human wisdom, but on God's power.
The apostle Paul

The people who crucified Jesus never...accused him of being a bore—on the contrary, they thought him too dynamic to be safe. It has been left for later generations to muffle up that shattering personality, and surround him with an atmosphere of tedium. We have very effectively pared the claws of the Lion of Judah, certified him "meek and mild", and recommended him as a fitting household pet for pale curates and pious old ladies.
Dorothy L Sayers

If thou take forth the precious from the vile, thou shalt be as my mouth.
Jeremiah

ACKNOWLEDGEMENTS

A number of people assisted me in this project, and for that I am profoundly grateful. In particular, about a dozen friends, family, pastors and associates were kind enough to read the first draft and make many enormously helpful suggestions. Among those were Dan Bassett, Dr Barry Chant, Dr Ken Chant, Peter Domorev, Tom Gordon, Ross Lee, Dr Jon Newton, Dr Rob Nyhuis, Trevor Pillar, Bruce Sharman and Hans Voortman. I marvelled at the perceptive ideas they put forward, and am humbly aware that to them belongs much of any final credit. Having said that, should you find anything that is not true, lovely and of good report, the responsibility is mine alone.

In addition to all those contributors, I am indebted to Kate Gordon who edited the final manuscript. I had an idea my English skills were wanting—Kate was able to show me, so graciously, just how much, and also make a number of wise suggestions regarding content on the way.

Above all, I am so grateful to my wife Nolene who has not only put up with my hiding away in my office for long hours and endless days, but patiently read all the first drafts, knocked them into shape, and encouraged me in the process. Her spiritual insight and faith have been a steady anchor throughout the process, in spite of some major health issues we had to tackle.

God is good. So many times have I seen his hand throughout this journey. Serendipitous moments, passing comments from friends or family, timely articles and books from here there and everywhere—have all appeared unexpectedly and often inexplicably through this process. The Christian faith is a wondrous thing. So many times have I looked back in deep gratitude for the day I found God, his son, Jesus, and our helper the Holy Spirit.

To my beautiful wife, Nolene, the love of my life, and my best friend

CONTENTS

ACKNOWLEDGEMENTS vii

INTRODUCTION xv

CHAPTER 1 1
A God-Sized Result

PART 1: THE FACTS

CHAPTER 2 7
Growth Rate Comparison

CHAPTER 3 19
Church Survey

CHAPTER 4 27
The Holy Spirit in Music

CHAPTER 5 37
Signs, Wonders and Miracles

PART 2: THE THEOLOGY

CHAPTER 6 83
Salvation and Spirit baptism—the difference

CHAPTER 7 89
Is Tongues the Evidence?

PART 3: THE HISTORY

CHAPTER 8 97
The Holy Spirit and the Renowned Revivalists

CHAPTER 9 121
*Tongues and Two Thousand Years.
What Happened in That Time?*

CHAPTER 10. 153
The Azusa Street Revival: Catalyst Charles Parham

CHAPTER 11. 177
The Azusa Street Revival: William Seymour

PART 4: THE CONCLUSIONS

CHAPTER 12. 209
Bringing It All Together

CHAPTER 13. 217
Stories from the Heart; Receiving the Holy Spirit

APPENDIX

APPENDIX A. 231
The Holy Spirit: Where He Ought to Be

APPENDIX B 241
The Neglect, and Why it Happened

APPENDIX C 251
Salvation And Spirit Baptism—the Difference (Expanded version)

APPENDIX D 267
The Fruit of the Spirit: Should Pentecostals and Charismatics Demonstrate More?

APPENDIX E 273
Is Tongues the "Evidence"? (Expanded version)

APPENDIX F 291
Questions and Objections

APPENDIX G 305
The Apostles' Creed: Towards a Twenty-First Century Version

APPENDIX H 307
Church Survey—Detailed Information

ENDNOTES 311

BIBLIOGRAPHY 323

By what authority are you doing these things, and who gave you that authority?

CHIEF PRIESTS TO JESUS

INTRODUCTION

This book uncovers information never published before—if it was even known. It has been simmering under the surface, waiting for someone to lift it out, hold it in their hands, understand its wonders, and tell the world. But it is contentious, and just about everyone has been too nice to rock the boat. However, those wonders are so rich and beautiful, I think they are worth the risk. So, I am taking hold of this, and following where it leads.

Such a subject calls for some background which, I trust, will establish my fitness for the task, and lay some foundations.

Here, briefly then, is my story, and the events that inspired this book.

I was riding my bike from Melbourne University, where I was studying Civil Engineering, to Ridley (Anglican) Theological College. The cheapest college around, Ridley took in a few secular students to keep the theologs' feet on the ground. That was a noble cause, and I was happy to help.

Riding back to college, I would sometimes take hold of a passing truck for a free fast ride. It worked lots of times, but not this day. I placed myself at the front, just behind the cabin, and the vehicle was long–very long. The driver, after gathering speed and apparently spotting me in his mirror, edged sideways, trapping me—at speed—between his truck and the rough, cobblestone gutter. If I had been at the back, I could have let go at any time. But not at the front. With the kerb on my left, the truck on my right, and my only escape at the rear, I couldn't let go. My path was so narrow, I had to hold fast to keep steady. So, there I was. Truck moving faster, my right hand on the steel tray, left hand gripping handlebars and bag of books, and cobbled gutter pounding my wheels like a jackhammer. I edged backwards down the length of the truck as fast as I could, the huge truck tyres drumming on the road inches away.

Eventually, my right hand came down onto space—I had reached the back of the truck. Without that support, I lost balance and careened out of control behind the truck. A car behind braked. I braced myself, extending my right arm, ready to hit the road at speed. Miraculously though, I regained my balance, still hurtling along behind the truck, which slowly drew away from me. With heart thumping, I pulled myself together and pedalled on.

It was lunchtime, and sitting beside a couple of theology students, I tuned in to their conversation. One was telling the other of his work in a mission to homeless men. After spending the last of his money on blankets for a troubled youth (who disappeared with them next morning), Len had no food money for the rest of the week. But that day, he received a cheque from his mother (about three hundred dollars in today's terms), and the next day the same from his brother. They had not communicated with each other, they had never done this before, and they hadn't done it since. Len was emphatic about those details. He saw this as God's approval, and his friend nodded enthusiastically, seemingly unsurprised.

Not me. Inside, I reeled. This was not coincidence. I had studied enough statistics to persuade me of that. It had to be God. I was shocked. But, above all, I realised Len and his friend had a link to God I didn't even know was possible. The bottom line exploded in my mind: when Len and his friend died, they would go to heaven. But I would go to hell! I would go to hell! I WOULD GO TO HELL!!!

I don't know where that came from. I had never been fixated on hell. The two students had certainly not mentioned it. But my truck near-miss reared like a monster. What if I had gone under those wheels? I closed my eyes and hell was everywhere. I had to do something. Too proud to ask for advice, I went to a bookshop and asked for a Bible. The price shocked me—almost as much as I earned in a day, selling menswear. But I gritted my teeth and handed over the money. Fortunately, it was a New Testament only, and I avoided getting bogged down in the Old Testament, where I would have begun if it was a complete Bible.

I was starting from scratch, except for one thing. I had heard a theolog say that the Bible is a spiritual book, so to understand it, you had to pray. Fair enough, so I prayed my first prayer, asked God for help, and began reading the gospel of Matthew. To shorten the story, I discovered, and embraced, the faith of these theologs. I was heaven-bound and I knew it. The peace and relief were profound for this 21 year old, as I changed direction, went to church, and opened my eyes to a new world.

However, another surprise awaited, and I need to explain that too.

I was struck by the authority and miracle power of Jesus. I had no idea he healed sick people and cast out demons and more. I tried to reconcile that with what I had seen in a few casual church visits, and was confused because they didn't seem to match. Then I came to the Book of Acts, which took my breath away. Fire, wind, noise, supernatural speech, Holy Spirit dynamic, hullaballoo, miracles, and booming growth throughout the world. A far cry from the conservative, structured church services I had seen. I was fascinated, but puzzled.

Warily, I asked God if I could have the same experience. Warily, because I didn't want to step out of line, but I felt the question was reasonable because my reading didn't match the reality. So, I prayed the prayer and left it at that.

Not long after, I decided to skip the Saturday night movies and visit a combined-church youth event I saw advertised. Guarded in my new faith, I sat near the back of the two or three hundred people and watched. All went well, until I noticed an odd "glow" creeping over me. I tried to dismiss it, but eventually realised it was serious, obviously God, and not going away. More than that, it escalated. Holy, glorious, liquid love, cascading, overwhelming; unprecedented in my life. I didn't know what to do. It was so overpowering, I thought I would collapse. I was helpless and horrified. What would people think? Everyone else was oblivious, and here I was about to crash on the floor. Knowing full well it was God, I begged him to hold it there, and he did.

I left in a daze, barely able to place one foot in front of the other. To my horror, an old friend rushed out of the crowd, amazed to see me there, shaking my hand. I could barely speak, filled with embarrassment and confusion. Driving home, I had an overwhelming sense of benevolence for everything out there. I peered into the headlights to avoid crickets on the road. Then I became aware of strange words running through my head. I wanted to get out, stand on the dark road and shout them into the sky. Thinking I was going mad, I composed myself, completed the drive and went to bed. That glorious glow diminished slowly over three or four days, leaving me profoundly affected, but mystified.

Today, I look back and realise that was the answer to my prayer. I had received what the Bible calls the baptism, or infilling, of the Holy Spirit (Acts 1 & 2), and the words I wanted to shout were the unknown language that came with it. But I told no one about it for several years, and let it lapse. Some years later, after I was married (to Nolene), a lay preacher came to our Methodist church and told us glowing stories of Baptist and Methodist ministers receiving this baptism in the Holy Spirit with speaking in tongues. Fascinated, we investigated and sometime later, a Pentecostal pastor prayed for us.

I was astonished to hear Nolene speaking fluently in a language that I knew she had never learned or spoken before. Nothing happened to me, but I continued praying at home and eventually spoke just a few words, experiencing once again that Holy Spirit glow. I persisted, praying with my few words, until one evening they seemed to naturally change, becoming fluent, natural and beautiful. It was such a surprise. I revelled in my new ability to interact with God. A rich new spiritual world opened up for both of us, where God was a tangible reality; the work of the cross clear, absolute and profound; and his Spirit of power and love so close. We learned more about experiencing the Holy Spirit on a daily basis, hearing the voice of God, learning his ways and experiencing the gifts of the Spirit, especially prophecy, healing, and discerning of spirits in confronting the demonic. It was the same Christian faith, but illuminated, expanded, empowered.

That was my spiritual journey introduction. Obviously, then, I approach this subject as a Pentecostal. It would be fair to say though, that my background prior to that gave me a reasonably clean slate. And regarding denominational influence, the college where I was converted was Anglican (I attended just one of their services). I joined my mother's Methodist church—the same denomination where I was married—then, after about four years, joined a Pentecostal church. And I spent many years in the YMCA—very interdenominational.

In the years following, Nolene and I published praise and worship resources which were widely used in Australian churches. About half our customers were Pentecostal, the rest were not. And we ran worship seminars in many churches across the spectrum. Sometime later, I served for several months in a traditional Baptist church as interim pastor. So, I have a reasonable grasp of the denominational scene.

I should add, my original training was in Civil Engineering, and that study, which included mathematics and statistics, has helped in areas needing statistical analysis.

So that is my background—why then this book?

It came about while preparing a sermon for Pentecost Sunday. I asked myself, has a century of Pentecostalism and its Holy Spirit emphasis made a difference? Or not? Why not crunch the numbers and see? To be truthful, I was a little nervous about the idea. I was a committed Pentecostal; what if I found it was really a flop? But I had long believed truth should not be feared, and the words of Socrates rang in my ears: "follow the argument wherever, like a wind, it leads us".

So, heart in mouth, I began my journey.

Sceptical scrutiny is the means, in both science and religion, by which deep thoughts can be winnowed from deep nonsense.

CARL SAGAN

CHAPTER 1
A GOD-SIZED RESULT

About 120 years ago, 40 students in a rag-tag Bible School in Topeka, Kansas, came up with a new and contentious belief that would sweep the world. That is probably an over-simplification—their "discovery" was really the culmination of a long series of events. But they pulled all that together, and it lit a firestorm of faith which raced through the Christian church, and continues to be a fiery subject today.

There were two parts to their new belief. The first was not really new. It had been simmering for a century among members of the American Holiness Movement (and others—more on that later). The second, however, was virtually a brand new idea.

The first part was this. The students embraced the belief that the biblical experience of baptism in the Holy Spirit (or the infilling of the Holy Spirit—e.g., see Matthew 3:11), was **not** the same as salvation. It was **not** the same as being born again, **not** the same as being regenerated by the Holy Spirit. It was a separate experience, to be received by faith—typically **after** a became a Christian. Salvation saved a person from their sins. The Spirit baptism, they claimed, was a different, dynamic experience of the Holy Spirit, for empowerment.

Why was that so controversial?

The traditional church (with a few exceptions) believed a person received the Holy Spirit baptism **when** they became a Christian. Being born of the Spirit, and baptised in the Spirit, they said, amounted to the same thing.

So, this new belief was a substantial shift, and the church does not easily embrace substantial shifts.

But the second part was the real eyebrow-raiser. The students claimed that, when the believer received the Holy Spirit baptism, they would speak in tongues, a language they'd never learned—just as the 120 disciples did long ago in Acts Chapter 2. That created a storm. So much so that the Christian church eventually divided into two streams on the issue.

Overall, their new idea had major ramifications. Think about it. Pentecostals claim to have discovered a discrete, empowering, tangible, dynamic and ongoing experience with a divine being, no less than the third person of the Trinity. They believe this gift is promised to all believers, after salvation, to empower them to spread the gospel. The unspoken implication, of course, is that **other Christians have *not* engaged the Holy Spirit in that way, and they could be much more effective if they *did*.**

That was not to say that other Christians did not *possess* the Holy Spirit. The new doctrine did not imply a wholly new impartation of the Holy Spirit, but rather the embracing of a *different kind* of relationship with the Spirit. Over many centuries, through the Holy Spirit working within them, millions of Christians had performed countless wonderful deeds, displayed divine character, and revealed Christ in their lives. Now, the students were saying, an additional dimension of the Holy Spirit had been (re)discovered. It promised unique power for evangelism, together with the unlocking of the supernatural gifts of the Spirit (1 Corinthians 12, 13 and 14).

Now here is the bottom line.

If that new belief is correct, then movements which have embraced it **ought to produce spiritual results that are glaringly obvious, measurably head and shoulders above others**. If not, we could reasonably conclude the idea is **false**.

On the other hand, **if they are** significantly above the rest, traditional Christians ought to **re-examine** their understanding of the Holy Spirit, for who would not want a God-ordained, God-sized boost to spiritual fruitfulness?

Obviously an important issue.

Note, however, while statistics and evidence do not **prove** the case for the baptism in the Holy Spirit (scripture is our ultimate guide), they may well justify a **rethink** of the doctrines that lie behind them.

For that reason, we will, after studying the statistics, turn to scripture. We will cover the case for two **separate or distinct** experiences—born of the Spirit and baptised in the Spirit—and the controversial speaking in tongues.

NOTE: The preferable expression to describe the "stand alone" Spirit baptism is "**discrete**", instead of "separate", or "distinct". I will mostly use that from now on.

As you can see, we will build the case by beginning with the facts and evidence around us. Is that reasonable? Think about these words from Paul:

> My message and my preaching were not with wise and persuasive words, but with a demonstration of the Spirit's power, so that your faith might not rest on human wisdom, but on God's power (1 Corinthians 2:4-5).

Paul was happy to build a case on God's power—the miracles God did through him. So, this is a reasonable approach, provided of course we ultimately make scripture our bedrock. And I will endeavour to do that.

As we proceed, remember this is not a fault-finding exercise. There are no first or second class Christians. I am contending, not for a denomination, but for the Holy Spirit—whether or not he has been given his place in the church. So, this is a statistical and factual analysis of fruitfulness, related to the Holy Spirit. No matter what the result, as Christians we are one in Christ. By the grace of God, we are his children, brothers and sisters, together.

If you do feel uncomfortable about that process, remember, this is an important issue. We have in our midst, clear disagreement on a vital issue. The ramifications are real and tangible. We must get it right, even if it bothers us on the way.

So let us now look at the facts on offer.

# PART ONE

THE FACTS

I have identified four measurable aspects of Christian life where the Holy Spirit has influence. There might be more but these four are important, and being measurable, lend themselves to factual analysis.

Here they are.

First: simple growth. The gospel must be preached. People must be added to the church. Statistics are readily available by which we can compare the growth of different groups. What will we find?

Second: church life. Does this Holy Spirit baptism produce authentic Christian life? The Australian National Church Life Survey, conducted each five years in Australian churches, examines issues considered important on this subject. One year, I decided to sort the data to enable a comparison between denominations, and to see how Pentecostals rated. I found some startling results, but kept them all to myself—until now. We will gather that information from the latest survey.

Third: praise and worship. Pentecostals seem to have led the way in the revolution that swept the church in recent decades. I have been heavily involved in that since 1981, publishing resources throughout Australia including music books, CDs and words books. That gave me a unique window on this aspect, and it has a surprising bearing on the subject.

Fourth: signs, wonders and miracles. Who is active in this type of ministry, so common in the Book of Acts? What are their backgrounds, and what is their experience of the Holy Spirit? Much of this is little-known, but illuminating.

God-sized, please

As mentioned above, effects of Holy Spirit power ought to be glaringly obvious. In the Bible, when the Spirit of God fell on people, it was not a small thing. Samson broke the ropes binding him and, with the jawbone of an ass, killed a thousand Philistines (Judges 15:13–15). You could call that a **God-sized result.**

When I first began this quest, and unsure of what I would find, I decided if there was evidence to support my theory, it ought to be "God-sized". It ought to be enough to make me say, "Wow!" Otherwise, I ought to revise my beliefs.

I invite you to come with the same expectation.

Be able to analyse statistics, which can be used to support or undercut almost any argument.

MARILYN VOS SAVANT

CHAPTER 2
GROWTH RATE COMPARISON

A Growth Story from My World

The knock on the door was Gwen, but it wasn't our usual Gwen. Her face was twisted with pain as she hobbled in, her little girl by her side. She had brought her daughter faithfully each week, in response to our letterbox drop promoting our Sunday School. We were planting a new church—in the home of my brother-in-law, Ray, and his wife, Margaret. Gwen sank gratefully onto the lounge suite, placing her foot gingerly up on a chair. She sprained it playing badminton and it would take several weeks to recover, the doctor had told her.

That Sunday our "congregation" consisted of Nolene, Nolene's parents and grandmother, Gwen, me, and maybe one other. Ray and Margaret were looking after the Sunday School (their four children and Gwen's daughter) in other rooms, and I led the adults in the lounge room. At one stage, I asked Gwen to read the Bible passage, but she declined. Her ankle hurt badly, but she was happy to listen. My study was about the lame beggar at the temple in Acts, chapter 3. When the beggar asked apostles Peter and John for money, they replied "Silver and gold I do not have but, what I do have, I give you. In the name of Jesus Christ, walk!", and hauled him to his feet. The man did more than walk; he jumped and praised God, and the crowds rushed to see what was going on.

My point was obvious—a favourite Pentecostal theme. In essence, Peter had told the crowd, "Don't look at me as if I am someone special. Faith in the name of Jesus brought this miracle, and anyone with faith can do the same". However, as I proceeded, it dawned on me that right under my nose lay my very own "lame man"—Gwen. And my faith was on the line. I wrestled for what seemed an eternity—what if it didn't happen? In the end, I paused the study and asked Gwen would she like us to lay hands on her and pray. She begged, "Please do", so we did. Then I told her to test it. She stood slowly, placing her bad foot gingerly on the floor. "Stomp it up and down", I told her. She did, then in a half surprised tone said "It's gone!" And it was, totally. We laughed and shouted. As I watched Gwen and her little girl walk home that day, I was filled with wonder and gratitude to God. There was not the slightest trace of a limp.

I would love to tell you that all Gwen's family and friends turned up at church next Sunday. But we never saw her again. The family, apparently suspicious of miracles, discouraged her from returning. Happily though, we had accumulated a number of people on the fringe of our little church and Gwen's story wrought wonders as we retold it. It was like a seed. It grew, and built faith that inspired others to pray and receive miracles, and activate their own spiritual gifts. Gradually, these newly-inspired people joined our little Sunday group and it blossomed.

A mid-week lounge room meeting and passionate worship also helped drive things along. Freshly baptised in the Holy Spirit, and enthralled by the gift, they loved to employ their new tongues in singing praise to God. As we sang the praise and worship songs, we often launched into singing in the Spirit and the room would erupt with glorious harmonies, weaving around and around. It became a signature part of our worship. One friend who visited from interstate said he would sit there and cry in those times. Worship seemed to bring down the glorious imprint of the Spirit of God.

So our numbers grew and, after three years, stood at about three hundred.

That was a small part of our experience of the Holy Spirit and church growth. In that way, we prayed and preached, explained God, Jesus and the Holy Spirit, and people were added.

Of course that rapid growth is not enough to prove my case. Many factors might have contributed. We need to spread the net more widely.

We need reliable numbers from across the Christian spectrum—Pentecostal and non-Pentecostal. We need to compare growth rates across different denominations.

So that is what we will do now.

Our logical starting point would be a denomination with doctrines closest to those of Pentecostals, but different on this issue of the Holy Spirit. That would be the Baptists, so we will begin there, and look at the numbers.

BAPTISTS

What do they believe?

Baptists believe the Bible is divinely inspired and has supreme authority. They believe Jesus died on the cross for our sins, and when we repent and embrace God's forgiveness, we are born again, put right with God and accepted into his family. They believe in baptism by immersion, they practise communion and they believe we ought to live holy lives. They believe in taking the good news about Jesus to the whole world. Pentecostals are at one with all those things.

BUT, as mentioned previously, most Baptists believe Christians receive the Holy Spirit baptism at salvation, not as a discrete experience afterwards. And they believe tongues either died out with the apostles or is a gift that just a few people receive from the Holy Spirit. Pentecostals, on the other hand, see the Holy Spirit baptism as a dynamic experience, distinct from salvation, with the initial evidence of speaking in tongues.

Has that belief made a difference for Pentecostals? Let us look at figures.

The World Baptist Alliance tells us there are 49 million Baptists in the world. However, Baptist churches are autonomous, and many choose to remain outside that Alliance, so 49 million understates the reality. It is hard to find a reputable source for the total of all Baptists, but 100 million seems to be commonly quoted so I have used that figure.

This 100 million was gathered over a period of 405 years, between 1609 and 2014 (the date of the given population estimate). But Pentecostals have been around for just over a hundred years and Baptist for some four hundred years. How can we compare these growth rates?

The best method would be to plot out the statistics for both groups and lay one graph on the other. Simple and obvious. But such statistics are hard to come by, and there are several other denominations we want to compare too. In the absence of such information, I will resort to a simple mathematical tool, which calculates **average** growth rates.

Knowing that some readers find mathematics challenging, I have put the maths in the following box for those so inclined to check, and then the result below.

Calculating *average* growth rates involves an assumption, of course. Growth rates are rarely constant, especially at the beginning of a movement, which can be explosive. Apart from that initial rapid growth, most denominations probably follow similar patterns, and we hope our method will not be influenced by too many bumps so that our comparisons will be meaningful. And, hopefully, the final results might be stark, and dwarf any bumps.

To allow for the common initial explosive growth, I will make an educated guess of initial growth of 10,000 in the first 10 years for all denominations, with an assumed uniform rate after that. If you don't make some assumption like that to allow for that initial growth, mathematicians will tell you the final figure can be significantly compromised. (If you think my assumption is unreasonable in any way, do some sums for yourself. It is not too hard.)

The standard population growth formula uses three pieces of data: number of people at the beginning (S: this will be 10,000 in each case), number of years (Y) since that beginning (less the initial 10 years assumed to reach 10,000), and number of people at the end (F). From these we calculate the growth rate, G. If this figure G comes to, say, 1.05, it means that after one year, 100 people will increase to 105, a 5% increase.

The formula is $G = (F/S)^{(1/Y)}$

Using that, for a Baptist population of 100 million accumulated over 405 years, we come up with:

$G = (100{,}000{,}000/10{,}000)^{(1/395)}$

> Baptist average annual growth rate comes to 2.4%.

For perspective on that figure, the world population growth rate is currently about 1%.

We can look now at the Pentecostals.

PENTECOSTALS

The Pentecostal movement can be traced back to an event in 1906. We will study that in a later chapter but, it can be argued, the Pentecostal Movements emerged from this date.

As at 2019, the number of Pentecostals worldwide is approximately 279 million.

Using our formula, with 1906 as our starting date, we come up with:

> Pentecostal average annual growth rate is 10.5%

COMPARING THE TWO GROUPS

Baptists have grown to 100 million in 405 years, an average growth rate of 2.4%.

Pentecostals grew to 279 million in 118 years, an average growth rate of 10.5%.

The graph gives us a feel for those numbers.

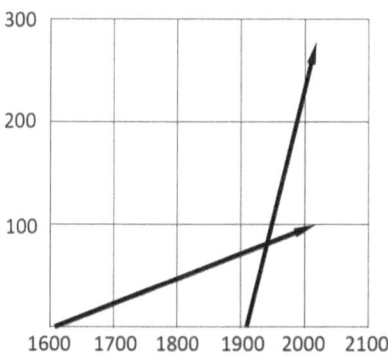

In other words:

The average annual growth rate of Pentecostals is 4.3 times higher than Baptists.

Or, for every 10,000 people joining the Baptists, 43,000 join the Pentecostals.

Or, in less than one-third the time, Pentecostals outnumbered Baptists more than three to one.

Two groups, so similar in so many ways, but differing on one major issue—the Holy Spirit.

Yes, we have made assumptions and approximations. Our statistics may be a little out in either direction. But these results are so significant, we can reasonably assume the effects of approximations and assumptions are dwarfed.

So this is a compelling set of results.

Of course, there are many denominations, apart from Baptists, which have not embraced the baptism in the Holy Spirit—that is our next step.

OTHER MAINLINE AND EVANGELICAL DENOMINATIONS

We will look at five more mainline and evangelical denominations: Anglicans, Lutherans, Methodists (as of 1977 the Uniting Church in Australia), Reformed and Salvation Army.

Commencement dates for denominations are sometimes not well defined, so information is included here to help locate the date used if you want to check it. And, for some, the actual number of adherents at the start may be significantly higher than the number assumed for the calculations. However, that effect is generous when it comes to calculating growth rates so, if anything, it will make the denominational picture rosier.

Reliable statistics for these denominations are not always easy to find. However, modest discrepancies have little if any effect on the final calculation, especially when you express the percentage in only two figures (as I have done).

Remember there are many variables in this exercise that might cloud results. To be convincing, we need a substantial result, so look for that.

Note also that, while Baptists are the closest to Pentecostals in belief and practice, most of these other denominations also have much in common with Pentecostals—especially in the fundamentals of the faith. But all differ from Pentecostals in their understanding of the baptism in the Holy Spirit and speaking in tongues.

I have not included Catholics or Orthodox churches. With their long history, and the impact of the Reformation, it is difficult to make meaningful comparisons. However, for your interest, if we assume Catholics began with 10,000 in 30 AD (a disputed date), and give them a figure today of 1,285 million, our formula provides an average growth rate of 0.6%. A very low figure but, again, not a realistic comparison.

Here now are the figures for the mainline and evangelical denominations.

DENOMINATION	COMMENCEMENT	NUMBER (millions)	GROWTH RATE (%)
ANGLICANS	1534 (Henry VIII declared Supreme Head of church)	85	1.9
BAPTISTS	1609 (Separatist, John Smith, fled to Amsterdam)	90	2.4
LUTHERANS	1521 (Luther, Edict of Worms)	80	1.8
METHODISTS	1738 (Wesley's Aldersgate experience)	80	3.3
REFORMED (includes Presbyterian)	1560 (Scottish Reformation)	75	2.0
SALVATION ARMY	1865 (Booth commenced in East London)	1.65	3.6
PENTECOSTALS	1906 (Azusa Street)	279	10.5

If you **average** the growth rates of the non-Pentecostal denominations, (all similar in size and from roughly the same time), we obtain an average result of 2.5%. The Pentecostal figure is 10.5%, more than four times that rate.

Now, you might argue that Pentecostal figures are from just one century, and the others could possibly have grown at the same rate in **their** first centuries. However, when you consider that Pentecostals grew to 279 million in roughly one century, and the others no more than 100 million in **several** centuries, it is clear that would not have happened.

What if Pentecostals were Baptists?

Here is a calculation which highlights the compounding effect of a significantly different growth rate. What if Pentecostals were Baptists? What if Pentecostals commenced in 1906 as previously noted, but grew at the Baptist rate of 2.4% instead of 10.5%? What would that do?

Using the same assumptions and formula we obtain a figure of 127,000: down from 279 million.

CHARISMATICS

We now need to consider two extraordinary Holy Spirit outpourings, without precedent in church history. They are Mainline Charismatics and Catholic charismatics, each a spin-off from the Pentecostal church.

In 1960, an American Episcopalian (Anglican) priest, Dennis Bennett, claimed to have experienced the baptism in the Holy Spirit with speaking in tongues. (His story is documented in his books *Nine O'clock in the Morning*, and *The Holy Spirit and You*.) Somehow he managed to withstand the subsequent storm, and remain in his denomination. Prior to that, most tongue speakers (i.e., Pentecostals) were considered cultish, and not accepted in mainline and evangelical churches. The Dennis Bennett incident launched what has become today, a worldwide movement of people, in almost every mainline and evangelical denomination, who have received the baptism in the Holy Spirit with speaking in tongues. Methodists, Anglicans, Baptists, Lutherans, Reformed—every denomination has been impacted, some more than others. Today, estimates put their numbers at an astonishing **200 million**.[1]

In embracing the experience, charismatics have added their unique flavour. And, while usually believing the Spirit baptism is an experience distinct from salvation, some believe tongues is not the only initial evidence, but just one of the nine gifts of 1 Corinthians 12. (More on this in Appendix E: Is Tongues the "Evidence"?)

Not long after Dennis Bennet's experience, some American Catholic priests came across a revolutionary book: *The Cross and the Switchblade*. It told the story of Pentecostal pastor David Wilkerson's remarkable work with drug addicts, and the key role of the baptism in the Holy Spirit in that ministry. This led to a number of priests receiving the Spirit baptism. In 1967, that news reached Notre Dame University in Indiana, which then became a centre for Catholic charismatic renewal. From there, the movement spread around the world, and today, estimates put the number of Charismatic Catholics at **160 million.**

> So, in addition to our 279 million Pentecostals, we have an additional 200 million Charismatics from mainline and evangelical denominations, and (in today's estimates) 160 million Catholic Charismatics.
>
> All of these people believe the baptism in the Holy Spirit is a discrete experience, different from salvation, given to empower us to spread the gospel, and that speaking in tongues (if not the unique defining element for some Charismatics) is alive and well.

How does that translate to growth rates?

Assuming the movement began with Dennis Bennett publicising his experience in 1960, the final number is roughly 200 million in 2019. With assumptions as before, we have a growth rate of 22.4%.

Fair comparison?

Is it reasonable to compare that figure with the previous rates? Probably not. Charismatics are typically churchgoing people who embrace the Spirit baptism and tongues. It is usually easier to persuade churchgoers of the Holy Spirit baptism than outsiders, who must first be persuaded to repent from sin and believe.

Adjusting for that effect requires surveys and calculations beyond my means. But bearing all that in mind, 22.4% is a significant number. It would be reasonable to say that no other new spiritual "thing" of any kind has ever brought such widespread recognition and change to the Christian church.

And remember, the stand out difference of the charismatic movement, which we can reasonably assume is the driver of this rapid growth, is the baptism in the Holy Spirit with speaking in tongues.

Now make the same calculations for Catholic charismatics.

Growth Rate of Catholic Charismatics

The commencement date is 1967 at Notre Dame University and, using our estimate at 160 million in 2019, we obtain a growth rate of 26%: another very significant number.

The Ethiopian Surprise

There is a particular episode worth attention. Pentecostal historian Cecil M Robeck noted that:

> Between 1985 and 2005, for instance, the Lutheran Church in Ethiopia has grown from two hundred thousand members to over four million members, and almost all of them describe themselves as charismatics.[2]

Quite a surprise! How does this compare with our rates above? Again, assuming a uniform rate of growth, when we apply our formula we have a substantial figure of 16.2 %.

Summarising this Chapter

Baptists have grown at 2.5%.

Pentecostals have grown at 10.5% (four times higher).

Or, in less than one-third the time, Pentecostals outnumbered Baptists more than three to one.

Anglicans, Lutherans, Methodists and Reformists have grown at about the same rate as Baptists.

If Pentecostals had grown at the same rate as denominational churches, their number would be 127,000 instead of 279 million.

Protestant charismatics numbered 200 million after 59 years—a renewal growth rate of 22.4%.

Catholic charismatics numbered 160 million after 52 years—a renewal growth rate of 26%.

Clearly, the growth rates of Pentecostal and charismatic churches are substantially higher than the others. We need, then, to ask the very subjective question: is the difference "God-sized"? If it is, of course, it is a compelling endorsement of the Pentecostal and charismatic belief of the baptism in the Holy Spirit.

So that's the first of our four measures: numerical growth.

NEXT:

While those statistics are compelling, we should ask the question: what about **quality**—God-quality? Are Pentecostals and charismatics **authentic Christians**? Do they demonstrate **authentic biblical Christian practice**, in their lives and in their churches? Can these things be **measured**?

In fact, yes! Church life has been surveyed regularly in Australia since 1991 and there are statistics which can answer this. We will look at that now.

Do people pick grapes from thornbushes?

JESUS

CHAPTER 3
CHURCH SURVEY

Every five years in Australia, NCLS Research conducts a National Church Life Survey to examine the health of Christians and churches around Australia. More than 20 denominations take part, involving about 3,000 churches, 260,000 adult attenders, and 6,000 leaders. They have done that since 1991, investigating "what vital and healthy churches look like".

The survey investigates spirituality, church health, leadership and how churches relate to their communities—obviously qualities considered important in authentic Christian faith.

The NCLS Board has representatives from Uniting, Anglican, Baptist and Catholic churches, all typically non-Pentecostal in their approach. That, of course, is ideal for the purposes of this book. Their findings ought to provide a fair and accurate assessment of the spiritual health of Pentecostal churches, which we can compare with others.

Of course, once again, we would prefer not to make comparisons. But, we remember again, this is a vital issue. Our understanding of the helper, the Holy Spirit, needs to be sound. The issue has potential to multiply the fruits of Christian ministry. That is clearly very important.

In comparing the qualities of Pentecostal churches, the survey should validate (or invalidate) the *authenticity* of the Pentecostal faith in these churches. Jesus warned us to be vigilant for wolves in sheep's clothing. Are Pentecostals authentic Christians?

Jesus provided a simple test for this: inspect their fruit (see Matthew 7:15–20).

A survey for all Christians, designed by non-Pentecostal Christians, ought to be a reasonable measure of such fruit (or lack of it). So what do we find here?

First, some information about the survey.

The survey measures performance on nine core qualities: personal faith, worship experience, sense of belonging, vision, leadership, innovation, community service, faith-sharing and integration of new people.

For each of those core qualities, respondents were asked questions on **33 specifics**, such as "How important is God in your life?", "How often do you attend church?", and "Does your church follow up visitors?"

Our goal is to find how well Pentecostals perform in these 33 specifics, in comparison with others.

How the survey works

The survey divides the results into two major sections:

- **Denominational groups or streams**: Participating groups are Catholic, Mainline Protestant, Other Protestant, All Protestant, and Pentecostal.
- **Individual denominations**: Participating denominations are Anglican, Baptist, Catholic, C3 Churches, Reformed, CRC Churches International, International Network of Churches, Lutheran, Salvation Army and Uniting.

The **Pentecostal** churches surveyed are: Australian Christian Churches (formerly Assemblies of God); C3 Churches (formerly Christian City Church); CRC Churches International, and International Network of Churches (formerly Christian Outreach Centre).

We will make **two** comparisons. We will compare Pentecostal results with **Mainline Protestant,** and with **Other Protestant**.

Complete results of such an analysis can be daunting for some readers, so I have placed more detailed tables in the Appendix and, for simplicity, provided here just the top scorer for each of the 33 qualities measured.

Following these tables, I have gathered the final results on three issues:

- The top score in the 33 qualities measured
- The comparison with Mainline Protestant
- The comparison with Other Protestant

Here are the results for the nine core qualities and the 33 specific questions asked. Figures are from the 2016 NCLS survey (the most recent as at time of writing). We will discuss the results at the end.

1. ALIVE AND GROWING *FAITH*

CORE QUALITY QUESTION	TOP SCORER
Importance of God in your life?	Pentecostal
Private devotional activity (prayer or Bible reading)?	Pentecostal
Much growth in faith over the past year?	Pentecostal

2. VITAL AND NURTURING *WORSHIP*

CORE QUALITY QUESTION	TOP SCORER
Preaching (very) helpful to your life?	Pentecostal
Appreciate the music?	Pentecostal
Inspired by the services?	Pentecostal
Experience a sense of God's presence?	Pentecostal
Have growth in your understanding of God?	Pentecostal
Challenged to take action?	Pentecostal

3. STRONG AND GROWING *BELONGING*

CORE QUALITY QUESTION	TOP SCORER
Usually attend church weekly?	**Baptist, Reformed**
Have strong and growing sense of belonging?	Pentecostal
Attend small study/prayer groups?	**C3 Churches (Pent.)***
Give 10% or more to your local church?	Pentecostal

*Pentecostals as a whole scored equal highest with Reformed here, but not the highest result. One of the Pentecostal churches (C3 Churches) scored a marginally higher result, so it is reasonable to include that here, and identify it as a Pentecostal church. The same happens a couple of other times below.

4. CLEAR AND OWNED *VISION*

CORE QUALITY QUESTION	TOP SCORER
Strongly committed to church vision?	Pentecostal
Fully confident vision is achievable?	Pentecostal

5. INSPIRING AND EMPOWERING *LEADERSHIP*

CORE QUALITY QUESTION	TOP SCORER
Gifts, skills greatly encouraged in the church?	Pentecostal
Leaders take ideas into account?	Pentecostal Uniting
Like to be more involved?	Pentecostal
Leaders inspire you to action?	Pentecostal
Leaders have a focus on wider community?	Pentecostal
Church has good and clear systems?	Pentecostal

6. IMAGINATIVE AND FLEXIBLE *INNOVATION*

CORE QUALITY QUESTION	TOP SCORER
Church willing to try new things?	Pentecostal
Leaders encourage innovation?	Pentecostal
Church (strongly) supports new ministry/mission initiatives?	Pentecostal

7. PRACTICAL AND DIVERSE *SERVICE*

CORE QUALITY QUESTION	TOP SCORER
Involved in church-based service activities?	Uniting
Involved in community-based service activities?	Uniting
Involved in informal helping—3 or more actions in last year?	Pentecostal

NOTE: If love is the first fruit of the Holy Spirit, and Pentecostals claim a unique experience of the Holy Spirit, shouldn't this be reflected in serving, and Pentecostals feature more prominently in this table? This important question is addressed in Appendix D, The Fruit of the Spirit: Should Pentecostals and Charismatics Demonstrate More?

8. WILLING AND EFFECTIVE *FAITH-SHARING*

CORE QUALITY QUESTION	TOP SCORER
Look for opportunities to share your faith?	Pentecostal
Invited people to church in last year?	Pentecostal
Involved in local church outreach?	Int. Network of Churches (Pent)

9. INTENTIONAL AND WELCOMING *INCLUSION*

CORE QUALITY QUESTION	TOP SCORER
Personal follow-up of new people very likely?	Pentecostal
Church always/mostly welcome new arrivals?	Int. Network of Churches (Pent)
Easy to make friends in this church?	Pentecostal

Summary

Gathering those results, we can now compare the Pentecostal denomination with the three groups: individual Protestant, Mainline Protestant and other Protestant.

Comparing with INDIVIDUAL Protestant churches: Pentecostals scored highest (or equal highest) in **30** of the **33** core quality questions. That is **91%.**

Comparing with MAINLINE Protestant churches as a group (Details in Appendix H): Pentecostals scored, on average, **47.5% higher.**

Comparing with OTHER Protestant churches as a group (Details in Appendix H): Pentecostals scored, on average, **31.5%** higher.

Are those results significant? Are they "God-sized"?

Imagine a marketing manager who produced sales figures like that. Would the boss be happy? You would have to think they would.

That being the case, two questions call for attention.

First, are there other stand-out distinctives in other denominations that might impact this result? Think of this.

The survey has analysed virtually every major denomination in Australia—each with unique differences and strengths which might make one stand out above another. For example, Baptists believe in full immersion, others believe in sprinkling. Presbyterians emphasise predestination, others emphasis free will. But if such things make a difference, the statistics certainly do not reflect it. Until you compare Pentecostals and others. And that difference is clear and dramatic.

Remember, the survey was designed by non-Pentecostals for churches of all kinds, and it examines issues considered essential for authentic Christianity. Assuming Pentecostals have responded in the same way as others did (and there is no strong reason to suspect otherwise), this is a very reasonable approach.

Second, what makes the difference?

As I expressed at the start, Pentecostals hold essentially the same underlying doctrines as the others, to which they have added their unique belief about the Holy Spirit. It seems reasonable to conclude that their experience of the Holy Spirit makes that difference.

> Note well: my purpose is not to promote Pentecostalism as a denomination. I am contending for the Spirit baptism. To evaluate that, it is necessary to evaluate the Pentecostal movement which has embraced it. Any glory goes to God alone.

NEXT:

The next measure of Holy Spirit reality is not what you might expect but, in my mind, is equally compelling, if not more so. It has to do with Christian music. How can you measure or make comparisons with Christian music? Read on.

"Do you like my new song?"
"Yeah. It's good."
"God gave it to me."
"Nah. It's not that good."

CHAPTER 4
THE HOLY SPIRIT IN MUSIC

This issue is very simple. It needs no statistical analysis, no in-depth theological study, and no intellectual gymnastics. In fact, just about anyone could dig around and find this for themselves. But I don't know anyone who has.

Here it is.

Many Christians today love to sing contemporary praise and worship songs. From about the seventies until the nineties, many, many churches made the transition from old hymns to contemporary songs. Uniting, Baptist, Pentecostal, Episcopalian (Anglican), Salvation Army, etc., even groups within Catholic churches, embraced them enthusiastically. This was a reality that Nolene and I lived and breathed for more than 20 years, compiling and publishing resources of the new songs. Twice a year, we sifted through some three hundred new songs, chose about 13 and published them in music books, CDs and other resources. We mailed millions of dollars' worth of these products, to thousands of Australian Christians of every kind. Our customers were, roughly, half Pentecostal, half non-Pentecostal.

Here is the thing. From all that activity, as far as I can determine, the overwhelming majority of the best loved contemporary songs **have emerged from Pentecostal or charismatic stables. Few, if any, came from the rest.**

When I tell Pentecostal and charismatic friends about this, they are surprised. None suspected it. Non-Pentecostal/charismatics are also surprised. But they ask questions. For example:

What about the grand old hymns?

I do not for a moment suggest our beloved hymns and sacred songs, penned well before the emergence of the Pentecostal movement, were not inspired. Hardly! All Christians have the Holy Spirit. When Handel completed *The Hallelujah Chorus,* his servant came in and found him weeping. All Handel could mumble was, "I did think I did see all heaven before me, and the great God himself". [3]. And the magnificent hymns of Charles Wesley emerged, as we will see in a later chapter, during an outpouring of the Holy Spirit in England. Thousands of old hymns and sacred songs, bear the unmistakable stamp of the Spirit of God.

What I am saying is this: in the Bible-believing, evangelical stream of **today**, that 'stamp' of inspiration lies overwhelmingly on songs from the Pentecostal and charismatic streams, and not the others. After many years in this ministry, that is my consistent observation.

Theology of new songs

At this point, I need to acknowledge the shallow theological content in many contemporary songs—in comparison with the great hymns, most of which encapsulate great doctrines of the faith in four or five profound verses. Several times over the years, I have written to songwriters, urging them to provide solid theological content. I even wrote a book on the subject: *Worship is a Bowl of Noodles OR What Would Jesus Sing*[4], and mailed a copy to more than 2,000 pastors. My message was "be selective", and avoid what I loosely described as "I, me, my" songs, which focus on ourselves and our wants, rather than on God and his works. However, while there is a general need for better theology in songs, wonderful exceptions can be found when you search for them.

Note that contemporary songs serve a different **purpose** from hymns. Contemporary songs feed the worshipper's hunger for intimacy with God; they are more personal. They talk *to* God instead of *about* God. They anticipate an experiential refreshing of the Holy Spirit, there and then. Worshippers expect to hear God's voice, either the still small voice or a prophetic spoken word. Hymns, more rigid in structure and more vocally demanding, do not suit this more personally engaging style of worship.

Note too, that contemporary songs are often shorter than hymns. They can't say as much. So, a comparison with the theology of hymns, with their many verses, is not always reasonable.

Nevertheless there is much room for improvement. Contemporary songwriters and worship leaders, while typically inspirational, young and passionate, are frequently a work in progress as far as theology is concerned. They tend to gravitate to the subjects they know best: their personal love for God and their experience of God. I would urge all songwriters to study the grand doctrines of the faith: salvation, God, Jesus, and the Holy Spirit, for a start. Interestingly, in a doctrinal analysis of several hundred songs, I found those that emerged as the most popular and long-lasting, were the ones which were most focused on God and his works. I was encouraged by this. It told me that many worship leaders were intuitively choosing the theologically better songs for their song lists.

What is the bottom line?

There is no doubt about the popularity and effectiveness of the new songs. The National Church Life Survey (mentioned last chapter) summed it up: "... churches making use of contemporary styles of music and worship are more likely to be growing numerically and attract newcomers from the wider community."[5]

But the focus of our investigation is this: while both streams of the church have gladly **embraced** these new songs, Pentecostals and charismatics are the ones who **write** them.

There must be exceptions to this rule, and I am sure there are. As I write this, there are some popular songs emerging from a non-charismatic evangelical church in Australia. But even assuming this has bucked the trend, my long experience has revealed that **well over 90%** of successful songs are from Pentecostal or charismatic stables. If the Pentecostal view of the Holy Spirit were false, you would expect a 50/50 split. That is certainly not the case.

Have the others tried to write songs? Yes they have. I have seen their efforts. They have produced CDs and posted songs on *YouTube*. But they are quietly ignored, even by their peers.

Are there special conditions favouring Pentecostal/charismatics? No. *This is a level playing field*. Anyone can compose a song, sing it at a church or conference, record it or post it on YouTube. Anyone can do that, and many do. What matters, is what follows: worshippers choose. Without being aware of it, worshippers cast votes—by downloads, credit cards and Sunday song lists. The best songs quickly emerge. The verdict? Songs composed by Pentecostal/charismatics are the most sought after—by all Christians.

But remember this. Those non-Pentecostal Christians are godly, Bible-believing, beautiful saints, praying, serving, giving, and loving. I have met hundreds of them, worshipped with them, conducted seminars in their churches. But the fact remains, while these wonderful Christians love those top songs, they seldom create them.

Why is this?

Only one possibility stands out. Writers of popular songs, Pentecostals and charismatics, have embraced the supernatural Spirit baptism. If my theory is correct, this Holy Spirit experience not only enhances evangelism results, but also empowers songwriters such that their songs carry that indefinable "essence". And that essence is apparent, not just to Pentecostal/charismatics, but to those who don't embrace that belief. If Spirit baptism is not the reason, we should urgently seek the real reason, for it is a wonderful treasure indeed.

Scripture Basis

Does the Bible speak about Holy Spirit inspiration of songs? Yes, there is a link between spiritual songs and the Holy Spirit in Ephesians 5:18–19:

> "Do not get drunk on wine, which leads to debauchery. Instead, be filled with the Spirit, speaking to one another with psalms, hymns and songs from the Spirit. Sing and make music from your heart to the Lord…"

Note that "songs from the Spirit" is probably the singing in tongues Paul mentions in 1 Corinthians 14:15:

> "I will pray with my spirit (i.e., in tongues), but I will also pray with my understanding; I will sing with my spirit (in tongues), but I will also sing with my understanding."

The Holy Spirit is active in worship. So, if the Pentecostal/charismatic understanding of Spirit baptism is correct, we should not be surprised to see it reflected in song writing.

A few factors now call for attention:

Inspiration of songs

Many songs are inspired by God, more or less. Most of the time, though, writers are unaware of that. When Luke wrote his gospel, he said, "...since I myself have carefully investigated everything from the beginning, I too decided to write an orderly account..." (Luke 1:3–4). He didn't know God was compiling a New Testament or that he was a big part of that plan.

Of course, songs are not on the same level as scripture. It is just that *God has not ceased inspiring his children.*

Is there a reliable measure of song popularity?

Yes indeed. The Christian Copyright Licensing International (CCLI) Top 100 listing.

CCLI liaises between churches and songwriters (and publishers), so that churches can use songs legally and writers can be rewarded for their work. Churches purchase an annual licence allowing them to use songs in a variety of formats, and they report their song activity so that revenue can be disbursed among songwriters. So CCLI has a quite accurate, up-to-date picture of which songs are chosen most. The top 100 songs are usually reported on their website.

How do you know if songwriters are Pentecostal/Charismatic?

For me, this began with inside knowledge accumulated over years. Rubbing shoulders with songwriters in our ministry, it began to dawn on me that Pentecostal and charismatic writers were the ones generating the top songs.

A few examples from that time span:

This is the Day, an early favourite, was written by Les Garrett, an Australian Pentecostal pastor. Jack Hayford wrote many, much-loved songs, of which *Majesty* was the stand-out, and he too was a Pentecostal pastor. Andre Crouch who wrote *To God be the Glory* and several other beautiful songs, also became a Pentecostal pastor. Graham Kendrick, a charismatic Baptist, burst on the scene from England. His signature song was *Shine Jesus Shine.* Then the Australian Pentecostal church, Hillsong, emerged and led the world, with a number of prominent writers churning out inspiring songs loved worldwide. Best known would have been *Shout to the Lord,* by Darlene Zschech. A great number of popular songs have been birthed from Bethel Centre, Pastor Bill Johnson's Pentecostal church. And so, it goes on.

I became bothered that non-Pentecostals were not producing successful songs, and began looking for CDs from non-charismatic churches. One leading, non-Pentecostal church released a CD of their new songs, so I slipped a copy to our selection team, saying nothing about it. *None of the songs made even the first cut.* And, confirming our selection team's judgement, in spite of that church's impressive pedigree, none made it to the CCLI top 100.

No one asks, no one tells

Songwriters often keep any Pentecostal affiliations low key, knowing it could be a turn-off.

A good example can be seen in the ministry of Graham Kendrick. Charismatic son of a conservative Baptist pastor, he buried his unambiguous Holy Spirit testimony on page 88 of his book *Worship.* And, before introducing the subject, he did his best to pour oil on contentious waters, saying cautiously: "It is worth relating my experiences here...to illustrate the 'ordinariness' of something that has become, in some people's minds, over-dramatised, 'scary' or seemingly out of reach".

He described his spiritual need, "I felt there must be more to Christianity than we knew", and his consequent visit to "a group of Spirit-filled Christians… who, for all I knew, at that very moment might be setting up the chandeliers for a swinging session". On returning home that night (after praying unsuccessfully for the Holy Spirit), he said, "I was half way through cleaning my teeth, quietly thanking God for hearing my prayer, but no more, when quite unexpectedly I found myself smiling…This was totally new, I'd never felt like this before; I was so full up with joy and peace that I spent the next hour right there (kneeling beside the bath) *enjoying* God for the first time in my life…my spirit had been liberated, and I remember lying at last in my bed, the fixed grin still on my face, praising and thanking God, and gingerly trying out a new spiritual language that had presented itself to my tongue with no regard at all for the objections thrown up by my incredulous brain!"[6]

In the years following, his songs brought blessing to Christians around the world, most unaware of any influence of the Spirit baptism and speaking in tongues in their creation.

The Ramifications

Many non-charismatic churches have considered Pentecostals "holy rollers", holding them at arm's length. They have written books, posted articles and preached sermons critical of Pentecostal ways. But amidst all that lies this contradiction. Such sermons are invariably preceded by enthusiastic singing of songs written by Pentecostals and charismatics. Songs that should also be composed by their own people. A different understanding of the Holy Spirit baptism seems to be all that is needed to open that door.

NEXT:

Now, a change in pace. The previous three chapters deal with facts and figures. Now we will look at signs, wonders and miracles. Jesus performed them—they were a significant part of his credentials. As Peter said, "…Jesus of Nazareth was a man accredited by God to you by miracles, wonders and signs..." (Acts 2:22). The apostles too performed miracles. Can we? Are they still valid today? If so, does our understanding and experience of the Holy Spirit affect that?

Surveys are lacking on this subject, but stories abound (if you look for them) of people who, by the grace of God, have worked convincing miracles. We will examine several, being alert for any link to the Spirit baptism. Stories call for more detail than facts and tables, so we spend more time here. I am confident that when you walk through them, you will find unexpected illumination and rich inspiration. Before we begin, we will briefly look at what lies behind a prevailing western reticence on the subject of miracles.

"...you call on the name of your god, and I will call on the name of the Lord. The god who answers by fire—he is God." Then all the people said, "What you say is good". (Elijah to the prophets of Baal, 1 Kings 18)

I came to you in weakness with great fear and trembling. My message and my preaching were not with wise and persuasive words, but with a demonstration of the Spirit's power, so that your faith might not rest on human wisdom, but on God's power. (The Apostle Paul, 1 Corinthians 2:3)

...biblical-quality healing miracles are not being performed today...After the time of the apostles, healings such as these ceased, and have never since been part of church history. John MacArthur [7]

CHAPTER 5
SIGNS, WONDERS AND MIRACLES

Many years ago, a friend of mine, while sitting in church with his parents, became disturbed by a comment from the minister. It welled up inside until eventually he could not hold it back and he dissolved into tears. "Jesus' miracles," the minister had said, "don't happen anymore today".

That story does have a happy ending, and I will finish it later. But before that, we need to ask the question: where did that idea come from, that Jesus' miracles are no longer for today?

In our western culture, so heavily moulded by science and rationalism, miracles are a magnet for scepticism. Expect eyes to roll when you raise the subject. Not so in Africa, Asia, South America, Pacific nations and more, where divination, witchcraft, magic, curses and other supernatural phenomena are well understood—by rich and poor, kings and servants, educated and uneducated. In fact the supernatural is so ingrained, that offering Christian prayer for a sick person is rarely a problem, and results can be spectacular. That difference between western and non-western cultures is well understood. The story is told, for example, of a sincere Indian Baptist pastor, who "complained that Americans he prayed for (in America) were rarely healed, but almost everyone he prayed for in India was healed".[8] I have heard that position described many times.

Two different world views. How did they come about?

Much western scepticism can be traced to the Enlightenment, (about 1750–1850AD), which brought a significant change to thinking in western countries. Prior to the Enlightenment, and throughout western Christian history, miracles were expected and experienced frequently.[9] They were not necessarily plentiful, but the supernatural work—of God or evil spirits—was not challenged as it is today.

The Enlightenment, which changed all that, was a philosophical movement that promoted reason and science over tradition and religion. Its benefits were seen in confronting the tyranny of absolute monarchies, and also the excesses of the established church, for which it advocated separation of Church and State. That process, however, together with emphasis on rational thought as the basis for authority and legitimacy, weakened church influence, and opened the door for atheism and, subsequently, liberal theology.

On this subject of miracles, the most prominent Enlightenment activist was the Scottish atheist, philosopher and writer, David Hume (1711–1776) who said:

> A miracle is a violation of the laws of nature; and [because] a firm and unalterable experience has established these laws, the proof against a miracle, from the very nature of the fact, is as entire as any argument from experience can possibly be imagined.[10]

In other words, he says, the laws of nature are set in concrete, making miracles impossible because they imply a violation of those laws. It follows then (he tries to convince us), that if something looking like a miracle occurs, no matter how convincing, or how many witnesses claim to have seen it, it is not a miracle.[11]

This is the reasoning undergirding much western "scientific" thinking today. I have debated atheists who still quote Hume. His argument is logically flawed, but, above all, it ignores the possibility that God created the laws of nature, and he can do as he chooses. Despite that, Hume's ideas have infiltrated Christianity too, robbing believers of a basic life instinct—the daily anticipation and experience of living with God and his supernatural interventions in their lives.

In its place is a scepticism, an unbelief, which casts a veil over our eyes, blurring our understanding of God's intentions. Non-western countries have escaped that scepticism, but that is not all to the good. Being open to spiritual things, but without the gospel and God's truth, they are vulnerable to the wiles of Satan. As a result, most of those cultures are steeped in some form of witchcraft or occultism. The good news is, that when they do hear the gospel and learn of its miracle power, they are quick to grasp it, and miracles are relatively plentiful, convincing them of the ability of God to forgive their sins.

The danger to western Christians is the felt pressure to conform to atheistic Enlightenment thinking, to make the Bible fit that mould. As a result, many Christians are blind to the abundance of passages unfolding God's power and desire to heal. Instead, they might justify their scepticism with a few isolated scriptures like Paul's thorn in the flesh (2 Corinthians 12:7), or his comment, "I left Trophimus sick in Miletus" (2 Timothy 4:20). They are unaware that their world view was not birthed from the pages of the Bible, but from the atheism and rationalism of the Enlightenment. The early church did not think that way, and the Bible was not written that way. A fundamental change of thinking is called for.

Miracles do occur today, a vital part of God's loving plan for us. The stories we will consider now, from the previous century, are a reflection of that fact. They are the blessings of God, brought to us through believers who rejected western scepticism, and placed their faith in scripture.

What are the scriptures that link miracles and the baptism in the Holy Spirit? First, Jesus, speaking to his disciples:

> ...Whoever believes in me will do the works I have been doing, and they will do even greater things than these, because I am going to the Father. (John 14:12)

> ...it is for your good that I am going away. Unless I go away, the Advocate will not come to you; but if I go, I will send him to you. (John 16:5–7)

In other words, Jesus returns to the Father, sends the Holy Spirit in his place, and the Holy Spirit empowers disciples to continue **his** works. That obviously includes miracles, because Jesus' works included miracles.

Here is Paul now, describing his own ministry:

> "...by the power of signs and wonders, through the power of the Spirit of God...I have fully proclaimed the gospel of Christ." (Romans 15:19)

> "My message and my preaching were not with wise and persuasive words, but with a demonstration of the Spirit's power, so that your faith might not rest on human wisdom, but on God's power." (1 Corinthians 2:4)

Clearly, signs, wonders and miracles, are linked to the power of the promised Spirit of God.

Luke's story of Philip the evangelist completes this section:

> "Philip went down to a city in Samaria and proclaimed the Messiah there. When the crowds heard Philip and saw the signs he performed, they all paid close attention to what he said. For with shrieks, impure spirits came out of many, and many who were paralysed or lame were healed. So, there was great joy in that city...Simon (a magician)...followed Philip everywhere, astonished by the great signs and miracles he saw." (Acts 8:5–8, 13)

Note the similarity to Paul's ministry: "by the power of signs and wonders... [Paul] fully proclaimed the **gospel** of Christ". Remembering that "**gospel**" means good news, and an "evangelist" is a bearer of good news, Paul could equally have said "by the power of signs and wonders...I **evangelised**."

Our question now becomes clear: in the Pentecostal/charismatic stream, with its emphasis on the Holy Spirit baptism, do we find *more* miracles, and/or *greater* miracles? If so, is the difference "God-sized"? Once again, we tread this path reluctantly, not wanting to be critical. But, once again, the answer is important, and we need to find out.

So, we will look at the lives of evangelists known for signs, wonders and miracles, particularly people over the last century, since the Pentecostal movement emerged. I will highlight their Holy Spirit experience, and subsequent healing ministry. Miracle ministry can be controversial, so I have also introduced them with a brief outline of their background, their calling, and any obstacles they faced, to give an idea of their character.

It needs to be said that, while we will read of remarkable miracles in these stories, not everyone is healed. We must remember, that was the case with Jesus too. He could not do mighty miracles in his hometown, and he healed only one of many at the pool at Bethesda. However, while not all are healed today, there are many occasions when wonderful, dramatic healings do occur in our time, and we will now turn our attention to those.

Smith Wigglesworth 1859–1947
"Only believe!"

From a poor English family, and with very little schooling, Smith Wigglesworth could barely read when he became an adult. He began work at the age of six, pulling turnips. Later, he helped his father in a woollen mill, and then learned the plumber's trade which he pursued until entering full-time ministry. A zealous Christian from childhood, he began evangelising as a small boy. As a young man, he spent much time with the Salvation Army. He said:

> ...it seemed to me they had more power in their ministry than anybody else at that time. We used to have all nights of prayer. Many would be prostrated under the power of the Spirit, sometimes for as long as 24 hours at a time. We called that the baptism in the Holy Spirit in those days.[12]

He used that term loosely, as we will see.

Smith was not a good preacher. Overcome by weeping he could not speak. But his wife, Polly, preached in Salvation Army and Methodist churches, with hundreds saved. Smith preferred to round up groups of people and take them to meetings, where they could hear the gospel. Eventually, just after they were married (when he was 23), they began a church of their own in Bradford.

In the late 1800s, Smith learned about healing meetings being held in Leeds. He was so enthused he gathered groups of sick people, paid their fares, and took them to receive healing.

Before long, he and Polly began to pray for the sick in their own church. At their first meeting, they prayed for 12 people and all were healed. One woman had an ulcer on her ankle, and a large sore that was continually discharging. Next day there was only a scar.

Polly tried to get Smith to preach but, he said, it took 20 years of open-air preaching before the Lord "began to give me more liberty".[13] Then, he said:

> My wife and I always believed in scriptural holiness, but I was conscious of much carnality in myself. A really holy man once came to preach for us, and he spoke of what it meant to be entirely sanctified. He called it a very definite work of grace subsequent to the new birth. As I waited on the Lord for 10 days in prayer, handing my body over to him as a living sacrifice according to Romans 12:1, 2. God surely did something for me, for from that time, I began to have real liberty in preaching. We counted that as the baptism in the Holy Spirit. And so, at our mission on Bowland Street, we stood for both healing and holiness.[14]

In 1907, Smith, then about 48 years old, learned about people in Sunderland claiming to be baptised in the Holy Spirit and speaking in tongues. He was puzzled, saying:

> According to my own opinion, I had been baptised in the Spirit. Thinking back to my 10 days of waiting on God and the blessings I had received as a result, I had called that the baptism in the Holy Spirit. So, I said to them (the people in Sunderland) 'I remember when I was baptised, my tongue

was loosed. My testimony was different'. But they answered, 'No that is not it'.[15]

Then followed four days in Sunderland, debating forcefully with other Christians, some of whom warned him, "That's the devil they are getting up there". He was also seeking, praying, even spending a night of prayer with a friend, but all to no avail. Heading home, he asked the vicar's wife, Mrs Boddy, to pray for him. Then:

> The fire fell. It was a wonderful time as I was there with God alone. He bathed me with power. I was conscious of the cleansing of the precious blood, and I cried out, 'Clean! Clean! Clean!' I was filled with the joy of the consciousness of the cleansing. I was given a vision in which I saw the Lord Jesus Christ. I beheld the empty cross, and I saw him exalted at the right hand of God the Father. I could speak no longer in English, but I began to praise him in other tongues as the Spirit of God gave me utterance. I knew then, although I might have received anointings previously, that now, at last, I had received the real baptism in the Holy Spirit as they received on the Day of Pentecost.[16]

When he arrived home his wife, forewarned, said:

> So, you've been speaking in tongues, have you?...I want you to understand that I am as much baptised as you are, and I don't speak in tongues...I have been preaching for 20 years and you have sat beside me on the platform, but on Sunday you will preach yourself, and I'll see what there is in it.[17]

When the time came he preached on Isaiah 61:1–3 ("The Spirit of the Lord God is upon me...") and:

> My wife was terribly disturbed. The bench on which she sat would seat nine people and she moved about on it until she

had sat on every part of it. Then she said in a voice that all around her could hear, 'That's not my Smith, Lord, that's not my Smith!'[18]

After the sermon, the secretary of the mission said he wanted what Smith had—then fell on the floor. Then his eldest son said he wanted what his father had, and he too fell on the floor. In a short time, there were 11 on the floor, laughing. Wigglesworth said:

> That was the beginning of a great outpouring of the Spirit, where hundreds received the baptism in the Holy Ghost and every one of them spoke in tongues as the Spirit of God gave utterance.[19]

Sometime later, Polly also received in the same way, and together they responded to many calls from people seeking the Holy Spirit. It wasn't always easy—they faced a good deal of persecution, together with remarkable success. Two extraordinary miracles followed. Firstly, a young man with a severe heart problem lay at death's door. After much prayer through the night and waiting on God:

> ...the moment I touched the young man, the power of God filled the room and was so powerful that I fell to the floor... Matthew in the bed was shouting, 'Lord, this is for thy glory!'...The bed simply shook, as did everything in the room, by the power of God. He was completely healed.[20]

Secondly, going from that place Smith was taken to a man in terrible pain from bladder cancer. He was healed immediately, his shouts of "Hallelujah" audible 50 yards away. Demand for Smith Wigglesworth's ministry became so great he abandoned his plumbing, and trusted God for his income.

He engaged two people to round up the sick for special banquets. After the meal, they would be entertained for an hour and a half with testimonies of others healed through prayer. Then the guests would be prayed for. The next week it would be their turn to testify at a similar banquet. Wonderful miracles followed.

Word spread and his ministry expanded into many towns, cities and countries. His message was consistent: God not only forgives all sin, but heals every disease.

Hundreds were saved and healed and baptised in the Holy Spirit. In Washington DC, he prayed for a young girl who had never walked, her "legs absolutely dangled, with the feet hanging vertically from them". Wigglesworth told her, "You are going to be a different girl when you leave this place". She was healed, and her uncle beside her "wept like a child". That night at home she walked up her stairs unaided. Her mother was also healed from a growth on her breast.[21]

During the same series of meetings:

> One brother testified to the healing of a cancer of two years standing. A poor, sick man whom the doctors had given up on, whose legs were useless except for slow motion, was healed and ran twice around the hall. When asked how many had been healed during the week's services, at least two hundred arose.[22]

Problems occurred in Sweden when doctors and ministers resisted him, and presented a petition to Parliament to shut down his ministry. As a result, he was forbidden to lay hands on people in public. To get around this, and with officials watching on as some 20,000 people gathered in a park, he asked those needing prayer to lay hands on themselves while he prayed for their healing. Many were healed. He called that "wholesale healing" and, from that time, often used the technique when crowds were too big to pray personally for everyone.

Smith sent handkerchiefs to many people seeking miracles—inspired by Acts 19:11–12: "God did extraordinary miracles through Paul, so that even handkerchiefs and aprons that had touched him were taken to the sick, and their illnesses were cured, and the evil spirits left them". His biographer describes the result:

> Volumes could be written containing nothing but answers to such cases…drunkards have lost appetite for strong drink; smokers have left off tobacco; wayward sons and daughters have been brought back to Christ; separated couples have been reunited. [The handkerchiefs] have been used for every conceivable kind of need, trouble and sickness.[23]

In Christiania (now Oslo), Smith wrote:

> I ministered for over three hours to the sick, after preaching for an hour and a half. Many coming were helpless. Hundreds were healed. A great pile of crutches and sticks and other helps have been left on the large platform. I ministered openly and the crowds looked on and shouted. The excitement was wonderful as the blind saw and the lame leaped. We are now in a place holding 5,000 and the people say it will be too small.[24]

Smith was a remarkable man, with a lifelong fiery zeal. He shed rivers of tears for the lost and needy, and revelled in all nights of prayer. The Bible was the only book he ever read. For years he lived this way, preaching the gospel. Then, late in life, he received the baptism in the Holy Spirit, and his world exploded into an international healing ministry, wonderfully blessing and restoring the lives of hundreds of thousands of grateful people.

We wonder how many more would have been healed and saved if he had learned of the Holy Spirit at the beginning of his ministry. And how many fewer, if he had never learned of it at all. And how many others today could, like him, bring healing and restoration if they experienced the same.

FF Bosworth 1877–1958

Author of the Christian classic, *Christ the Healer*.

Born in Utica, Nebraska, Fred Bosworth was a capable and ethical man who, in his life as a healing evangelist, touched more than a million people, and paved the way for other healing evangelists. He had links to Azusa Street, the 1906 birthplace of the Pentecostal movement, and also with the healing evangelists of the 1940s and 1950s. He systematically documented healing miracles, was careful that seekers would not be carried away by emotionalism and, over the years, accumulated 250,000 letters from people healed and touched by his ministry. The Chicago Daily News even reported that, when Bosworth visited a school for the deaf, so many students were healed that the school closed its doors.[25]

Fred was soundly converted in his late teens at a Methodist church. As a result of his new life, he left his sales job, unhappy with the dishonest methods he had been asked to use.

Contracting tuberculosis at 19 and told he would not survive, he went to a Methodist Revival where healing evangelist, Miss Mattie Perry, was ministering. Knowing nothing about him, she told him he was too young to die, and God still had work for him. She prayed, and in a matter of days Fred was completely healed.

Marrying at 23, he heard about the famous healing evangelist, Alexander Dowie, and Zion City—a Christian community Dowie had built in Illinois. So, he and his wife moved there to learn more.

It was there, at the age of 29, that he learned about the baptism in the Holy Spirit and speaking in tongues. Dowie had opposed this new belief, but Bosworth and another evangelist, John G Lake, were interested. When Charles Parham (more on him later) came to Zion City to preach about it, they welcomed him into their home for meetings, and both received the gift. Reflecting on this, and past instabilities in his life, Bosworth later said:

> I wish someone at that time had told me about being baptised in the Holy Spirit. I did a great deal of drifting not knowing what the right place was for me.[26]

The experience brought dramatic changes to Bosworth. In Zion City, he had lived with a fear that God would call him to preach. After his Spirit baptism, he feared the opposite—that God would *not* call him to preach!

So, he and his family departed Zion City on an itinerant ministry, trusting God to provide for their needs. Eventually, they settled in Dallas, Texas, where they conducted tent meetings, introducing people to the power of the Holy Spirit.

In 1910, Bosworth established the first Assemblies of God Pentecostal church in Dallas, Texas. Crowds came, and many were baptised in the Holy Spirit, speaking in tongues. Diligent in his Bible study, his ministry broadened from evangelist to teacher/evangelist. In 1912, he held a series of meetings at his church with prominent healing minister, Maria Woodworth-Etter. Many were saved, healed and baptised in the Holy Spirit. He became well known through those meetings and was influential in the formation of the new Assemblies of God movement that arose from these beginnings.

However, he began to doubt the scriptural validity of the new doctrine of the Holy Spirit. He came to believe tongues were not the only initial evidence of receiving the baptism in the Holy Spirit and, as a result, in 1918, quietly withdrew from the Assemblies of God. He continued, nevertheless, in his healing and evangelising ministry.

Tragically, in 1919 his wife contracted tuberculosis and died, leaving him with two daughters to care for. But his faith remained strong, and he returned to preaching, and in the 1920s conducted many successful campaigns.

His first was in Lima, Ohio, where a pastor invited him to preach on healing. Apprehensive about the idea, he spent much time studying healing passages in the Bible. Hundreds came and were healed—the deaf, the blind, the lame. Doctors brought patients for healing. The most remarkable was Alice Baker, whose face had been eaten away by cancer—so much so her teeth were visible. After first embracing Christ as her Saviour, she asked for prayer. She said:

> As they prayed for me, it seemed a rubber cap was drawn over my face, and it gradually slipped off, and I knew I was healed. I told a lady to remove the bandages and God blessed my soul, so I could not help shouting, and I shouted many times. It is so good to be without pain…Oh, I am so happy all the time…Many have come from other towns to see me… and hear about my healing.[27].

In Pittsburgh, results were even more remarkable. The *National Labor Tribune* reported:

> All denominations crowd the hall...Several hundred seekers after God crowd the platform daily...Doctors, lawyers, financiers, merchants, professional men of all types and calibre...nurses, and head nurses from the hospitals and sanatoriums, all seeking soul salvation or bodily healing. It is a sight that astounds the onlookers to see those multitudes seeking their way to God...Beyond belief are the results.[28].

One of the miracles concerned a man named John Sproul. Suffering continuous pain from WW1 mustard gas, and after 14 operations, he was unable to talk. As a returned soldier, his tragic story had become widely known, filling the papers. But he was completely healed at a Bosworth meeting, and a simple but remarkable newspaper headline shouted the news to the world: "John Sproul can talk!"

And so, Bosworth ministered throughout the 1920s in the USA and Canada, to huge crowds, becoming the most prominent and respected of the healing evangelists of that time. Because of the huge demands on his ministry, he ventured into radio broadcasts, which he continued very successfully along with his normal healing meetings, until the 1940s.

In his early seventies, he teamed up with another healing evangelist, William Branham. This put him before vast crowds outside the USA. He would teach healing during the day, and Branham would conduct miracle meetings at night.

In 1952, he left the Branham campaigns, and spent several years preaching in South Africa, Cuba and Japan. After more than 50 years of preaching ministry it is believed he brought more than a million people to Christ.

As mentioned at the start, Bosworth had once lived with a fear God would call him to preach, but after his baptism in the Holy Spirit, he feared God would *not* call him to preach. What would have happened had Bosworth never learned about the Holy Spirit? How would people like Alice Baker and John Sproul have ended their days?

And how many other capable, godly "Bosworths" have never heard the message of the baptism in the Holy Spirit that set Bosworth on his path? How many sick and lost have been denied healing and knowledge of God as a result?

Fair questions.

Reinhard Bonnke 1940–2019

Around the beginning of the twentieth century, a German Lutheran named Luis Graf migrated to America to make his fortune. There he received the baptism in the Holy Spirit through the Azusa Street revival—the birth of the Pentecostal movement. On retiring, he returned to Germany, touring for four years in his shiny Mercedes, and preaching the gospel. In the little village of Trunz, he asked the baker if there were any sick people he could pray for and was directed to a man whose agonised cries could be heard throughout the village. Following prayer, the man was instantly healed, leaping and shouting and weeping. His name was August Bonnke, and his son, Hermann Bonnke, subsequently became pastor of a small Pentecostal church in the area. In time, he also had a son, Reinhard, who became an evangelist to Africa.

In his life, Reinhard built the world's biggest tent, and saw more than 80 million people converted. A million of these came from just one meeting. (For perspective, Billy Graham saw 2.2 million conversions in his lifetime.)[29] He ministered personally to Presidents and their parliaments, and witnessed countless extraordinary miracles. He was jailed once, received a death threat from Osama bin Laden (prior to 9/11), shut down a crusade because land mines had been planted there, was whisked away from snipers at an airport, and rescued by armoured cars from city-wide Muslim riots in Nigeria. Truly a modern-day Paul.

What lay behind this extraordinary life?

As a small boy, he was zealous for God. Sometimes he and a friend would go into the forest and practise preaching. His mother's baptism in the Spirit impacted him strongly. Discouraged after seeking the Holy Spirit without success, one night in bed she...

...felt herself falling into the loving arms of her Lord. Flooded with waves of divine love, another language began to pour from her mouth like a fountain. She wept and praised God, and spoke in tongues for hours, completely exhilarated by the experience.[30]

The change was dramatic. Seeing her the next day, Reinhard said:

I ran to meet her. The closer I got, the more astonished I became. My mother was glowing. Her eyes sparkled. Her step was like the step of a young girl...I could feel the love pouring from her like I had never felt before...Above all, I knew that I wanted to have what she had. [31]

Though soundly converted at eleven, Reinhard still found himself struggling with feelings of unworthiness. One day, he and his father heard a speaker, well known for helping people receive the Holy Spirit baptism. When invited with others to kneel, Reinhard...

...was overwhelmed with an incredible sensation. No one needed to lay hands on me to pray. I received the gift of speaking in tongues spontaneously and burst out in a heavenly language... My mind began to receive a stream of pure light and love from the very throne of God. It flowed over me and went straight through me at once...Forgiveness [of others became] as easy as breathing, and it flowed from me on a tide of tears. Every form of fear, self-consciousness, and natural self-centredness was blown away like chaff as God poured his love through me...At the age of 11, the Spirit baptism began to lead me on an adventure of faith that has not ended. I literally took off like a rocket ship, and no one could stop me. I continue to be empowered by it to this very day. [32]

The miracles flowing from the Holy Spirit baptism are not, of course, limited to healing alone. The prophetic gift was also important in Bonnke's life. Here are some examples.

The Bonnke's church was small and different, an oddity in a German Lutheran stronghold. Nevertheless, for those who made it their home, it was a spiritual oasis, with all night prayer meetings and gifts of the Spirit a common occurrence. One of the ladies with prophetic gifts was Eliese Kohler. One day, Reinhard's father (the pastor) had unjustly rebuked him. Eliese was unaware of that, but during a prayer meeting she spoke out:

> I see a shepherd with his sheep...but his shepherd's crook is upside down...the crook, which is meant to protect the sheep, has injured one of the lambs. Reinhard's father began to sob, crying, "Forgive me Reinhard. I am sorry, son. Forgive me."[33]

On another occasion, her prophetic insight saved him from a tempting but unwise change of ministry direction. Then, some time later when Reinhard was in Africa, he became ill after drinking contaminated water—a sickness that led to the deaths of many missionaries. He said:

> After three terrible days of delirium...I saw something like a...dark shroud floating down over me... Death was very near...Then, somehow I could see through the blanket. On the other side, I saw the face of Jesus, and a wonderful peace flooded my heart...In the next moment, I heard the voice of dear sister, Eliese Kohler praying for me... I heard her crying out to God to spare my life. In that moment, the fever broke...

He learned later that, before dawn that day, the Holy Spirit woke her saying, "Pray for Reinhard. Intercede for his life because he is dying in Africa". So, she prayed most of the day until the burden lifted.[34]

Events like these were a normal part of life for Reinhard and built strength, character and faith that stood him in good stead throughout his African ministry.

On the advice of a charismatic English pastor, he enrolled in a non-Pentecostal Bible School in Wales—an unconventional move for a Pentecostal. It had been founded by renowned Christian leader, Rees Howells. Reinhard failed the preaching subject, but gained much from the college emphasis on learning to trust God for financial and other needs. Those lessons became invaluable when he was later called to believe God for gigantic tents and massive crusades.

The college was birthed in the Welsh Revival, so it was spiritually dynamic, but tongues were off limits—they were not allowed to discuss the subject in the school. Nevertheless, even the lecturers would discreetly ask Reinhard about his experience. One day a Dutch friend said, "I want what you have. I want the baptism in the Holy Spirit…but I do not want the speaking in tongues". Puzzled by that, Reinhard eventually agreed to pray for him. He said:

> We prayed for about ten minutes. Then lightning struck. He fell from his chair and began rolling on the floor. He was not just speaking in tongues, he was trumpeting in tongues. On and on he went until finally, after several minutes, he calmed down.[35]

Embarrassed by the result, his friend denied he had spoken in tongues. To Reinhard's amusement, he said, "I just spoke unspeakable words".

When Bible School was finished, Reinhard set off for home. Passing through London, with time on his hands, he noticed a nameplate on a house reading, "George Jeffreys". On discovering it was the famous healing evangelist (more about this man shortly), he asked to see him but was firmly refused. But the elderly Jeffreys happened to be coming down the stairs, and said, "Let the young man in". Reinhard said:

> What happened next was extraordinary. All of a sudden he took me by the shoulders and fell to his knees, pulling me to

the floor with him. He placed his hands on my head and began to bless me as a father blesses a son, as Abraham blessed Isaac, who blessed Jacob, and so on. The room seemed to light up with the glory of God as he poured out his prayer over me. I was dazed by that glory. I do not remember the words with which he blessed me, but I do remember their effect. My body felt electrified, tingling with divine energy.

After that prayer—which took about half an hour—Reinhard stumbled away "like a drunken man", wondering what it all meant. What were the chances of this happening to a "21-year-old Bible college graduate, on his way home to serve a practicum at the smallest church in all of Germany?"

A few months later, George Jeffreys died. Reinhard wrote, "As I absorbed the news, I realised something wonderful had happened in London. I had caught Elijah's mantle that day...I could not yet dream of what it would mean".[36]

Tent ministry was a major feature of his work. It began in Germany when a pastor asked him to conduct a three-week evangelistic campaign in a 250 seat tent. That campaign was a success, with people converted each night. Eventually, he launched out with a tent to plant his own church in Flensburg, northern Germany. Oddly, a circus set up a big top right beside theirs, and the circus director asked Reinhard to preach there on a Sunday morning. Impressed by the big structure, Reinhard prayed:

> Father... someday I want a circus tent as big as this one just for preaching the gospel. And I want to see it full of people who have come—not to see a circus—but expecting to meet Jesus.[37]

That prayer was eventually answered—his biggest tent was eight times larger than the largest circus big top.

He moved to Africa and, though his evangelistic work proceeded well, he was distressed because miracles were not happening, in spite of his fervent believing and prayers.

So, he asked a prominent healing evangelist to hold meetings for him in Lesotho. But at the end of the first night, the evangelist refused to pray for the sick, and departed, saying the Holy Spirit had told him to leave. Next day a huge crowd came expecting prayer, and the stunned Reinhard was forced to fill in. However, as he preached, the Holy Spirit power became so strong that his interpreter fell to the floor. In that interlude, God said to him, "My word in your mouth is as powerful as my word in my mouth".

Encouraged by that, he prayed, "In the name of Jesus, blind eyes open!" Immediately, a blind woman received sight, and rushed through the crowd screaming. Then a young boy with twisted limbs was healed in Reinhard's arms, fell to the floor, and began running around. There was pandemonium. That meeting ran all day, with many more miracles. Reflecting on this he said:

> I saw the pattern for the future. *This is how all Africa shall be saved*, I thought. *Not by might, nor by power, but by my Spirit, saith the Lord of Hosts.* It was not a natural calling. It was not a natural enabling. It was supernatural.
>
> Nothing was the same in the days ahead. It was as if I was catapulted from one level to another...We acquired a second-hand tent and began to set it up at various locations and hold meetings. Soon a storm ripped the tent to shreds... We began to seek another.[38]

After renting a number of tents which soon became too small, he commissioned a tent to seat 10,000. But the crowds outgrew this too, so he commissioned another to seat 34,000—a cavernous monster—the biggest in the world.

After just one use, however, a huge storm destroyed the fabric. Remarkably, there were stories of people taking pieces of that fabric to the sick, who were healed, again reminiscent of Paul's handkerchiefs and aprons in Acts 19:12.[39]

While the team was extremely discouraged by the disaster, publicity from that incident and the widely publicised spectacle of the biggest tent in the world, caused an astronomical increase in the crowds. As a result, the repaired tent became too small. So Reinhard donated it for use as a hospital, and ran his meetings in stadiums and outdoor areas.

Miracles became an everyday thing. In Gaborone, Botswana, after commencing a campaign with just 100 people, the miracles attracted huge crowds, and he moved to the 10,000 seat Botswana National Sports Stadium. At one of those large gatherings, he felt God say, "I want you to pray for the people to receive the baptism of the Holy Spirit". So, he asked his African helper, more familiar with the language, to explain it to the people. But the African mentioned nothing about tongues, so Reinhard rose to explain that aspect. Sensing a check from the Holy Spirit, however, he refrained, and simply prayed for the Holy Spirit to fall on the almost one thousand people who came forward. As he prayed:

> I saw a transparent wave coming from the right to the left, sweeping over that stadium. As it hit those people, it was as if a mighty rushing wind blew them to the ground en masse. All of them were speaking in tongues and prophesying as the Spirit gave utterance. This confirmed to me that I had indeed heard the voice of the Spirit in my heart. I had heard him true. It also demonstrated the reality of speaking in tongues without any hint of suggestion or manipulation.[40].

That powerful event was compelling evidence indeed, of the value of miracles in drawing people to hear the gospel, and the link between speaking in tongues and the Spirit baptism.

SOME ANECDOTES FROM HIS MINISTRY

A campaign was held in Conakry, Guinea, that had an 85% Muslim population. They were fortunate to gain permission for the event but one of the President's wives, a Christian, influenced her husband. Reinhard's custom, after preaching, was to gather the sick and pray for them, beginning with the blind. A group of young Muslim men made a pact that, if their blind friend was not healed, they would stone Reinhard with stones hidden in their robes. After the prayer, "In the name of Jesus, blind eyes, open!" the blind man suddenly shrieked, "I see! I see!" The young men let their stones fall to the ground.[41]

At a campaign in a slum area of Nairobi, a local 'madman' wandered through the vast crowd, naked and filthy, his hair matted and full of vermin. At the prompting of the Holy Spirit, Reinhard interrupted his sermon to say, "In the name of Jesus, I break every witchcraft curse here tonight". The man was immediately shaken, as if hit by lightning, and said to those around him, "Why am I here? Why am I naked? How did I get here?" The next night, clean, clothed and in his right mind, the crowd roared as he shouted into the microphone, "Jesus has set me free!"[42]

Reports of the incredible crowd sizes and many conversions were often met with scepticism. However, in the early days when numbers began to explode, a church historian encouraged Reinhard to make accurate counts, and they devised methods to do that. Helpers were also trained to counsel converts, provide follow-up literature, and report back on every commitment made. That follow-up process was mammoth. In Nigeria, 200,000 workers were trained, $1.2 million spent on follow-up material, 1000 ushers prepared for crowd control, and 1000 police officers were in attendance. On the final night, 1.6 million people attended, with 1,093,000 registered decisions.[43]

Two wonderful miracles of healing from other events were caught on camera, and are accessible on YouTube.

Firstly, an English woman, Jean Neil, had suffered terrible pain with a severe back condition and hips permanently disconnected from their sockets. One night, she was warned in a dream not to have another operation and, in a second dream, saw herself being healed by an evangelist in a vast auditorium. That miracle came to pass at a youth meeting in England, with almost 12,000 in attendance. Raised from her wheelchair she ran around the building, to the astonishment of all who knew her. A video clip of the healing includes interviews with people who had known her during the long illness. Google "Reinhard Bonnke Jean Neil miracle", or youtube.com/watch?v=SS5MQLWPoEU.

Secondly, an African pastor was killed in a car accident when his brakes failed. His wife and others prayed for him to be raised from the dead. After three days, he was taken from the morgue to a Bonnke meeting, and placed in the basement below as the meeting proceeded. After persistent prayer, he came back to life. The video follows the whole saga in solemn detail, with testimony from doctors and others, and an interview with the man. Watch it on youtube.com/watch?v=SroD02bP120.

Reinhard was keen to teach the world that anyone could preach the gospel and perform signs and wonders by the power of the Holy Spirit. He ran "Fire Conferences" in many places for that purpose.

He was a German Pentecostal evangelist, preaching by the power of the Holy Spirit to millions of Africans, and created a story that, in so many ways, is a mirror to the Book of Acts.

Carlos Anacondia 1944 –

It was the last meeting of a 60-day crusade in Cordoba, Argentina. As the exhausted evangelist finished and made his way out, he was asked to pray for a demented man lying on a stretcher. Animal-like, the man had lived in the mountains, half naked, talking to himself, his nails long, his hair unwashed and matted. Wearily, the evangelist placed his hands on him, and commanded the demons to go. Immediately the man sprang to his feet and ran out of sight. The evangelist left, trusting God to do the rest.

Six months later, that same man, in his right mind and properly dressed, told his story at a special Day of Pentecost meeting. After that prayer, he had run to the middle of a field, and screamed for five days as demons left him. On the fifth day, he returned home, completely normal.

The evangelist was Carlos Anacondia.

Commencing ministry in 1982, his impact has been so great that, when Argentinians speak of the church in Argentina, they often use the term "**before** Anacondia" or "**after** Anacondia". Missiologist, Peter Wagner has said, "Anacondia may well be the most effective city-wide interdenominational crusade evangelist of all time".[44] It is estimated that more than two million people have accepted Christ as Saviour in his crusades.[45]

Born in Argentina in 1944, married to Maria, and raising nine children, Anacondia also flourished in his business—the largest of its kind in

Argentina. But his wealth and success did not bring peace and, when he attended an evangelical meeting in 1979, both he and his wife were saved and dramatically changed.

Ten days later, he received the baptism in the Holy Spirit. He said:

> The night I received the baptism in the Holy Spirit marked my ministry and me forever... We started to pray and worship God. In a few minutes, most of the people in the place were speaking in new tongues... From the depth of my soul, I wanted to receive the baptism they were receiving. I started to cry out with all my heart, "Lord baptise me or I will die!" I had only known him for a week, and I was already experiencing incredible things...
>
> [Then] lightning fell over me from heaven. It was God's power. It threw me to the ground, and I started to speak in tongues. I was speaking one language after another, all throughout that night... [The Lord] gave me a vision that night. I saw myself in a large stadium, three stories high, speaking to 150,000 people. I was shouting at them, trying to explain what was happening to me—the baptism of the Holy Spirit... [Of course] God was giving me a vision of what was going to be "my call to preach the gospel".

From that time, he experienced the supernatural, and felt a burden for the lost. Every day, he would cry over a map of Argentina, "laying my hands on each province as I prayed for the lost souls there".[46]

In 1982, a man invited him to speak at a three-day crusade in a shantytown. The preacher's wife had, in a vision, seen Anacondia preaching, so they called him. Twenty five people turned up. The area was dangerous and, on the first night, several gang members came. But, before the night was over, they were rolling around on the ground, foaming at the mouth as they were delivered from demons. The next night, there were more deliverances, miracles and people saved. Two of the men present then invited

Carlos to run a crusade in their church in another city. And so, his crusade ministry began.

Like many other evangelists, Anacondia gathered churches of all denominations to pray and provide helpers for the campaigns, which might run as long as 60 days. Peter Wagner has noted that, while many evangelists use similar organisational methods, "the major difference is Carlos Anacondia's intentional, premeditated, high energy approach to spiritual warfare." He explained:

> ...literally hundreds of individuals are delivered from demons each of the 30 to 50 consecutive nights of a crusade. The 150 foot deliverance tent, erected behind the speaker's platform, is in operation from 8 pm to 4 am each night. Scores of teams [have been] trained to do the actual hands-on ministry...Many miraculous healings occur, souls are saved, and so great is the spiritual power that unsuspecting pedestrians passing by the crusade meeting have been known to fall down under the power of the Holy Spirit. [47]

In crusades in the city of Mar del Plata in 1983 and 1984, out of a population of four hundred thousand, there were 83 thousand converts—some 20% of the city. The most common miracle witnessed, and seen from time to time under Anacondia's ministry, was healing of teeth. It was estimated that in the Mar del Plata crusade, at least one member from every household had a tooth miraculously restored.[48]

Many different miracles occurred. On one occasion, a veteran from the Falkland Island war was healed. Half his skull had been lost in a battle, and doctors had replaced it with a platinum plate. During a meeting, the platinum plate miraculously disappeared, and bone was created in its place. When people are healed, they are asked to testify, and the stories lead to many conversions.

Signs and wonders are crucial to Carlos Anacondia. He said:

> I didn't hear about [the Lord] until somebody told me about the supernatural signs taking place in the crusade where I

was converted. It was these signs that drove me to the place where I met the Lord. Then I understood, if there were no signs of God in Argentina, people would not believe. In the gospels, supernatural signs are not for the *believers,* but for the *unbelievers*. In my country, "seeing is believing" is a must.[49]

One pastor, who had previously been involved in follow-up during crusades with other ministries, noticed a difference in Anacondia's new converts. He said:

> Before, as we visited them, they would say, "Yes, I went (to the crusade), but I'm not really interested..." or "I went to the meeting, but I don't want to change my religion..." Now, instead, when the brothers introduced themselves as coming from Carlos Anacondia's crusade, the response invariably was "glory to God!" and immediately the people would start telling some amazing story about the miracles they had received. We realised that, when the people were called to the altar to give their lives to Jesus Christ, their hearts were truly converted.[50]

Lasting, tangible fruit followed the crusades. Peter Wagner wrote:

> Several pastors showed me new sanctuaries they had constructed to contain the growth after Anacondia's crusade in their city. One showed me a basketball stadium they had been leasing for six years. Another church now holds 17 services a week in five rented theatres. Another pastor reports "a notable change of attitude among the people of our city as a result of Anacondia's ministry".[51]

The emphasis on deliverance from demons and confrontation with spiritual forces might seem strange to the western Enlightenment mind. But the similarity between the ministries of Anacondia and Philip the evangelist is obvious. And, centre stage in Anacondia's ministry, is the baptism in the Holy Spirit, and speaking in tongues. This opened the door for the "supernatural experiences" that marked his meetings, and his burden of prayer for the lost.

> NOTE CAREFULLY: In understanding the effectiveness of the Spirit baptism in these healing evangelists, we need to also recognise their unique gifts and callings, which contributed to their remarkable success. The Spirit baptism is available to everyone, but gifts and callings vary from person to person. For example, Bonnke would have had exceptional skills as entrepreneur, motivator, organiser, financier, and so on. Anacondia had a unique calling in intercessory prayer for his nation. Because our gifts and callings are different, we cannot expect everyone to be like those described here. Nevertheless, we have seen that these ministries were powerfully impacted by their own personal experience of the Holy Spirit. And we understand that each one of us has access to the same Spirit baptism, which enhances the unique gifts and abilities we possess.

The ministries we have seen so far were introduced to the baptism in the Holy Spirit typically by others from the Pentecostal movement. It is fair to ask, if the Spirit baptism is from God, couldn't he send the Spirit without human influence? Couldn't he step into, say, an untouched culture, by a sovereign act?

Well, here is an example of that—very different from the previous examples.

The Prophet Harris c1860–1929

In 1923, a young, British, Wesleyan Methodist missionary, the Rev WJ Platt, arrived in the African Ivory Coast to discover "the most wonderful and soul-stirring story in the history of Christian mission".[52] News of it created a sensation when it broke in England and France.

When Platt ventured into the Ivorian bush and its many villages, he found some 100,000 Ivorians who had abandoned idolatry, fetishes and occult practices, embraced the Christian faith, tidied up their villages, built churches and obtained a Bible (which they could not read). They faithfully observed the Sabbath, sent their children to government schools and cooperated meaningfully with the French administration.

But, most extraordinary of all, these tens of thousands had all been waiting—some for as long as ten years—for **a white man to come and teach them from their Bible.**[53]

When Pratt arrived with his Bible, they welcomed him as that white man. He was embarrassed by their display of affection. He said, "Village bands, whole villages bedecked with flags, street arches of palm-leaves, all formed part of the outward signs of the people's enthusiasm and longing".[54] He rose to the task and took the story back home, and missionaries were sent to teach the people from their Bibles, as they had asked.

How did all this happen?

The answer lies in the extraordinary ministry of one man, William Wade Harris, a Liberian Grebo tribesman. He achieved all this, without outside support, IN LESS THAN TWO YEARS!

Born to illiterate parents in about 1860, Harris was raised from the age of 12 by a Grebo uncle who, under the influence of British missionaries, had become a minister in the Methodist church. Harris became literate in Grebo and English, and committed to Christianity at 21. He worked for a while as a sailor on cargo ships, then as a bricklayer. He married in 1885, had six children, and found employment as a teacher and catechist at mission schools.

In 1909, at the age of about 50, he was jailed for political activity during unrest between the settled black Americans (former American slaves), the French colonists and indigenous tribesmen (who wanted British rule). Languishing in prison, the angel Gabriel appeared to him. Extraordinary as it may sound, academics and historians who write about Harris all record this as fact. Dr Gordon Halliburton, who, in the 1960s, devoted his PhD thesis to a study of Harris, described that visitation:

> Gabriel said, "You are not in prison. God is coming to anoint you. You will be a prophet..." Then, as [Harris] heard the words, "You are not in prison; you are in heaven", he felt the Spirit descend on him with a sound like a jet of water. It

came on him three times. He believed it was the same Spirit that came down at Pentecost, and later told [a Methodist missionary] that, just as men had then been made to talk with tongues, so now he was able to talk with tongues...⁵⁵

Gabriel had more to say. Harris was to abandon his western dress, don a white robe and turban, burn his fetishes, and compel others to burn theirs. (A fetish is a spiritual object, worshipped in many cultures because of the belief a spirit resides in it.) His message was to be: repent, be baptised, follow the true God, and receive instruction from missionary teachers and churches—both Protestant and Catholic.

Harris also taught principles he had learned as a Methodist: morality, the Sabbath, the dignity of labour, obedience to authority and living at peace with one another. And, finally, he instructed each village to build a church, obtain a Bible, and wait for a white man to come and teach them.

Burning fetishes was perilous—powerful evil spirits were associated with worship of these objects. Every village was ruled by a tribal chief, elders, a fetish priest, witches, healers, travelling fetish prophets and others. All were steeped in fetishism, and their interactions with the spirits were real. Spirits ruled all aspects of life, from placing curses to protection from curses, from healing to calling down rain. These occult practices were so real, and the fear they engendered was so great, that missionaries had enormous difficulty winning converts.

So Harris began the angel's commission in this world, so foreign to western eyes, but so familiar to his own. With flashing eyes, long beard and white robe, he walked barefooted, carrying a two metre bamboo cross, a bowl of water for baptising, a Bible, and a calabash (which rattled when shaken, and was used for singing). Several women accompanied him, some converted fetish priestesses. They also dressed in white, and assisted in singing hymns.

His method was simple. On entering a village, he and his helpers would quickly draw a crowd by singing, dancing and rattling their calabashes. Then he would preach: "Burn your fetishes and idols or fire from heaven will be upon you".⁵⁶ He would command them to repent, be baptised and believe in the one true God. Having done that, he would promise to return in the morning, to burn their fetishes and baptise them.

That, of course, was an outrageous challenge to priests and witchdoctors, and they would go away and pronounce curses to make Harris sick, mad or die. But they always failed. Harris was never known to be sick in this ministry. So, when they found him alive and well next day, the majority would acknowledge—before all—that Harris' God was greater. Piling up their fetishes, they would allow Harris to burn them. The village people, seeing their leaders convincingly subdued, would meekly follow suit. This extraordinary pattern was repeated, in village after village.

But it was rarely without incident. Once a man hid his fetishes in a bush—just in case. But "a strange fire consumed them there, and this increased the awe inspired by Harris".[57] Another man "hid his fetishes but his head began to hurt and, in a few days, he was obviously demented".[58] When another convert kept his fetish, a thunderbolt struck his room and destroyed it.[59]

Sometimes Harris would order the fetish priests to take hold of his cross. Evil spirits would manifest, and the priest would begin to shake. With a loud voice, Harris would drive out the spirits, touch his Bible on their head and, when they were free, baptise them.[60] Often, when the Bible touched a man's head, he would confess the names of people he had killed through witchcraft. Harris would then tell them to throw away all their medicines, saying, "If you go back to these medicines, YOU will die!"[61]

In one case, a man sought baptism, but Harris warned him he must first return home and destroy his fetishes, otherwise he would die when he returned. He insisted he had none, and was baptised. But, just as Harris predicted, he collapsed and died on the way home.[62]

Harris always baptised the people as soon as they had burned their fetishes, in contrast to Catholics and Protestants, who would not baptise until the convert was taught and settled in the faith. Harris said Christ told him to do this, as a safeguard against the fetishes they had destroyed. On one occasion, the Catholic priests asked Harris to stop baptising. His response was to bring hundreds of people to their mission for them to baptise.[63]

Amazing stories abound. For example:

> Megnan... a noted fetish practitioner and on intimate terms with gods and spirits [came to Harris] when his fetish spirit

told him, "I am not powerful now because God brings a man who is more powerful, so I cannot live here but must go to another country". Megnan sought out Harris and was baptised, and... remained a strong and prayerful Christian for the rest of his days.[64]

Local papers reported Harris' activities. *The Gold Coast Leader* wrote, "Those who would not harken to him but kept their fetishes from being burnt run mad on the spot, some dying under his prayers". It described how his prayers for thunder were answered, and "not less than seven-eighths of the inhabitants" were converted after throwing their fetishes into the sea or into dustbins.[65]

They continued:

> A man had been converted at Ayinose, the seat of demons, by Harris and, within two days [of] his conversion after surrendering his fetishes, he is now in possession of a Harris Bible and a cross and this fetish priest who has no knowledge of English language can now speak English language very well, abandoning the use of his mother tongue, everyone appreciates the work of Wonderful Harris."[66]

In Fresco, a British outsider, Mr Morgan, an agent for a company named Woodin and Co., wrote this report:

> Folks... were sunk in debased superstition and fetish worship, and had been so for years. In three days, this prophet-fellow—I heard him myself—changed all that. Their fetishes were burnt and what was an ordinary African coast village, steeped in superstition, became nominally a Christian town.[67]

Other supernatural incidents abounded. In the coastal village of Kraffy:

> When he touched with his (baptismal) water anyone who was hiding fetish objects or was possessed by evil spirits,

this person would become crazed and run off into the bush or struggle on the sand. Harris would drive the spirit out by putting his sheepskin scarf on the person's head and his Bible on top of that. By the same actions, Harris healed all those who were sick, and people paralysed for many years were permanently cured by him.[68]

Regarding the miraculous gift of speaking in tongues, Harris told an Irish missionary, Father Peter Harrington, that, "The gift of tongues had enabled him to preach in French—but he might 'exercise this great gift only for the preaching of the Word, and it comes and goes as the Spirit wills'".[69]

A consistent comment from old men who had witnessed the work of Harris was, "He taught us to live in peace".[70]

Why did Harris' extraordinary work remain unknown until Pratt came? The main reason was Harris' polygamy—a deeply entrenched custom throughout much of Africa to this day. Harris' first wife, on learning of the Gabriel incident and the change in Harris, thought he had gone mad, and died of grief.[71] Harris believed polygamy was culturally permissible for Africans (provided the husband loved and cared for his wives). So he took several who accompanied him in his ministry. The Methodist missionaries consistently and fiercely opposed him on this. As a result, in spite of Harris' tremendous successes, the missionaries held him at arm's length, and did little to help him or publicise his work.

Many missiologists and observers have written about Harris, astounded by the numbers of converts, the demolition of fetish worship, and the extraordinary miracles.[72] They typically link his success to the social and political issues of the time, and Harris' grasp of local customs. But there were other indigenous preachers and prophets of that time, whose work did not enjoy the same spectacular results.

Those commentators are typically conservative, missionary based, non-Pentecostals. They gloss over Harris' spiritual prison encounter, and the significance of his Holy Spirit baptism and speaking in tongues. But, in fact, that dramatic experience is the issue that set Harris apart from other African evangelists of that time. All of them, while very aware of the problems of fetish worship and occultism, were virtually powerless to deal with it. Harris went straight for that 'jugular', in the power of the Spirit and, in that power, conquered it decisively.

Note that Harris, instructed by his Methodist missionary-trained uncle, would not have received teaching on the baptism in the Holy Spirit and speaking in tongues. His experience came unexpectedly, and he had no theology to go with it. So he did not preach it and, as far as I can see from the reports, the Spirit baptism with speaking in tongues was not evident among his converts.

Harris' commission and equipping was a sovereign act of God. A committed and educated Christian, languishing in a cell, Harris was chosen by God, commissioned by Gabriel, and equipped by the power of the baptism in the Holy Spirit, with speaking in tongues. The result was very consistent with the experiences we find in the Book of Acts.

Wigglesworth, Bosworth, Bonnke, Anacondia, Harris: all received the baptism in the Holy Spirit and speaking in tongues. All were revolutionised by that experience.

There are many more, who would fill as many pages but, for the sake of space, here is a thumbnail sketch of just a few others.

Oral Roberts 1918–2009

Born in Oklahoma to godly parents of part Cherokee heritage, as a young man, Oral Roberts was miraculously healed of stuttering and tuberculosis. He began preaching at 18, and about a year later, was baptised in the Holy Spirit and spoke in tongues, at a camp meeting in Sulphur, Oklahoma.

Roberts was deeply stirred by 3 John 2 (KJV), "Beloved, I wish above all things that thou mayest prosper and be in health, even as thy soul prospereth." He became convinced God's desire was for people to be healed and prosper, and that his message must be "God is a good God".

But, after 12 years of ministry, he became restless in his faith. Over several months he fasted and prayed, until eventually he heard God say, "From this hour you will heal the sick and cast out devils by my power."[73]

So he did, and many were healed and saved at his meetings. Miracles included healing from deafness (a number of children from a deaf school were able to hear for the first time), tuberculosis and much more. He obtained a large tent and transported it from town to town, becoming known as the nation's "faith healer". Laying his right hand on sick people, he would pray for thousands, the prayer line sometimes more than a mile long. After this, he would be so exhausted that he had to be carried away. He was featured in both *Look* and *Life* magazines, America's most popular magazines of the time.

He came to Australia in 1956. The wife of my pastor told me she saw a goitre disappear from the neck of a woman as he prayed. Another lady told me she and her twin sister had been born with eyes crossed. But, as very small girls at the time, within a week of prayer from Roberts, their eyes became straight. Unfortunately, the press gave Roberts appalling and fabricated reviews and, in the face of threats to burn down the tent and pressure from his insurance company, he left, vowing never to return.[74]

Oral Roberts was also well known for building the first Christian University (Billy Graham gave the prayer of dedication), and a hospital where staff ministered both medical and spiritual healing.

George Jeffreys 1889–1962

Born in a Welsh mining village, George Jeffreys was converted during the Welsh Revival of 1904–05. In 1910, he heard of people speaking about the baptism in the Holy Spirit and speaking in tongues in Sunderland. Initially sceptical, he became convinced when he saw the change it brought to his nephew. So, he too was baptised in the Holy Spirit and, at the same time, was healed of a debilitating speech impediment and facial paralysis that had hindered him from preaching.

In 1913, he began preaching and witnessed his first healing miracle: a woman with a diseased foot that was to be amputated was healed. That miracle brought widespread attention.

With a band of helpers, he formed a movement called Elim, which later linked with another healing evangelist, Aimee Semple-McPherson. In 1926, from Portsmouth, he wrote to a friend:

"I am having the time of my life. Souls are continually flocking to Christ, most startling and marvellous healings, while yesterday hundreds were turned away from the Town Hall an hour before the starting time".[75]

Those crowds increased through the late 1920s and early 1930s. Jeffreys:

"...began his 1930 campaign in Birmingham in a Congregational church in the city. Within five days, the church was filled to capacity, and so the meetings were moved to the Town Hall, then to the Embassy Skating Rink which sat eight thousand. In the final weeks of the campaign, they moved to the massive Bingley Hall Exhibition Centre, which had seating for 15,000. Jeffreys preached 26 meetings in that hall, and the number of converts during the entire campaign was recorded at ten thousand."[76]

A comprehensive 200 page book, *Healing Rays,* presents Jeffreys' theology of divine healing. He builds a solid scriptural case, and adds the witnesses of early church leaders such as Justin Martyr, Irenaeus, Tertullian, Origen, Clement, the Waldenses, the Moravians, Zinzendorf, the Huguenots, Martin Luther, Wesley and Dr E Stanley Jones. He concludes with many stories of miracles seen under his own ministry including healings from insanity, sleeping sickness, blindness and seizure, epilepsy and cancer. As we read earlier, shortly before his death he prayed his mantle would be passed on to Reinhard Bonnke.

John G Lake 1870–1935

An early Pentecostal leader, Lake was influential in bringing Pentecostalism to Africa, where he established the Apostolic Faith Mission, now found in 29 countries. He wrote of his baptism in the Holy Spirit:

When the phenomena had passed, the glory of it remained in my soul. I found that my life began to manifest a varied range of the gifts of the Spirit. And I spoke in tongues by the power of God, and God flowed through me with a new force. Healings were more of a powerful order...

Tongues have been to me... the making of my ministry. It is that peculiar communication with God... [that] reveals to my soul the truth I utter to you day by day in the ministry.[77]

Lake studied divine healing under John Alexander Dowie, and many were healed under his ministry. Queen Wilhelmina of Holland asked him to pray for her after six miscarriages and, a year later in 1909 she gave birth to her only child, a daughter, who became Queen Julianna, ruling from 1948 until 1980. In Spokane, Washington, Lake set up healing rooms where people could be prayed for. It was reported that as many as one hundred thousand people received healing as a result.[78] Because the results were so controversial, a government investigation was launched, but was soon called off when interviews with healed people soon verified the reports.

John Wimber 1934–1997

Founder of the Vineyard Movement, Wimber was a prominent healing minister from the early 70s until the mid-90s. Having experienced the baptism in the Holy Spirit, he endeavoured to walk a middle line between Pentecostals and evangelicals, focusing on the gifts of the Spirit (healing, prophecy, tongues etc.) and the baptism of the Holy Spirit, but was of the view that speaking in tongues was not the only evidence of receiving the Holy Spirit. It is hard to nail down his doctrine, but *Direction, A Mennonite Brethren forum,* noted that "in [Wimber's] teachings, he suggests that those who speak in tongues are liberated and have power". I include Wimber here because he and his followers certainly had experience with the Holy Spirit. Speaking in tongues was an accepted part of their ministry, and they were influential in demonstrating what this chapter is all about: signs, wonders and miracles by the power of the Holy Spirit.

Francis MacNutt 1925–2020

Francis MacNutt was one of the first Catholic priests to be involved in the Catholic Charismatic Movement. Before his charismatic days, he was already a prominent figure, standing at six feet four inches (1.93 m), with a bachelor's degree from Harvard, a master's from the Catholic University of America, and a PhD from The Dominicans' Aquinas Institute of Theology. During his time at Catholic University, he felt called to the priesthood. He was especially interested in preaching, joining the Dominican Order (the Order of Preachers), and was ordained in 1956. Teaching the subject for seven years at the Dominican Seminary in Dubuque, Iowa, he also wrote three books on preaching, and helped establish the (now defunct) Catholic Homiletic Society.

In 1967, 11 years after his ordination, and the year the Catholic Charismatic Movement began, he was invited to a week-long Charismatic Protestant retreat. There he met two charismatic leaders, Agnes Sanford and Tommy Tyson. Agnes Sanford was the daughter of a Presbyterian missionary and, in spite of having been taught that spiritual gifts were no longer available, became prominent on the subject of inner healing, a decade before the charismatic movement emerged. Tommy Tyson was a Methodist pastor/evangelist, who was baptised in the Spirit in 1952 and later took a position as director of spiritual life at the new Oral Roberts University. Through their prayers, McNutt received the baptism in the Holy Spirit, bringing a dramatic change to his ministry. Sanford prophesied McNutt would be used by God to bring healing ministry back to the Catholic Church, and that was soon fulfilled.

He began to focus on healing through prayer, and soon saw people healed from many kinds of sicknesses: asthma, allergies, cancer, mental and demonic issues and more. Resigning from his teaching position, he travelled and, in a few years, had ministered in 31 countries among both Catholic and Protestant churches. He also became a founder of the Association of Christian Therapists, encouraging the medical profession to engage in Christian healing ministry. A prolific writer, he wrote two books on this subject. His first, *Healing* (published in 1976), became a classic, selling more than a million copies.

Controversially, he left the Catholic Church in 1980 to marry. He and his wife ministered healing together for many years, under the name Christian

Healing Ministries (christianhealingmin.org). In 1993, their marriage was given dispensation by the Catholic Church, and their ministry expanded further into the Catholic arena. In fact, in 2007, the Vatican renewal office even sponsored a six-day conference with him in Jacksonville, to bring healing to the worldwide church. Some 450 Catholic leaders from 42 countries attended.

Many people around the world owe a debt of gratitude to this dedicated Catholic man—for miracles of healing from physical and emotional suffering. Few of them would know that the spiritual gifts that brought their healing, were birthed in a week-long charismatic Protestant retreat in 1967, where he was baptised in the Holy Spirit.

Our final story has a different emphasis. We need to ask the question, is healing the realm of only the specialists, or can everyone play a part? This couple provides an answer.

Charles and Frances Hunter 1920–2010; 1916–2009
God, I'll make a deal with you. I'll give you all of me...in exchange for all of you.
Frances Hunter

Charles and Frances Hunter brought a shift in the way healing ministry was performed. Prior to their day, much of the ministry of divine healing was left to prominent healing evangelists such as we have seen. The Hunters taught everyday Christians that they, themselves, could lay hands on the sick and expect healing.

The Spirit baptism was the key that opened the door to their far-reaching ministry. Prior to that experience, they had already enjoyed a successful preaching ministry in non-charismatic churches. But when they received the Spirit baptism and spoke in tongues, their upcoming bookings were cancelled.

However, they did retain one engagement with a Christian men's group— The Full Gospel Businessmen's Fellowship International. Frances was their first ever woman preacher. More than five hundred were baptised in the Holy Spirit that night. Invitations then flooded in, as the Hunters connected with the booming charismatic movement.

In 1973, they ministered at a Southern Baptist church whose pastor, and his family, had been baptised in the Holy Spirit. During one of the services, the Hunters announced that God had just instructed them to conduct a healing service—something they had never done before—and to bring the sick. Two days later, an 11 year old girl was healed from deafness in one ear, the pastor's son was healed from stuttering, and another young girl born with cerebral palsy was able to walk. Her legs straightened with no further need for braces or crutches.

From that time, healing became an integral part of their ministry, particularly by encouraging and training Christians to pray themselves for the sick. Their slogan was, "If we can, you can". In 1980, to spread the message worldwide, they prepared a 14-hour series of videotapes, teaching people to administer divine healing.

Next, with the help of a Pittsburgh Christian TV station, they ran a "Healing Explosion" workshop in a 10,000-seat auditorium. More than a thousand people were trained to be part of the healing team. During the event, more than 5,000 people sought prayer for the Spirit baptism after which the healing team prayed for the sick. There were many healing miracles, with doctors on hand to verify them.

Over the next five years, they ran more than a 150 Healing Explosions throughout America and then overseas where crowds sometimes numbered 40–60,000. There were many, many miracles, and multitudes were baptised in the Holy Spirit.

Charles and Frances Hunter: an everyday couple, baptised in the Holy Spirit, who offered God everything they had, enjoyed many supernatural things God offered them, and passed them on to anyone who would listen.

Lay People

I began with the story of a friend who, as a little boy, cried when the minister said Jesus' miracles happened no more. His name is Peter. A sad story, but fortunately Peter's passion didn't die. As an adult, he experienced the Spirit baptism and later began to pray for healing miracles. One day, he prayed for an elderly lady as she entered our church with a walking frame. The pain left her and she no longer needed the frame. She continually sang the praises of God and my friend, and became a devoted member of the congregation.

Peter is a quiet, unassuming person. He doesn't preach or draw attention to himself but is typical of millions of lay people throughout the world who quietly move around in the power of the Holy Spirit, praying for miracles. Here are a few more of his stories.

In Fiji:
A brother and sister, about 10 or 11 years old, had never been able to speak because their tongues rolled back in their mouths. Both were instantly healed after prayer.

A seven year old boy had a very painful wrist. Peter prayed about seven times, and nothing happened. He called a friend to join him and they prayed several more times. Then the boy's hand and arm became strong. The following day he was completely well, and could be given "whizzies"—held by the hands and spun around.

While praying for a young mother, her non-Christian husband became terrified when he saw two huge shining angels, one on each side of Peter. The man later gave his life to Jesus, and was baptised at the beach.

In Sri Lanka:
Peter went into a gift shop and saw the owner limping around on crutches. She agreed to receive prayer, and she and her husband were completely astonished when she was immediately healed. They were not Christians.

In Melbourne:
He prayed for a woman at a church in Wyndham Vale. An operation had been scheduled to remedy plantar fasciitis, which caused unbearable pain in her heel. After prayer, she stomped her foot again and again, and shouted out to her husband to come and see, saying, "I've been healed!"

A friend in another city had pneumonia, and agreed to Peter's offer to pray—over the phone. As he was praying, he heard his friend take a huge gasp of air. He hadn't been able to do that for weeks, and went away amazed and grateful.

At an Awakening meeting in Melbourne, Peter prayed for a young man in his mid-20s. He was instantly healed of a longstanding hamstring strain. He yelled out to his friends, and was doing squats and running about, "showing off".

Summarising

We began with western scepticism towards miracles, and the influence of Enlightenment rationalism. Then we traced the lives of healing evangelists from the last century, and the close link between their remarkable miracles and Spirit baptism. After that, a short story of a lay person who, despite a setback as a boy, quietly goes about in the power of the Holy Spirit, ministering divine healing.

Now here is my point. Evangelists or lay people in *non*-Pentecostal/*non*-charismatic circles **rarely demonstrate this type of miracle ministry.** Signs, wonders and miracles are **conspicuous by their absence.** There are many wonderful, godly evangelists in these church streams, but they are certainly not known for miraculous healings. Similarly there are godly pastors, and insightful teachers. But Paul's "demonstration of the Spirit's power", is absent.

Once again, we note that the difference between the two streams is their view of the baptism in the Holy Spirit. So, we have what you could reasonably call, a "God-sized difference".

— — —

That concludes the analysis of our four measures, and **Part One, The Facts**.

This, then, is a good point to reflect. We have seen that:

- Numerical growth of Pentecostals is four times that of mainline and evangelical denominations.
- Praise and worship songs are almost exclusively from Pentecostal and charismatic sources.
- Pentecostal churches recorded the highest result on 30 of the 33 NCLS criteria.

- The healing and miracle ministries of the last century came, with few exceptions, from Pentecostal and charismatic ministries.

Each of these measuring sticks revealed stark differences between the two streams. We need to ask the question: "Is this exceptional, or are there other outstanding differences between denominations? Earlier, I referred to characteristic differences between denominations: Baptists practise immersion, others sprinkling; Presbyterians emphasise predestination, others don't; and so on. But if those things make any difference it is not apparent. There are no unambiguous differences—until you compare Pentecostals and Protestants. There are always anomalies, of course but, measured across the board, the results are unequivocal.

If we consider those results to be God-sized, we must look for a God-sized reason. The Pentecostal belief in the baptism in the Holy Spirit, God's provision of spiritual power, is surely the logical candidate.

NEXT

The next section is simple: what does the Bible say about all this? If results from our four measuring sticks don't find foundation in the Bible, there is something wrong, and we need to fix it. That is where we must go now—to Part Two, the Theology.

PART TWO

THE THEOLOGY

What the Bible says

Before we tackle this, we need to remember that the church holds two conflicting views on the Holy Spirit. As explained in Chapter 1, Pentecostals (and some others) believe the baptism in the Holy Spirit is given to those who ask, **after salvation**. Others say the gift is given to all, without exception, **as a part of salvation.**

As you would expect, readers with the second view will question the Pentecostal view, and those questions call for replies that can be very lengthy. But those holding the Pentecostal view don't usually need those lengthy answers so, to cover both bases, I will proceed as follows:

In the next chapters, I will provide just a **simple, brief** biblical explanation of:

- the Spirit baptism as a separate experience from salvation (Chapter 6)
- the link between Spirit baptism and speaking in tongues (Chapter 7)

And you will find a **detailed discussion** of the important and more controversial issues in the Appendix, as follows:

APPENDIX A: The Holy Spirit–where he ought to be. An illuminating compilation of New Testament Holy Spirit verses.

APPENDIX B: How and why knowledge of the Holy Spirit was kept in the dark for centuries.

APPENDIX C: Explaining the Spirit baptism as a discrete experience: a detailed study.

APPENDIX D: Fruit of the Spirit–should Pentecostals and charismatics demonstrate more?

APPENDIX E: Is "tongues" the "evidence"? Includes compelling Old Testament insight.

APPENDIX F: Common questions: Do Pentecostals neglect Christ? Are tongues authentic languages? Are tongues linked to the occult? Health and wealth teaching. Is Pentecostalism divisive? Did Church Fathers believe gifts had ceased?

If you are not sure which way to go, I suggest you just proceed with Chapters 6 and 7, then go to the Appendix if you need more.

God is going to call you to do something that is beyond yourself, so you will rely on his power.

A WOMMACK

The Lord is slow to anger but great in power.

NAHUM 1:3

CHAPTER 6

SALVATION AND SPIRIT BAPTISM–THE DIFFERENCE

When you join the army, two important things happen. First, on enlistment, a formal agreement, a signed paper, makes your place in the army **official**. Second, a weapon placed in your hands makes your task **effective**.

You join up, then you are equipped.

God works that way too.

First, a spiritual agreement between you and God makes your place in his kingdom **official**. Then a 'weapon' is offered to you: the glorious, incomparable power of the Holy Spirit, to make you **effective** in his service.

This pattern is the same in Old and New Testaments–with a couple of important differences. Here it is in more detail:

Our entry: To secure our entry to the kingdom of God, we repent from our sins and receive God's forgiveness, by faith. A substitute/proxy takes the punishment for our sin. In the Old Testament, an animal was that substitute; in the New Testament Jesus became the substitute.

Our weapon: the Holy Spirit. This power is provided because God's unchanging method of operation is to give us tasks beyond our natural ability. The Old Testament establishes this approach, laying an important foundation for the New.

Holy Spirit incidents in the Old Testament can easily be found using a search for the word, "Spirit". We find that, over a several thousand years' time span, they were not plentiful. There were enough, though, to give us a picture, as follows.

In Exodus 31:30, Bezalel was filled with the Spirit to make artistic designs for the temple. The Spirit of the Lord came on Othniel to equip him for war (Judges 3:9–11). Similarly for Gideon (Judges 6:34). David, too, was equipped by the Spirit to be king (1 Samuel 16:13). Three times the Spirit of the Lord came on Samson—to defeat a lion, to kill 30 Philistines and, later, 1000 Philistines (see Judges 14 and 15). And the Spirit of the Lord came on Ezekiel and told him to prophesy to the people (Ezekiel 11:5–9)

In each of these cases, we can see three things: a specific **purpose** for the outpouring, a tangible **experience** of the Spirit, and a dramatic **result**. We might expect a similar pattern in the New Testament. Look for it when we get there.

Before we do, there are two other different but important Old Testament outpourings which set a pattern for the New Testament. The first occurred when Moses' 70 elders were equipped for service (Numbers 11:16–26), and the second when King Saul (and his men) were similarly set apart and empowered (1 Samuel 10:5–6 and 1 Samuel 19:20–23). Moses was worn out with the task of leading the people, so God took the Spirit that was on him, and placed it on 70 elders to share that burden. Note that, when this happened, they all prophesied as did two of the 70 still in the camp. Saul's story was similar as God was calling him to serve as king. Twice the Spirit fell on him and his men, and they also prophesied. These two incidents set the scene for the rest of our story.

A key prophecy in Joel 2: 28-30 prepares us for changes in New Testament Holy Spirit outpourings. Joel declares boldly "[In the last days] I will pour out my Spirit on all people... Even on my servants, both men and women, I will pour out my Spirit in those days."

Note the promise: I will pour out my Spirit on ALL people. In the Old Testament the Spirit fell on SOME people: Bezalel, Othniel, David, etc. Now a promise of an explosion of this power, the Spirit available to **ALL**: a vast and exciting shift that embraces you and me.

Another difference also becomes obvious. In the Old Testament the Spirit fell on people who were **not expecting it**– a sovereign act of God. In the New Testament, while the **promise** is to **all** believers, it now becomes incumbent on the believer to **ask** for the Spirit (Luke 11:13: "... your Father in heaven [will] give the Holy Spirit to those who ask him!"). We are to ask and receive this gift by **believing** "(Galatians 3:5: does God give you his Spirit ... by the works of the law, or by your **believing** what you heard?") A universal promise, it is conditional on our asking and believing. That is the pattern we must follow.

We now need to establish from the New Testament that salvation, being born of the Spirit, is indeed a separate experience from that of receiving the baptism of the Holy Spirit. A number of passages do this but, for this brief analysis, we will use just two. (See Appendix C for more.)

The first is Acts 8:5-17. (Read this through, this is an important passage.) Philip the evangelist went to Samaria and preached. Miraculous signs followed him. The paralysed and lame were healed, and demons were cast out, creating amazement and joy in the city—as you can imagine. We are then told that the people **believed** Philip as he preached the gospel, and they were **baptised**. Clearly they were saved at this point (see Mark 16:16), born of the Spirit (John 3:16). However, several days later, the apostles came down and prayed for them to receive the Holy Spirit for, we are told, "the Holy Spirit had not yet come on any of them; they had simply been baptised in the name of the Lord Jesus." (Acts 8:16) Obviously, for these Samaritans, receiving the Spirit was quite separate from their salvation experience several days prior.

The second example unfolds in Acts 19:1-6. Paul found some disciples in Ephesus, and asked an important question: "Did you receive the Holy Spirit when you believed?" The question clearly implies that it is possible to believe and not receive the Holy Spirit; otherwise it does not make sense. In addition, after further interaction with the twelve men, we learn that "when Paul placed his hands on them, the Holy Spirit came on them, and they spoke in tongues and prophesied." (Verse 6) There was an interval, however small, between their believing and baptism, and then Paul laying hands on them to receive the Spirit. Again, two separate experiences.

Note also that the **purpose** of the Holy Spirit is different from salvation. Jesus told the disciples, "You will receive **power** when the Holy Spirit comes on you; and you will be my witnesses..." (Acts 1:8) Salvation provides forgiveness of sin, and entry to the Kingdom of God. The Spirit baptism is an empowering weapon, making us effective in service.

One more thing. As I mentioned above, the **tangible and dramatic** Old Testament outpourings ought to set the stage for the New Testament. Do they? Are New Testament outpourings tangible and dramatic? Yes indeed. Look at the above examples. When the apostles prayed for the Samaritans, a wily magician named Simon was watching on. So entranced was he by what he saw that he offered money so that "everyone on whom I lay my hands may receive the Holy Spirit" (Acts 8:19). He had already seen deliverance from demons and healing miracles, so receiving the Holy Spirit must have been something very striking and tangible indeed. And, when Paul prayed for the Ephesians, as we have seen, they spoke in tongues and prophesied. Clearly tangible, dramatic experiences.

Those supernatural experiences are, of course, quite unlike those anticipated at salvation. Yes, the new birth is a regenerating work of the Holy Spirit and brings with it the indwelling Holy Spirit. Paul makes this plain in Romans 8:9: "You... are in the realm of the Spirit, if indeed the Spirit of God lives in you. And if anyone does not have the Spirit of Christ, they do not belong to Christ." Clearly, belonging to Christ, being born again, means having the Holy Spirit. But, as explained in chapter one, the **baptism** in the Holy Spirit, the **filling** of the Holy Spirit, is a different kind of relationship with the Holy Spirit. It is a dramatic and tangible empowerment for evangelism, and it unlocks the miraculous gifts of the Holy Spirit.

So there it is. As in the army, our place in God's kingdom is secured by a formal, spiritual agreement. In that process, God deals with our sin which had separated us from him.

Having done that, God provides us with our weapon, the incomparable power of the Holy Spirit, a glorious, sufficient provision, to make our lives effective in all he calls us to do.

— — —

NEXT: We are now faced with an essential, but profoundly simple question: We can't see the Holy Spirit; how do we **know** when we have received him?

The answer is straightforward, but controversial.

Here we go.

If speaking in tongues were taken out of the Pentecostal movement, perhaps nine-tenths of the opposition would disappear; Pentecost might possibly become the most popular religious movement in the Protestant world.

CARL BRUMBACK

Extraordinary claims require extraordinary evidence.

CARL SAGAN

CHAPTER 7

IS TONGUES THE EVIDENCE?

Six hundred million people claim to have been baptised in the Holy Spirit. How do they know?

The Spirit baptism is a personal experience between us and God the Holy Spirit. You can imagine that individual impressions of such a dramatic experience might differ from person to person; different personality types and life experiences can colour the way people interpret what has happened. To understand it all, we need a reliable, unchanging guidebook. That, of course, has to be the Bible, and that is where we go to tackle this.

Once again, we gather references to the Spirit of God falling, looking for evidence. If we find a pattern it is reasonable that we should expect the same today, for God is unchanging. And, once again, we will begin in the Old Testament to lay our foundation.

In a nutshell, when we collect evidence in this way, we discover that Old Testament outpourings fall into two groups:

- outpourings for specific, one-off events
- outpourings for ongoing service

In both groups, we always find tangible confirming evidence.

In the previous chapter, we examined a number of Old Testament outpourings and their effects: Bezalel, to make artistic designs for the temple, Othniel and Gideon to equip them for war, Samson to fight a lion and the Philistines, and Ezekiel to prophesy.

All were called to tasks beyond their natural abilities and God provided the Holy Spirit for that. In each case, we saw vital, tangible, confirming evidence of the Spirit's power.

Now the crunch. The pattern of the other two outpourings (for ongoing service) is different. The immediate, outward, confirming evidence is **supernaturally inspired speech**.

Here are the passages–study them for yourself.

- "When the **Spirit** rested on [Moses' 70 elders, for service], they **prophesied**" (Two others in the camp also prophesied.) (Numbers 11:16–26)
- "The Spirit of God came powerfully on [Saul] and he joined in [the prophets'] prophesying." Similarly on his men. (1 Samuel 10:5–6 and 1 Samuel 19:20-23)

We see that the tangible evidence of these outpourings was prophecy–occurring several times. When the Holy Spirit fell, its astonishing effect was such that the men spontaneously broke into inspired speech.

And that is the pattern unfolding in the New Testament.

Fascinating confirmation now emerges in Joel 2: 28-30, which we looked at in the last chapter. Joel prophesies boldly: "And [in the last days], I will pour out my Spirit on all people. Your sons and daughters will **prophesy**..." Prophecy is the first thing that comes to Joel's mind when he proclaims the outpouring of the Holy Spirit.

How does this pattern develop in the New Testament? It commences with three incidents surrounding the birth of Jesus.

Firstly, in Luke 1:41-43. Mary, pregnant with Jesus, visits Elizabeth who, "filled with the Holy Spirit", declares Mary to be "the mother of my Lord". That statement, "mother of my Lord" is prophetic, inspired by the Holy Spirit. Elizabeth could not have known that fact. Her infilling with the Holy Spirit immediately led to prophecy. Secondly, in Luke 1:67-76 we read Zechariah "was filled with the Holy Spirit and prophesied". A clear link. And, thirdly, in Luke 2:27-35 Simeon "moved by the Spirit", took baby Jesus in his arms and spoke words that were clearly prophetic. Three different people, all under the Spirit, break into prophecy.

Now the final section–the Day of Pentecost and subsequent events.

On the Day of Pentecost, the Holy Spirit fell on the disciples–more than 120 of them. The evidence? A sound of a violent wind from heaven, tongues of fire resting on the people, and "All of them were filled with the Holy Spirit and began to speak in other tongues as the Spirit enabled them." Noise, fire and tongues.

It is significant that Peter addressed the bewildered crowds by quoting Joel: "I will pour out my Spirit on all people. Your sons and daughters will **prophesy**..." Peter equated Joel's promise of "prophecy" to speaking in tongues, and this became the characteristic New Testament evidence of receiving the Holy Spirit. It is seen in two more passages as follows.

Firstly, Acts 10:45-46: The disciples preaching to Gentiles "were astonished that the gift of the Holy Spirit had been poured out even on the Gentiles. For they heard them speaking in tongues and praising God." Speaking in tongues was the defining characteristic of the experience. It was so compelling that it persuaded the sceptical disciples that God had now welcomed the once despised Gentiles into the fold–a radical turn around for them.

Secondly, Acts 19:6: Paul, with some disciples at Ephesus: "When Paul placed his hands on them, the Holy Spirit came on them, and they spoke in tongues and prophesied." Once again, tongues and, in this case, alongside prophecy.

Two other passages describe receiving the Holy Spirit, but confirming evidence is not quite as strong. In Acts 8, the Holy Spirit fell on the Samaritans with no mention of supernatural evidence, except that the wicked Simon the magician "saw that the Holy Spirit was given at the laying on of the apostles' hands". (Acts 8:18) It must have been visible and appealing, however, for he offered money "so that everyone on whom I lay my hands may receive the Holy Spirit". (Verse 19) Most Bible commentators suggest it was speaking in tongues. The second incident relates to Paul in Ephesus, described in Acts 9:1-17. The disciple, Ananias, was sent by Jesus to pray for Paul's sight and for him to receive the Holy Spirit. We are not told what happened right then but we do know that Paul said later: "I thank God that I speak in tongues more than all of you." (1 Corinthians 14:18) So, in the light of the other events, it was likely he received the ability when Ananias came to him.

A table summary of all the above events brings out a clear trend:

WHO	EVIDENCE
70 elders	Prophecy
2 other elders	Prophecy
Saul	Prophecy
Saul's men	Prophecy
Saul another time	Prophecy
Joel	Prophecy
Elizabeth	Prophecy
Zechariah	Prophecy
Simeon	Prophecy
The Pentecost 120	Tongues, wind, fire,
Cornelius	Tongues, praise
Ephesians	Tongues, prophecy
Samaritans	Tongues probable
Paul	Tongues plausible

Summarising all that, we can now say the infilling of the Holy Spirit is a dramatic, observable, spiritual experience, the effect being such that the recipient responds with **Spirit-inspired speech**.

In the **Old Testament** the Spirit-inspired speech was **prophecy**.

In the **New Testament** it became **tongues**.

Now the big question.

From that information, can we say, categorically, that you **must** speak in tongues to be filled with the Spirit or that, if you have not spoken in tongues, you have not been baptised in the Holy Spirit? Obviously there is no clear, direct Bible statement like that.

However, one incident goes close. When the Gentiles received the Spirit and spoke in tongues:

> The [Jews] who had come with Peter were astonished that the gift of the Holy Spirit had been poured out even on Gentiles. **For** they heard them speaking in tongues and praising God. Acts 10:44-46

It was tongues that convinced the sceptical Jews that the despised Gentiles had received the Spirit and were now accepted by God. Gentile conversion was an extraordinary shock for the church, and an extraordinary measure was needed to convince them it was God's doing.

That incident, together with the above table, is clearly compelling, and must not be ignored. We have no good reason to expect that receiving the Holy Spirit today should be different, and should have a high expectation that the same thing will happen when we seek the Holy Spirit. It also follows that a person who claims to have the experience without speaking in tongues ought to have a rethink, acknowledge that something is missing, and pursue this wonderful, confirming, God-ordained and God-given blessing.

Have you received the baptism in the Holy Spirit? If not, maybe you can right now. A helpful practical and biblical guide is located at the end of Chapter 13.

— — —

NEXT:

We have looked at the dramatic effects of the Spirit baptism, and its scriptural foundations. What about its *pedigree*? Is this truly a *newcomer*, after an absence of almost two thousand years? What was happening all that time?

John MacArthur says: "Today's [Pentecostals and charismatics], largely unaware of the history of the practice, seem to think of glossolalia as more or less a mainstream practice dating back in an uninterrupted line of succession to the apostolic era of the church. Not so."[79]

Is he correct? What does history tell us?

That's where we go now.

PART THREE

THE HISTORY

In this section we will address these questions:

- How did giants of the faith see the Holy Spirit?
- Was there any speaking in tongues in the 1800 years before Pentecostalism emerged?
- How did the Pentecostal understanding come about?
- How did it spread through the world?

First, giants of the faith.

Since the Reformation, there have been many famous revivalists and faith giants: Wesley, Booth, Moody and others, who had wide and dramatic spiritual influence in their day. They would have read about the baptism in the Spirit in the Bible many times. Did they experience it? How did they understand it?

A fascinating journey, filled with intriguing stories and facts, much of which has rarely seen the light of day.

The future is unknowable, but the past should give us hope. ... Study history, study history. In history lies all the secrets of statecraft.

WINSTON CHURCHILL

CHAPTER 8
THE HOLY SPIRIT AND THE RENOWNED REVIVALISTS

GEORGE FOX 1624–1691

George Fox was a prophet, outspoken and uncompromising. He called the church of his day, "The false church, ruled upon the beast and dragon's power" and criticised its leaders for their "second-hand faith, sin-excusing doctrine, hireling ministry, and compromise with political powers".[80] For that stance, Fox was imprisoned about a hundred times. His followers were imprisoned too, and literally hundreds died in prison.

His disciples became known as Quakers, or the Society of Friends–friends of Jesus, as in John 15:15.

Fox consistently taught that the leading of the Spirit should be preeminent in every Christian life. He called it the "inner light", based on John 1:4, "In him (Jesus) was life, and that life was the light of all mankind." He believed that, just as writers of scripture were inspired by the Spirit, in the same way, those who wish to understand the scripture must rely on that same Spirit. Because of these convictions, Quaker meetings were run simply by listening to the Spirit. And today, in the same way, Friends Societies have no order of service. The congregation sits in silence until a person is moved by the Spirit to pray, read a scripture, prophesy (give a revelation) or sing.

Fox and his early followers also experienced dramatic activities of the

Spirit including healing, deliverance from demons, divine judgment on persecutors, resurrection from the dead, visions and speaking in tongues. He kept a journal, which recorded many of these events. He said:

> "Many great and wonderful things were produced by the heavenly power in those days; for the Lord made bare his omnipotent arm, and manifested his power to the astonishment of many; through the healing virtue of the power, many were delivered from great sicknesses, and the devils were made subject through his name; of which particular instances might be given, beyond what this unbelieving age is able to receive or bear."[81]

Here are some of his journal extracts describing healing and deliverance from demonic spirits:

> While I was in [Guildford, Surrey], James Claypole of London ... was suddenly taken very ill with so violent a kidney stone attack that he could neither stand or lie down; and with extreme pain cried out like a woman in childbirth ... I was moved to lay my hand upon him and prayed the Lord to rebuke his infirmity. As I laid my hand on him, the Lord's power went through him; and by faith in that power, his pain eased quickly and he soon fell into a sleep. When he awoke, the stone passed from him like dirt; and he was so well, that the next day he rode with me twenty five miles in a coach, though each previous kidney stone attacks forced him to bed for two to four weeks at a time.[82]

> ...a woman with two others came to me (while imprisoned in Nottingham jail) and said that she had been possessed for thirty-two years; and the priests had kept her and had kept fasting days about her, and could not do her any good ... When I came out of prison, I told Friends to bring her to

> Mansfield ... [where] the poor woman would make such a noise in roaring, and sometimes lying along upon her belly upon the ground with her spirit and roaring and voice, that it would set all Friends in a heat and sweat. [They prayed around her and eventually] ...it was done ... she lifted up her hands and said, 'Ten thousand praises to the Lord' ... And then the world's professors, priests, and teachers never could call us any more false prophets, deceivers, or witches after, but it did a great deal of good in the country among people in relation to the Truth and to the stopping the mouths of the world and their slanderous aspersions.[83]

Fox also experienced many visions. During one of his imprisonments, God revealed to him a great plague was about to fall on London, followed by a great fire. The terrible bubonic plague of 1665 struck while he was in prison, and the Great Fire of London broke out on the day of his release in 1666.[84]

He also mentioned speaking in tongues in their meetings. He wrote:

> And while waiting upon the Lord in silence ...in our diligent waiting and fear of his name, and hearkening to his word, we received often the pouring down of the spirit upon us, and the gift of God's holy eternal spirit as in the days of old, and our hearts were made glad, and our tongues loosed, and our mouths opened, and we spake with new tongues, as the Lord gave us utterance and as his spirit led us, which was poured down upon us, on sons and daughters ...[85]

Fox's Legacy

Fox, though totally familiar with the power of the Spirit, did not formalise a doctrine about the Spirit baptism, or the evidence of receiving the Holy Spirit. That extraordinary aspect of his ministry seems to have been lost. Quaker meetings have continued now for more than 350 years in the same form, waiting quietly on God, allowing the Spirit to move and following his leading.

Meetings are generally silent, with the occasional prayer, scripture reading, hymn or prophecy. Anything leaning towards emotion is discouraged.

How has that group fared? Jesus said, "...you will receive power when the Holy Spirit comes on you; and you will be my witnesses...to the ends of the earth" (Acts 1:8). Has that Quaker emphasis on the Spirit been effective in spreading the gospel?

In 2017 there were about 400,000 adult Quakers in the world. That equates to a growth rate of close to 1.0%. If Pentecostals had grown at the same rate, today there would be less than 20,000 instead of the 279 million we see.

THE WESLEY BROTHERS AND GEORGE WHITFIELD

The Wesleys were first labelled Methodists in 1729 when John began to meet "methodically" with like-minded students to study, pray and be discipled. However, he was unsure of his salvation and fell for a time into asceticism. He also suffered a failed ministry in America.

His Aldersgate experience of 24 May 1738 is well known:

> I felt my heart strangely warmed. I felt I did trust in Christ, Christ alone for salvation; and an assurance was given me that he had taken away my sins, even mine, and saved me from the law of sin and death.[86]

Seven months later, on New Year's Day 1739, the evangelist George Whitfield joined them and about 60 others for a love feast. At about 3 am the power of the Holy Spirit came upon them in an unusual and dramatic way. They all fell down, crying, weeping for joy and praising God together. George Whitfield spoke of that time as follows:

> It was a Pentecost season indeed: sometimes whole nights were spent in prayer. Often have we been filled as with new wine; and often have I seen them overwhelmed with the Divine Presence, and cry out, "Will God indeed dwell with

men upon the earth? How dreadful is this place? This is no other than the house of God and the gate of heaven".[87]

It is significant that, from that time, the Wesleys and Whitfield carried a renewed compassion for the lost, taking them to new levels of ministry. With this new emphasis on the ministry of the Holy Spirit, they became known as "enthusiasts", a common term then, equivalent to our "fanatic". Later that year, after the Church of England shut them out, they began their phenomenal outdoor preaching ministry. It is worth noting that John's first outdoor sermon to 3,000 people was taken from Luke 4:18–19:

> The Spirit of the Lord is on me, because he has anointed me to proclaim good news to the poor. He has sent me to proclaim freedom for the prisoners and recovery of sight for the blind, to set the oppressed free, to proclaim the year of the Lord's favour.

The great Methodist Revival that followed is renowned. It swept England, changing the course of history. Driven by preaching to vast outdoor crowds, it was sustained by small, well-organised, meetings in homes.

It is important to note this: it was not until 10 years after beginning his "methodical" groups that his ministry exploded, and that explosion was preceded by the above 1739 New Year's Day experience with the Holy Spirit.

There seems to be no record of the Wesleys or Whitfield speaking in tongues, but there are many instances of healing and casting out of demons in their ministry. Here are a few of them.

- A weaver, John Hayden, criticised Wesley's ministry but, after reading one of his sermons, he was tormented by an evil spirit, and fell to the ground screaming. The Wesleys were called and cast it out.[88]
- At Horsley on Tyne, an acquaintance, Mr Meyrick, caught a violent cold and the doctor said he would not live. After prayer over several days, he was healed. Wesley said, "I wait to hear who will either disprove this fact, or philosophically account for it."[89]

- Wesley once wrote that God had justly (but temporarily) withdrawn his power from them because he and others had been (among other things), "blaspheming his work among us, imputing it either to nature, to the force of imagination and animal spirits, or even to the devil".[90]

All these miracles seemed incidental to Wesley's preaching ministry. They just happened as the Holy Spirit fell around them. The meetings were often unruly. People would cry for mercy, fall to the ground, shout for joy and shake under the influence of the Holy Spirit. All this happened in spite of the fact that he didn't teach his followers about the Spirit baptism and signs and wonders. His central message was salvation.

CHARLES FINNEY 1792–1875

Finney was born in Warren, Connecticut, a year after the death of John Wesley. He brought more than half a million people to salvation and pioneered a new way of evangelism. When preaching, he would give a clear explanation of salvation, then place responsibility firmly on the listener to decide to believe there and then. This technique clashed with the prevailing Calvinist philosophy, "if God wants to save people He will", and brought severe persecution from newspapers and rabble-rousers, and harsh criticism from ministers. But he said:

> "Show me a more excellent way. Show me the fruits of your ministry; and if they so far exceed mine as to give me evidence that you have found a more excellent way, I will adopt your views."[91]

Finney was a lawyer, initially sceptical of Christianity. But he was intrigued that the legal profession was so dependent on Old Testament laws, and that led him to study the Bible. Eventually, one Saturday in October 1821, in great anguish that he might go to hell, he went to the woods and wrestled with God, finally gaining peace and assurance of salvation. That evening, as the last person left his office, he said:

> "...as I closed the door and turned around, my heart seemed to be liquid within me... it seemed as if I met the Lord face to face. It did not occur to me then, nor did it for some time afterward, that it was wholly a mental state. On the contrary, it seemed to me that I saw him as I would see any other man. He said nothing, but looked at me in such a manner as to break me right down at his feet...I fell down at his feet and poured out my soul to him. I wept aloud like a child, and made such confessions as I could with my choked utterance..."

Then, after a little time, he was about to sit down when:

> "I received a mighty baptism of the Holy Ghost. Without any expectation of it, without ever having the thought in my mind that there was any such thing for me, without any recollection that I had ever heard the thing mentioned by any person in the world, the Holy Spirit descended on me in a manner that seemed to go through me, body and soul. I could feel the impression, like a wave of electricity, going through and through me. Indeed, it seemed to come in waves and waves of liquid love: for I could not express it in any other way... I wept aloud with joy and love; and I do not know but I should say, I literally bellowed out the unutterable gushings of my heart. These waves came over me, and over me, one after the other, until I recollect I cried out, "I shall die if these waves continue to pass over me."[92]

What were these "unutterable gushings" of Finney's heart? Were they speaking in tongues? We cannot be certain. But over the next few days, almost everyone who met him was profoundly impacted by God. The town was astir, and people gathered at the church. The minister asked the congregation for forgiveness for his unbelief that Finney could be saved. Finney preached, and every person in the church except one was saved. He said, "I was every day surprised to find that a few words, spoken to an individual, would stick in his heart like an arrow".[93]

And so began his remarkable ministry.

Finney was systematic in his approach, and taught a number of principles for revival which, he believed, would work anywhere. The principle of prayer was a major factor. Finney called it, "a spirit of prayer", "real travail of soul", "groaning out their heart's desire". Also, as mentioned earlier, he would demand on-the-spot response to his message of salvation. Finney's teaching focused on conversions, not the power of the Holy Spirit, but he was nevertheless convinced of the necessity of the Holy Spirit in preaching. He wrote:

> When Christ commissioned his apostles to go and preach, he told them to abide in Jerusalem until they were endued with power from on high. This power, as everyone knows, was the baptism of the Holy Ghost poured out upon them on the Day of Pentecost. This was an indispensable qualification for success in their ministry. I did not suppose then, nor do I now, that this baptism was simply the power to work miracles. The power to work miracles and the gift of tongues were given as signs to attest to the reality of their divine commission. But the baptism itself was a divine illumination, filling them with faith and love, with peace and power; so that their words were made sharp in the hearts of God's enemies, quick and powerful like a two-edged sword. This is an indispensable qualification for preaching Christ to a sinful world. Without the direct teaching of the Holy Ghost, a man will never make much progress in preaching the gospel.[94]

Finney taught emphatically that the Holy Spirit baptism was a discrete experience. His method of receiving was, first, to understand that God is more willing to give the Holy Spirit to us than we are to give good gifts to our children (quoting Luke 11:13). Then, he said, we should make it a constant subject of prayer. Recognising that few were successful in this, he gave reasons:

- We are not *willing*, on the whole, to have this,
- We are self-indulgent (he listed about 20 common sins),
- Because of unbelief.

He then addressed a common question, "If we first get rid of all these forms of sin, which prevent our receiving this enduement, have we not already obtained the blessing? What more do we need?" To this he then replied:

> There is a great difference between the *peace* and the *power* of the Holy Spirit in the soul. The disciples were *Christians* before the Day of Pentecost, and, as such, had a measure of the Holy Spirit. They must have had the peace of sins forgiven and of a justified state, but yet they had not the enduement of power necessary for the accomplishment of the work assigned them. They had the *peace* which Christ had given them, but not the *power* which he had *promised*. This may be true of all Christians, and right here is, I think, the greatest mistake of the church and of the ministry. They rest in conversion, and do not seek until they obtain this enduement of power from on high.[95]

While Finney often referred to his own experience of receiving the Holy Spirit, and tells many stories of remarkable conversions under his ministry[96], his biography does not describe any instances of his followers successfully receiving the Holy Spirit as he had done. (Though he did speak much of "a Spirit of prayer" in his meetings, when people had devoted themselves to fervent and prolonged prayer.) And, while he acknowledged the speaking in tongues on the Day of Pentecost, he made no further comment about that, nor his "literally [bellowing] out the unutterable gushings of my heart".

Finney's methods of evangelism, especially the calling for conversions on the spot, and systematic prayer beforehand, have been enthusiastically embraced by other evangelists since then, some with very good success. But his theology of the Holy Spirit, in spite of clear instruction and strong exhortation, did not include any method of conveying its reality to others, and that aspect did not succeed.

DWIGHT L MOODY 1837–1899

Born in Northfield, Massachusetts, Moody and his eight siblings were raised in poverty by their widowed mother. But he was an entrepreneur, a 'mover and shaker', and eventually became wealthy as a shoe salesman and property investor.

Converted at 18, he immediately began inviting unreached people to church, but was particularly moved by the needs of children in the worst slums of Chicago. He organised Christian classes for them, for which he was nicknamed "Crazy Moody". By the age of 23, he was ministering to 1,500 children. He even received a visit from President Lincoln. The YMCA assisted him in this ministry and, through that YMCA link, Moody had opportunity to minister to soldiers in the Civil War.

A driven man, Moody tended to rely more on his considerable natural ability and fierce ambition, and less on spiritual power. But he was puzzled by an incident not long after his conversion. After speaking effectively (as he thought) at a Sabbath school, he was approached by an old man. Moody wrote:

> He caught hold of my hand and gave me a little bit of advice. I didn't know what he meant at the time, but he said, 'Young man, when you speak again, honour the Holy Ghost'. I was hastening off to another church to speak, and all the way it kept ringing in my ears—'Honour the Holy Ghost'. And I said to myself. 'I wonder what the old man means.'[97]

Several years later, two women approached him in a similar way and told him, "We are praying that you may get the power". RA Torrey, the first superintendent of Moody Bible Institute said, "(These two women) told him about the definite baptism with the Holy Ghost. Then he asked that he might pray *with* them and not they merely pray *for* him".[98]

They met on Fridays and one of the ladies, Sarah Cooke, later wrote of an experience with him on Friday, 6 October 1871:

> At every meeting, each of us prayed aloud in turn but, at this meeting, Mr Moody's agony was so great that he rolled on the floor and, in the midst of many tears and groans, cried out to God to be baptised with the Holy Ghost and fire.[99]

Roberts Liardon says of that time, "Dwight, however, reports that he left this meeting unchanged. He felt near his breaking point."[100] However, a few months later, as he was preparing for his second and most important trip to England, something happened. Moody later wrote:

> I was crying all the time that God would fill me with his Spirit. Well, one day, in the city of New York—oh what a day!—I cannot describe it, I seldom refer to it; it is almost too sacred an experience to name. Paul had an experience of which he never spoke for 14 years. I can only say that God revealed himself to me, and I had such an experience of his love that I had to ask him to stay his hand. I went to preaching again. The sermons were not different; I did not present any new truths, and yet hundreds were converted. I would not now be placed back where I was before that blessed experience if you should give me all the world—it would be as the small dust of the balance.[101]

Moody shared the story with Torrey, who later wrote:

> ... the power of God fell on him as he walked up the street and he had to hurry off to the house of a friend and ask that he might have a room by himself and, in that room, he stayed alone for hours; and the Holy Ghost came upon him, filling his soul with such joy that, at last, he had to ask God to withhold his hand, lest he die on the spot for very joy.... when he got to London... the power of God wrought

through him mightily in North London, and hundreds were added to the churches; and that was what led to him being invited over to the wonderful campaign that followed in later years.[102]

In an 1875 campaign in London, he conducted 285 meetings, speaking to 2,500,000 people. (England's population at that time was about 30 million.)

Many were soundly converted under Moody, and lives were transformed. The "Cambridge Seven" (seven university students who famously left all to evangelise in China) were inspired to their missionary task by Moody. But there is little, if any, record of the miracle power of God. In fact, Moody organised his meetings in such a way that there was little room for the dramatic experiences seen under Wesley or Finney or William Booth. Finney's "anxious seat" was replaced by an "enquiry room" where counsellors would answer questions and pray for them, rather than the previous wrestling for assurance of salvation, and crying out for the "touch of God".

Having said that, Robert Boyd wrote about a campaign in Sunderland, UK, as follows:

> When I got to the rooms of the YMCA, I found the meeting on fire. The young men were speaking in tongues and prophesying. What on earth did it mean? Only that Moody had been addressing them that afternoon.[103]

However, a new movement from England, named Keswick, began to teach the idea of a second blessing—the baptism in the Holy Spirit. In the 1870s, it began what were called Higher Life conferences, to spread this message (more on this later). Moody became involved with them in England, and conducted many Higher Life seminars in the USA. But they did not include the miraculous element, or speaking in tongues. Rather, they presented the idea of a second blessing which people should pursue. There was no certainty of how the believer could be assured it had come, but the importance of the experience, and the encouragement to pursue it, were both there.

WILLIAM AND CATHERINE BOOTH
(1829–1912 and 1829–1890)

The Salvation Army

The Booths began their ministry in England at the height of the Industrial Revolution. Earnest contenders for the poor and marginalised, they brought the compassion and power of the gospel of Jesus Christ, with extraordinary results.

William Booth was a fervent advocate of the Spirit baptism, and it leaps from his writings. For example:

> The chief danger of the twentieth century will be religion without the Holy Ghost, Christianity without Christ, forgiveness without repentance, salvation without regeneration, politics without God, and heaven without hell.

And, in 1869, about 30 years before the birth of the Pentecostal Movement, he wrote this:

> Success in soul-winning, like all other work, both human and divine, depends on certain conditions… first and foremost, I commend one qualification which seems to involve all others. That is, the Pentecostal baptism of the Holy Ghost. I would have you settle it in your souls for ever this one great immutable principle in the economy of grace, that spiritual work can only be done by those who possess spiritual power. No matter what else you may lack, or what may be against you, with the Holy Ghost, you will succeed; but without the Holy Spirit, no matter what else you may possess, you will utterly and eternally fail.
>
> Many make mistakes here. Aroused by the inward urgings of the Holy Spirit, they endeavour to comply with the call which comes from the Word and the necessities of their

fellow men; but being destitute of this power, they fail, and instead of going to the Strong for strength, they give up in despair. Again aroused, again they resolve and venture forth, but having no more power than before, they are as impotent as ever. And fail they must, until baptised with power from on high. This I am convinced, is the one great need of the church.

We want no new truths, agencies, means, or appliances. We only want more of the fire of the Holy Ghost....

You do desire to see signs and wonders wrought in the name of Jesus. To see a great awakening among the careless crowds around you... This baptism then, is your first great need. If you think with me, will you not tarry for it? Offer yourselves to God for the fullness. Lay aside every weight... Hold on! Though your feelings are barren, your way dark, and your difficulties be multiplied, steadily hang on the word of God.

Expect the baptism every hour; wait if he tarry.

'This kind goeth not forth but by prayer and fasting'; and 'the Lord whom you seek shall suddenly come to his temple'.[104]

Catherine Booth was one with her husband. She said:

> ...whatever success or blessing I may attribute to the efforts and measures of the Salvation Army, I always pre-suppose a pre-existing qualification—[the] Equipment of the Holy Ghost...We deem it a great mistake to suppose that any human learning, any human eloquence, any human qualification whatever, fits a man or woman for ministering God's word or dealing with souls. Whatever else there is or is not, there must be the equipment of the Holy Ghost, for without him all qualifications...are utterly powerless for the regeneration of mankind... [105]

That belief was not just academic. When it came to action at the coalface, out where the sinners are, powerful conversions and dramatic manifestations of the Holy Spirit were the order of the day. A biography of an early Salvation Army leader, Elijah Cadman, *The Happy Warrior* by Humphrey Wallis, paints the picture.

> At one o'clock in the morning, the Holy Spirit came upon us, and suddenly 30 fell down and cried out to God for the Blessing of a Clean Heart. Some lay as though they were dead for a time. Oh, may God give us more and more of his Sanctifying Power, the complete armour for the people of the Salvation Army.[106]
>
> The course of the regular meetings began to be interrupted by Salvationists falling into 'Glory Fits'. In one of Elijah's meetings at Bradford, about a hundred persons were in 'Glory Fits'. Soldiers came up to officers to say, "I don't believe in this", and, while speaking, fell under the strange manifestation of the Divine Presence.
>
> The 'Glory Fits' were ecstasies during which the individuals affected were insensible, usually silent, and remained thus for one or many hours...
>
> People fell suddenly where they stood or sat, many crying out, as with a last breath, 'glory to God!' On returning to consciousness, no coherent account was given of what had taken place. A few described their withdrawal from material sense as 'bliss', 'great happiness', 'like Paradise', 'walking into heaven in a rainbow', 'joy the body was unable to bear', and a 'sense of the love and glory of Christ'.
>
> Said Elijah, "I have seen them lying about all over the platform and Hall, but never once in an unseemly posture. Their bodies were, as a rule, quite stiff. We had our own people carry them out of the Meeting—that was the strict regulation—and take every precaution for them. Men

carried men and women carried women. They were placed in different ante-rooms adjoining the halls, and several elderly, trusted soldiers of the same sex left in charge until they recovered. Frequently, doctors attended them. None ever became indisposed, ill, or died. It was often the most peaceful and composed of our people who were affected. There were never, in my experience of the 'Glory Fits' any warning signs. A Meeting might be 'hard', that is, very difficult to pray in and to get others to pray; a lot of sinners making trouble, perhaps, and then, in an instant, the power of God would descend on us, sinners be hushed into awe, and be overcome by the sense of his majesty and his love, through his Son, to us all, and all the world...

I have led meetings where the Holy Spirit was manifest in such power that half the soldiers present were in 'Glory Fits' and I had to cling, nearly helpless, to the platform rail, lifting my heart and crying inwardly all the time to God to shepherd my people. Conversions always took place in such meetings".[107]

Media reports are illuminating. A reporter from the *Newcastle Daily Chronicle*, on 21 May 1879, described a similar meeting in the Handyside Hall in Gateshead. He wrote:

> When I came away, people were swooning all over the place. I had to step over a man in a fit in order to reach the door.
>
> When I reached the street and the pure air, it was a fresh grey morning... 'Is this a common sort of thing here?' I asked of the policeman outside. 'Very', he said, 'but it has reduced our charge sheet, and I haven't had a case for two months'.[108]

Booth was obviously well acquainted with the work of the Holy Spirit and, from the passages above, he obviously believed the Spirit baptism was an experience to be received after salvation. He urged his leaders to seek that—in comparison to mostly silence from the other renowned preachers we have just considered. So, it is interesting to note that, after Booth's death, the Salvation Army had an average growth rate roughly double the mainline and evangelical denominations we looked at.

But while Booth spoke fervently about its importance, and that power was convincingly present in his ministry, you will search his writings in vain for systematic instruction on how to receive that gift, how we know when it has happened, or how to release that power. "Tarry" is what he tells them, be a holy vessel, and get on your knees and pray for it.

Interestingly, Booth's grandson, William Booth-Clibborn, was taken by his father to Pentecostal meetings in England in 1908, and there he received the baptism in the Holy Spirit. In 1930, he moved to Australia, where he had great success. In a campaign in Mackay, Queensland, the numbers grew from about 50 on the first night to 700 at the end, with many conversions and healings. A dynamic and controversial character, he once attempted to gather all the Sydney Pentecostal churches together under his leadership. For two years, he preached in a 2,000-seat tent, but eventually established a Pentecostal church in Brisbane, which became known as the Glad Tidings Tabernacle, affiliating with the Assemblies of God in 1940. While obviously a beneficiary of his grandfather's Salvation Army fire, Booth-Clibborn was nevertheless drawn to the Pentecostal teaching and experience of the Holy Spirit.[109]

JONATHAN GOFORTH 1859–1935
Canadian Presbyterian missionary to China.

Under this man's remarkable, sacrificial ministry, many thousands of Chinese were converted, amid scenes of heart-rending confession of sin, and earnest seeking after God. General Feng, leader of the Chinese army, became a Christian, and Goforth was given free access to preach to his soldiers. On one occasion, after 13 days of meetings, they baptised 960 soldiers, and gave communion to 4,600. Less than 11 years before that, they had all been heathen. A Chinese report said:

> [Soldiers from other armies] when they came, seized our houses and public buildings and made off with anything

> they took fancy to, and our wives and daughters were at their mercy, so that the people called them soldiers of hell. Now General Feng leads his men through the city, and nothing is disturbed, and nothing is molested. Even the General lives in a tent, as his men do, and everything they need they buy, and no one is abused. The people are so delighted the people call them the soldiers of heaven...[110]

Today, the largest percentage of Christians in China are located in the Henan Province where Goforth ministered.

Goforth's remarkable success came at the age of 45, after he became restless and dissatisfied with his progress in China. He was sent pamphlets about the Welsh Revival, and also a copy of Finney's *Lectures on Revival,* which he devoured. His wife wrote:

> Again and again, he read the passage (Concerning Finney's belief that when correct methods of evangelism were employed, revival inevitably followed). The children became hushed and gathered about us, sensing something unusual. At last, my husband said, "It simply means this: the spiritual laws governing a spiritual harvest are as real and tangible as the laws governing a natural harvest" (That is, a crop will be reaped when seed is sown.) Then, solemnly, almost as if making a vow—"If Finney is right, and I believe he is, I am going to find out what these spiritual laws are and obey them, no matter what the cost may be".[111]

Goforth then set himself to an intensive study of the Holy Spirit, marking key passages in a wide-margin Bible, and pursuing it with such intensity that his wife became worried about him, saying, "I fear you will break down". She described his response:

> ...putting his hands on my shoulders, he faced me with a look I can never forget. I can only describe it as 'glorious' and yet

sad, as he said, "Oh, Rose, even you do not understand! I feel like one who has tapped a mine of wealth! It is so wonderful! Oh, if I could only get others to see it!" From that time on, I could only step aside, as it were, and watch.[112]

That process led to an expansion of his ministry and, not long after, his preaching brought about a remarkable revival in Manchuria. His wife wrote that, while he had gone there as an unknown missionary, he returned with the limelight of the Christian world upon him.

Miracles sometimes occurred in his meetings. He wrote:

> A wonderful testimony meeting was held on the last evening. Spontaneous resolutions to new obedience were heard from many. One remarkable thing about these testimonies was the great number who claimed that... when the Spirit's fire had swept so irresistibly through the audience, they had been healed of their bodily ailments. In my address, I had made no special mention of divine healing. Yet here was the testimony of these people that suddenly, at some crucial moment, the illness which ailed them passed away.[113]

Goforth was remarkably fruitful. He was obviously impacted by what he had learned from Finney (a "spirit of prayer", and to challenge the audience to believe there and then), and also from the results of his passionate search for the Holy Spirit. But his legacy was not such that his followers could reproduce that same experience of the Holy Spirit. He left no clear theology that others could embrace and experience in the same way.

SUMMARISING THIS CHAPTER

I introduced this chapter with these words:

> Since the Reformation, there have been many famous revivalists and giants of the faith: Wesley, Booth, Moody and

others. They had dramatic and widespread spiritual influence in their day. They would have read about the baptism in the Holy Spirit in the Bible—many times. Did they experience it? How did they understand it?

Let us now gather extracts about the Holy Spirit from their stories and look for a picture:

George Fox:

> ...his understanding of the "inner light" of Jesus Christ...led by the Spirit of God.
>
> ...many remarkable instances of supernatural work of the Holy Spirit... divine healing, deliverance from demons, divine judgment on persecutors, resurrection from the dead, visions and speaking in tongues.

The Wesleys and Whitfield

> At about 3 am, the power of the Holy Spirit came upon them... they all fell down, crying, weeping for joy and praising God together.
> ... from that time, the Wesleys and Whitfield carried a renewed compassion for the lost, taking them to new levels of ministry.
> ... Later that year, after the Church of England shut them out, they began their phenomenal outdoor preaching ministry. John's first outdoor sermon to 3,000 people...
> ...People would cry for mercy, fall to the ground, shout for joy and shake under the influence of the Holy Spirit.

Finney

I received a mighty baptism of the Holy Ghost. Without any expectation of it... the Holy Spirit descended on me in a manner that seemed to go through me, body and soul.... Indeed it seemed to come in waves and waves of liquid love...I wept aloud with joy and love... I literally bellowed out the unutterable gushings of my heart...until I recollect I cried out, "I shall die if these waves continue to pass over me".

... over the next few days, virtually everyone coming in contact with Finney was radically impacted by God.... Charles preached and every person in the church except one was saved. Finney said, "I was every day surprised to find that a few words, spoken to an individual, would stick in his heart like an arrow".

Moody

"Young man, when you speak again, honour the Holy Ghost"

"We are praying that you may get the power"

I was crying all the time that God would fill me with his Spirit. Well one day, in the city of New York—oh what a day!... and I had such an experience of his love that I had to ask him to stay his hand. I went to preaching again. The sermons were not different; I did not present any new truths, and yet hundreds were converted. I would not now be placed back where I was before that blessed experience if you should give me all the world—it would be as the small dust of the balance.

The Booths

> The chief danger of the twentieth century will be religion without the Holy Ghost...

> Success in soul winning, like all other work, both human and divine, depends on certain conditions...first and foremost, I commend one qualification which seems to involve all others. That is, the Pentecostal baptism of the Holy Ghost.

> ...the Holy Spirit was manifest in such power that half the soldiers present were in 'Glory Fits' and I had to cling, nearly helpless, to the platform rail, lifting my heart and crying inwardly all the time to God to shepherd my people. Conversions always took place in such meetings.

Jonathan Goforth

I feel like one who has tapped a mine of wealth! It (the Holy Spirit) is so wonderful! Oh, if I could only get others to see it!

These giants of the faith had something special in common: a dramatic experience of the Holy Spirit. It took their ministries to levels far beyond what they had ever imagined.
Did they successfully impart knowledge of that experience to others?
Not really.
In spite of their experiences, and passionate conviction about our need for God's power, none of them left a definitive method which would enable followers to experience that power, and know they had received it.
What is that definitive method?
We find it in Acts 8:17; 9:17, and 19:6, and it is simple.
After conversion, new converts are prayed for to receive the Holy Spirit. And there is immediate, tangible confirmation.
That process, the laying on of hands and expecting the dramatic infilling of the Holy Spirit there and then, was not in the toolbox of these great leaders.

Yes, they had personally experienced wonderful activity of the Holy Spirit. But they hadn't 'put two and two together' and worked out how it happened, and how others could confidently expect the same. That mystery remained, waiting for someone else to find it.

We are close to seeing just how that came about. But before we get there, think some more about this Pentecostal ancestry.

We just looked at Holy Spirit experiences of a few faith giants, dating from the 1600s to the late 1800s. Were there more? What about lay people? And what about *prior* to those times? Little is spoken of those 1500 years–what happened there? And were there unusual spiritual conditions in the 1800s that pre-empted the Pentecostal explosion?

More important questions, and history gives answers. What are they? What do ancient and recent Christian writings tell us?

That is where we go now. Hold onto your chair. This is fascinating.

History is philosophy teaching by examples.
THOMAS JEFFERSON

People without the knowledge of their past history, is like a tree without roots.
MARCUS GARVEY

Life is divided into three terms—that which was, which is, and which will be. Let us learn from the past to profit by the present, to live better in the future.
WILLIAM WORDSWORTH

CHAPTER 9

TONGUES AND TWO THOUSAND YEARS. WHAT HAPPENED IN THAT TIME?

The Pentecostal tongue-speaking movement exploded onto the scene soon after 1900 with the extraordinary phenomenon of speaking in tongues. Why not before then? What happened during the previous 1800 years? Were there no records of tongues during that time? What does history tell us?

This is an absolutely fascinating story, and we will look for incidents of tongue speaking and other supernatural gifts of the Spirit in the early church, medieval and other records through the years. Little-known, extraordinary, and intriguing.

In a nutshell, the picture we find is as follows.

After the death of the apostles, and in the following centuries, formal ecclesiastical structures emerged which stifled spiritual gifts. So much so that some, at that time and today, believed the gifts had ceased—a view called cessationism. Occasionally, however, pious individuals would receive Holy Spirit infillings and experience tongues and other gifts. Many such stories can be found throughout history. However, as we have seen, with no effective theology of the Holy Spirit, their experience would go with them to the grave until someone else stumbled on the same thing and the cycle repeated. Eventually, though, a new idea emerged: the baptism of the Spirit was a powerful, discrete experience, to equip the believer in his service to God. That discovery was slow in coming, but eventually culminated in the powerful Pentecostal event at the beginning of the twentieth century. There, a theology of the Holy Spirit baptism was formulated which, when explained to others, could be replicated. With that tool plus a band of committed people and a remarkable outpouring of the Holy Spirit, the Pentecostal movement exploded.

That was the journey, here are the milestones.

THE FIRST THREE HUNDRED YEARS

Among the church fathers, at least three reported active supernatural gifts of the Spirit in their time, including prophetic gifts and tongues. They were Irenaeus, (Bishop of Lyons, France, 130–202 AD), Justin Martyr (about 165 AD), and Tertullian (North Africa, about 155–240 AD). Tertullian wrote of his involvement with a significant group called the Montanists.

The Montanists (About 150–400 AD) and Tertullian

Named after their founder, the Montanists were a large movement which commonly practised the supernatural gifts. Unfortunately, in their zeal, inexperience and lack of theological understanding (remembering that the New Testament Canon was not finalised until 397 AD), the Montanists adopted a number of unorthodox (or maybe misunderstood or even heretical) practices, for which they were shunned. For example, they forbade fleeing from martyrdom—Jesus had said martyrdom would happen so they believed it was God's will. Women were not allowed to wear ornaments, and virgins were required to wear veils. Second marriages were forbidden—they believed marriage was for eternity. Placing emphasis on prophetic gifts, they incorrectly predicted the descent of the Heavenly Jerusalem in 156 AD in Pepuza, Phrygia. Eventually, in 230 AD, a church Synod denounced them as a heresy and their followers were virtually excommunicated. Church leaders who wrote about them were harsh and critical. For example, Eusebius said Montanus, "was filled with spiritual excitement and suddenly fell into a kind of trance and unnatural ecstasy. He raved, and began to chatter and talk nonsense..."[114] That "chattering" would almost certainly be speaking in tongues, but Eusebius obviously considered it spurious.

Surviving records of Montanists were written by their critics, and need to be studied through that filter. However, in spite of Montanist persecution, they found a good friend in Christian scholar, apologist and lawyer, **Tertullian**. We see it in an essay he wrote against the heretic, Marcion:

> Let Marcion then exhibit, as gifts of his god, some prophets, such as have not spoken by human sense, but with the Spirit of God, such as have both predicted things to come, and have made manifest the secrets of the heart; 1 Corinthians 14:25 let him produce a psalm, a vision, a prayer 1 Corinthians 14:26—only let it be by the Spirit, in an ecstasy, that is, in a rapture, whenever an interpretation of tongues has occurred to him; let him show to me also, that any woman of boastful tongue in his community has ever prophesied from among those specially holy sisters of his. Now all these signs [of spiritual gifts] are forthcoming from my side (i.e., the Montanists he related to) without any difficulty, and they agree, too, with the rules, and the dispensations, and the instructions of the Creator...[115]

Obviously Tertullian was not slow to condemn heresy but, in this instance, we can see he was happy to overlook any Montanist peculiarities, and tell the world their supernatural gifts (including tongues) were authentic.

The fact that there were doctrinal differences between Montanists and the established church does not necessarily prove Montanists were heretics. Heaven knows there have been multitudes of doctrinal conflicts between Christians over the centuries on many issues. And that same conflict between Montanists and the established church has been repeated many times during the last century—between Pentecostals and the mainstream church.

For a time, Montanism was the majority group in North Africa, where Tertullian was mostly situated. It is often compared with the Pentecostal movement today. It was not 'a flash in the pan', continuing for several centuries. So their record of speaking in tongues is significant in this study.

A comment by John Wesley is illuminating. In 1750, after reading a book in support of Montanus, Wesley wrote:

> I was fully convinced of what I had once suspected: 1) that the Montanists...were real scriptural Christians; and 2) that the grand reason why the miraculous gifts were so soon withdrawn was not only that faith and holiness were well-nigh lost, but that dry, formal, orthodox men began even then to ridicule whatever gifts they had not themselves, and to decry them all as either madness or imposture.[116]

The established church of the time apparently had a 'hands-off' attitude to the miraculous gifts. Their observations of Montanism would have further entrenched that stance, and some believe this set the course for the centuries that followed. Yes, prophetic and supernatural gifts did occur over the centuries, as we will see, but mostly among "holy" men and women (typically canonised saints), often in monasteries and caves. Common belief was that these saints were gifted with a unique holiness, a holiness inaccessible to most others. As a result supernatural gifts were limited to a few of these exalted individuals and leaders.

Before we look at these saints, we need to lay some background.

SAINTS FROM EARLY CHURCH AND MEDIEVAL (about 476 – 1453 AD) PERIODS

Xenoglossia

Some of the following stories introduce another element to speaking in tongues. It is called xenoglossia, the miraculous, instantaneous ability to speak, read, write or understand a foreign language. Just as the languages spoken by the 120 disciples were recognised by the crowds on the Day of Pentecost, so too we have stories of people miraculously recognising languages they never learned, in a number of different situations.

Reliability of information sources

Many saints from the medieval period had supernatural experiences. However, the reliability of evidence from those times can be uncertain. Information comes mainly from two sources: hagiographies and vitas. A hagiography (literally "holy story") is the biography of a saint which presents that saint as a hero without failings. A vita is a record of the life of the saint, formally prepared for the canonisation process. Its purpose is to assist the canonisation authority to decide whether or not the person is worthy of sainthood.

Our problem with vitas is that many ancients, keen to see their saint canonised, might have embellished the facts. Some are definitely farfetched. The problem escalates when records are compiled well after the death of the saint. Some tell of miracles that are clearly folklore, apparently intended that way. For example, one monk was said to hang his clothes on a sunbeam. The Ethiopian saint, Takla Haymanot, supposedly died and returned to life forty times during conflict with magicians; he raised a thousand men from the dead who had died from lightning strikes twenty-five years previously; and his monks and nuns could sleep in the same beds without succumbing to temptation.[117] These stories are clearly fanciful and implausible, and not intended to be taken at face value.

However, as we consider the following stories, of saints miraculously preaching in languages never learned, we remember that supernatural speech is entirely plausible because it happened in the Bible. On one occasion, God also spoke through an ass (Numbers 24:28). And, in the New Testament, speaking in tongues is mentioned more than twenty times.

Note too, that these stories are typically found amidst fervent, godly evangelism or pastoral care. In other words, they don't smack of fraudulence. And, we will see, they are *plentiful and consistent*. So there is good reason to believe they are authentic.

Protestant/Catholic issues

A few of the miracles described in hagiographies are related to visions of Mary and the saints. Protestants have problems with the veneration of Mary and saints, a practice which arose late in the fifth century. To avoid controversy, I have chosen to exclude such stories, and concentrate on those involving just supernatural tongues and the prophetic gifts, which are the focus of this book.

It is probably because of the above issue that most Protestant books about Spirit baptism and tongues avoid the stories you are about to read, and they remain little-known. Get ready for some surprises.

One clarification: a number of the saints are referred to as *mystics*. Pentecostals and charismatics would, probably, instead use the (biblical) term *prophet*.

Tongues: Recognised, not recognised, and miracles of HEARING

Most of these Catholic (and Orthodox) stories involve a supernatural tongue, *recognised by the hearer*, which solves a communication problem. That has a precedent at Pentecost when 120 disciples spoke languages instantly recognised by many different people groups (Acts 2:1–41). Peter followed up by preaching to that mixed crowd in his own language. We should recognise that there is a possibility here that the multilingual crowd all (miraculously) understood him. If so, we have a miracle, not in the speaking, but in the *hearing*.

An enlightening story on this subject concerns the Tower of Babel, in Genesis 11. When the people (of one language) tried to make a name for themselves, God scattered them by confusing their language. Now, today, for humble believers, under the unifying favour of the Holy Spirit, it seems that can be reversed.

Now here are some stories of saints who spoke in tongues that were recognised.

The Stories

St Patiens (died about 150 AD) Fourth Bishop of Metz, France. Entering Gaul and unable to speak their language, St Patiens was given the same "miraculous token" as the Apostles—the "knowledge of tongues". "And so, with this certain sign, 'Blessed Patiens' came to the city of Metz."[118]

Pachomius (died AD 346) An Egyptian Coptic Christian, Pachomius was asked by a Greek-speaking Christian from Rome to hear his confession. Unable to speak his language, Pachomius found an interpreter. But the Roman refused, saying, "I only want you after God, and nobody else, to know the evils of my heart". Telling the Roman to wait, Pachomius went away and:

> ... prayed for three hours, entreating God earnestly for this. Suddenly, something like a letter written on a piece of papyrus was sent from heaven into his right hand. Reading it, he learned the speech of all the languages. Having sent up praise to the Father, the Son and the Holy Spirit, he came back to that brother with great joy and began to converse with him faultlessly in Greek and Latin. When that brother heard it, he said that the Great Man surpassed all the scholars in that language.[119]

St Ephrem (born about 306 AD, in Mesopotamia, modern-day Turkey) One of the most significant fathers in the Syriac-speaking Orthodox Church, St Ephrem was a theologian and prolific writer of popular sermons, hymns and poems. On a trip to Egypt, he met with the famous Saint Bishoy, in a cave in the desert. A biography of St Ephrem records:

> The holy Bishoy did not know Syriac, and neither did the holy Ephrem know Egyptian. They asked from God and was granted to Bishoy so that he uttered words in Syrian and Ephrem, Egyptian. And Ephrem, the holy saint, was greatly affected by the appearance and conversation of the great man of God, Abba Bishoy. The Lord promised him, while on the mountain of Edessa, "that your reward in the kingdom is as the great man Abba Bishoy is being rewarded". And the blessed master Ephrem dwelled with the great man of God for a week, and they abounded in the company of each other.[120]

Andrew the Fool (died 936 AD) An Eastern Orthodox saint, Andrew was known for his commitment to live as a 'fool for Christ', in humility and patience, and for his remarkable visions and experiences with God. One night, in the home of a wealthy disciple's father, he was approached by a tearful servant who wanted to leave his master and follow Andrew as his disciple. Then:

> The righteous man understood in his spirit what the boy wanted to obtain and, as he wished to speak with him in private, through the power of the Holy Spirit changed the boy's language to that of the Syrians and sat down and talked with him in fluent Syriac.

Then, when the other servants "driven by ardent love" sat around him, Andrew was able to see the sins of each one, and he spoke in parables to them:

> They, on their side, gave ear to the holy man's words, some turning red as fire for shame, others becoming dizzy and trembling while still others were ashamed and went away, for the righteous man's plain speech bluntly exposed the sins of each, revealing why and how and where they had committed them. And the most wonderful of all; each one understood what he said in his own language. They all assumed, "This man is speaking about me!"[121]

St Norbert of Xanten (About 1075–1134 AD) A Catholic Bishop, born in Germany. He became an itinerant preacher throughout northern Europe, encouraging the priests. He was credited with a number of miracles, including the following:

> ...he gave a sermon to the people, clearly hardly knowing or understanding this Romance language until now because he never learned it. But then he was without despair, so he began to address in his mother tongue (German). The Holy Spirit, which had formerly taught the 120 people different

languages, then made the uncivilised German language and the difficulty of the eloquent Latin language suitable to be understood by the hearers.[122]

St Dominic (1170–1221 AD) A Spanish priest who founded the Dominican Order (The Order of Preachers). Known for his fasting and asceticism. Two stories relate his miraculous speaking of another language:

> Once, on a journey, the servant of God happened to meet a certain religious whose saintly manner he could see but whose speech and manner were utterly foreign to him. Saddened by the fact he could not refresh himself by conversing about divine things with this holy person, he prayed and obtained from the Lord the favour that each one would speak in the language of the other. By thus conversing, they were able to understand each other for the three days they were together.[123]

In this next story, Dominic is travelling with Friar Bertrand when they meet a group of German Christians in France.

> One day, blessed Dominic said to his companion, "Brother Bertrand, I feel terrible eating the food provided by these pilgrims and giving them no spiritual food in return. If it is agreeable to you, let us kneel down and ask the Lord to make us understand and speak their language so that we may be able to speak to them about the Lord Jesus Christ". Then, to the amazement of the pilgrims, they began to speak intelligibly to them in German and, for the next four days, they went with them, speaking about the Lord Jesus until they reached Orleans.[124]

St Anthony of Padua (1195–1231 AD) From a wealthy family in Lisbon, Portugal; renowned for his powerful preaching (said to have drawn crowds of up to 30,000), his knowledge of the Bible, and compassion for the needy.

When called to address a gathering of the Pope and cardinals, with men from different countries:

> Greeks and Latins, French and Germans, Slavs and English and men of many other different languages and idioms... being inflamed by the Holy Spirit and inspired with apostolic eloquence, he preached and explained the word of God so effectively, devoutly, subtly, clearly and understandably that all who were assembled at that consistory although they spoke different languages, clearly and distinctly heard and understood every one of his words as if he had spoken in each of their languages.... In amazement they said to one another, "Is he not a Spaniard? How then are we all hearing him in the language of the country where we were born...?"[125]

St Bernadino of Sienna (1380–1444 AD) Popular preacher (said to have preached to as many as 50,000), Italian priest and Franciscan missionary. At the 1439 Council of Florence, convened for the reuniting of Greek and Roman churches, he was said to have miraculously addressed the Greeks in their language, which he did not know.[126]

St Vincent Ferrer (died 1419 AD) Said to have converted tens of thousands of Jews and Muslims to Christianity. Spoke the native dialect of Valencia, Spain but, while preaching, he was understood by a multilingual crowd as follows:

> Many Greeks, Germans, Sardinians and Hungarians, and others born in other places... when they came to the places in which Vincent was preaching... when his words came to an end, they revealed that they had understood the words of the man of God no less than if they had heard him speaking in their own language.[127]

St Louis Bertrand (1526–1581 AD) (Post-Reformation, but I have included it with these similar stories.) A Spanish Dominican friar, known as the "Apostle to the Americas" (South and Central America), he was responsible for the conversion of tens of thousands of South Americans. He preached in his native Spanish language and was understood there by many different language groups.[128]

CATHOLIC (AND ANGLICAN) WOMEN WHO SPOKE IN RECOGNISED TONGUES

I have treated the women as a separate group. The church did not allow women to preach, so miracles of inspired preaching were not part of their world. However, the supernatural ability to speak in other languages did occur but in a different way, as we shall see.

St Lutgard (1182–1246 AD) A Flemish-speaking mystic and Benedictine nun from the Belgium/Netherlands, area. One day, a distressed French-speaking woman arrived at the nunnery. When the nuns were unable to console her, she tried to leave. However, they persuaded her to wait for Lutgard who took her aside. She returned from that meeting "to the fullest confidence and hope". The woman said to the nuns:

> "Why did you say that this most holy lady was Flemish? Indeed, I have found by experience that she is quite French."... It is no wonder that the two women could communicate for a while without knowing each other's language, for Lutgard was filled with the same Spirit that filled the assembled disciples with a variety of tongues.[129]

St Clare of Montefalco (or St Clare of the Cross; 1268–1308) Italian Augustinian nun and Mother Superior of her abbey. Clare had prophetic gifts and sometimes would predict the arrival of pilgrims and the reason for their coming. One French-speaking visitor, Marguerite, was surprised when Clare told her she was expecting her. And:

> ... another wonderful thing was that Clare understood her speech. The nuns who were with Clare at the grill could not

understand what Clare was saying. Clare, on the contrary, understood, grasped her meaning completely and answered in an entirely appropriate way. But why was it wonderful or surprising? He who had enabled Clare to see the woman before she came, also saw to it that the speech was understood.[130]

Margery Kempe (Born 1373) An English Christian mystic and mother of 14 who, late in life, embarked on pilgrimage to Jerusalem, Rome and around England. She was renowned for her very loud weeping in church (for which she was misunderstood and harshly treated) and profound spiritual experiences. Unable to read or write, she dictated her life story to a scribe, giving us the oldest known autobiography in the English language. (Her story is thus unique, because it did not originate from hagiographies or vitas.)

While in Rome, Margery tried to converse with a priest who knew only German and Latin. Frustrated at having to use an interpreter, she asked the priest to pray that God would give them both the ability to communicate. So, the German priest and his friends prayed for 13 days after which:

> ...the priest came back to her to test the effect of their prayers, and then he understood what she said in English to him and she understood what he said. And yet he did not understand the English that other people spoke; even though they spoke the same words that she spoke, he still did not understand them unless she spoke herself.[131]

Margery's cynical British companions didn't believe this was possible, and complained to an English priest who happened to sympathise with her—in spite of her odd ways. He agreed to Margery's suggestion that they all dine together with the German priest to test this phenomenon. As they dined, Margery spoke in English to the priest and:

> Then (speaking in Latin), they asked [the German priest] if he understood what she had said, and he straightaway in Latin told them the same words that she said before in

English, for he could neither speak English nor understand English except from her tongue. And then they were astonished, for they knew that he understood what she said, and she understood what he said, and yet he could not understand any other English person.[132]

St Colette of Corbie (1381–1447 AD) Mother Superior of a French abbey; set out to restore the Franciscan Second Order to its original ideals of poverty and austerity. Her vita, prepared by Pierre De Vaux shortly after she died, compared her with the apostles as follows:

> The apostles were speaking in various tongues and understood all languages. In the same way she herself understood all languages, namely Latin and German and the rest.[133]

She was also given the gift of a foreign language when confronted by armed men whilst on a journey. She spoke in their language, which was foreign to her, and in such a way that "their evil designs are transformed into 'amour et charite'" (love and charity).[134]

St Jeanne Delanoue (Blessed Joan of the Cross) (1666–1736) From France; devoted her life to caring for orphans, the poor and the needy.

> Two Muslim slaves were given to her convent, but no one was able to convert them to the Christian faith. Joan, however, was given the gift of Algerian—their native language—and persuaded them. On other occasions, she was heard speaking in languages she had not learned, including Latin and Arabic and others.[135]

MIRACULOUS LATIN

The next stories are a little different. The medieval church had a problem. The Bible, the Psalter and other important books were all in Latin. But many women were uneducated and could not understand the Latin liturgy. So, they sought God's help, and God was gracious. It is not quite speaking in tongues, but closely related, as you will see.

St Hildegard of Bingen (1098–1179 AD) An influential German mystic, composer, writer, botanist and preacher. A number of her musical compositions have regained popularity in recent years, and she was well known for her knowledge of herbal and natural cures for sickness. She claimed never to have learned Latin, but said:

> When I was 42 years and seven months old, a blazing fiery light came from the open heaven and poured over my whole head and heart and breast like a flame... Immediately I knew how to explain the books of the Psalter, gospel and other Catholic volumes of the Old and New Testament. However, I did not know how to interpret the words of their text, nor the division of syllables, nor the knowledge of cases and tenses.[136]

In addition to this, and consistent with her prolific music abilities, "She was reported to have exercised several spiritual gifts, including singing in unknown tongues".[137]

Christina the Astonishing (1150–1224 AD) A Belgian holy woman. Following a massive seizure at the age of 21, she was assumed dead but, to the astonishment of all, rose from her open coffin to go on and lead a remarkable (though excessively ascetic) life. (She was sometimes tied to trees to curb her exuberance.) It was said of her:

> Although she had been completely illiterate from birth, yet she understood all Latin and fully knew the meaning of Holy Scripture. When she was asked very obscure questions by certain spiritual friends, she would explain them very openly. But she did this most unwillingly and rarely, for she said that to expound Holy Scriptures belonged to the clergy and not the ministry of such as her.[138]

There is also a record of Christina singing in her supernatural Latin language. While staying with a woman recluse on the border of Germany, she:

> ... went to the vigils of matins every night. Then, after everyone had left the church and the doors were locked, she would walk around the church floor and utter a song so sweet that it seemed to be angelic rather than human singing. This song was so marvellous to hear that it surpassed the music of all instruments and the voices of all mortals...[the song was] in Latin and wondrously adorned with harmonious phrases.[139]

St Catherine of Sienna (1347–1380 AD) An outstanding author and mystic, a lay member of the Dominican Order, and the first woman to be declared a Doctor of the Church. Unable to understand the Latin Psalms and Divine Office, she set out to learn Latin. After several frustrating weeks, she prayed to God:

> "If you want me to learn to read so that I can say the Psalms and sing your praises...deign to teach me what I am not clever enough to learn by myself. If not, thy will be done, I shall be quite content to remain in my ignorance and shall be able to spend more time in meditating on you in other ways." Then a marvel happened—clear proof of God's power—for during this prayer, she was so divinely instructed that, when she got up, she knew how to read any kind of writing quite easily and fluently, like the best reader in the world...I (Raymond of Capua, her spiritual mentor) was flabbergasted...though she could read so fast she could not read separate syllables; in fact she could hardly spell the words... From then on Catherine began to hunt for books of the Divine Office and to read the Psalms and anthems...[140]

Summing up this time period

In her book, *The Gift of Tongues, Women's Xenoglossia in the Later Middle Ages* (her PhD dissertation), Christina Cooper-Rompato says this supernatural gift (which she calls "sapientia") in the Latin language was experienced by a wide range of people. She observes:

> Miracles of sapienta occur in both men's and women's lives and are extremely popular ways of demonstrating people to be divinely inspired. The gift is reported to have been experienced by a range of recipients, from illiterate nuns and lay brothers and sisters to the most learned of male clerics and theologians.[141]

What caused the explosion of recorded tongues incidents in the 12th to 15th centuries? Cooper-Rompato suggests the following:

- Miracle accounts were being more frequently recorded as the Middle Ages progressed
- Mission efforts increased, employing public preaching to people of diverse linguistic backgrounds
- Learning about the miracle built an expectation for the gift
- Medieval preaching emphasised the sins of the tongue and this gift related to that "tongue" theme
- More Latin works were being translated into the language of the people, making them more aware of the gift

Note the first point – miracle accounts were more frequently recorded. That suggests there were more incidents prior to that time that we don't know about.

Also, there was a rising expectation for the gift as a sign of authentic ministry. Those preparing vitas might have felt a pressure to establish that tongues were genuinely experienced by the proposed saint, or justify the absence of the gift. Cooper-Rompato observes that:

> ...the vita of the Franciscan St Peter of Alcantra (d 1562) states quite emphatically that Peter did not receive the gift because he did not need it since he preached only in Liberia.[142]

The many incidents described above were clearly supernatural miracles of speech. But just how these instances related to the baptism in the Holy Spirit we do not know. It is possible they were just simple miracles. Or they may have accompanied a dramatic baptism of the Holy Spirit. What we do know is that speaking in tongues had certainly not ceased over these centuries.

THE REFORMATION (1517–1648)

Instances of xenoglossia, **recognised** tongues, seem to dry up after the Reformation. Prior to that, most of the tongues incidents are recognised by hearers, or they are a miracle of understanding Latin. (One Protestant group, the Camisards, also enjoyed that gift, as we will see shortly.)

So the next examples, following the Reformation, mostly describe tongues which were unrecognised, and consistent with the tongues experienced in Acts 10:44–46 (the Gentiles) and 19:1–6 (the Ephesians).

George Fox (1624–1691 AD). We looked at the life of George Fox in Chapter 12. As we saw there, he relied heavily on the Holy Spirit in his ministry, and made this reference to tongues:

> And while waiting upon the Lord in silence... in our diligent waiting and fear of his name, and hearkening to his word, we received often the pouring down of the spirit upon us, and the gift of God's holy eternal spirit as in the days of old, and our hearts were made glad, and our tongues loosed, and our mouths opened, and we spake with new tongues, as the Lord gave us utterance and as his spirit led us, which was poured down upon us, on sons and daughters...[143]

The Camisards (Late 1600s and early 1700s)

Poor and mostly uneducated, the Camisards were Huguenots (French Protestants) living in the isolated and rugged Cévennes, a mountainous area of France. It is important to note that they spoke Occitan, a language quite unlike the native French of their country.

The Camisards have an extraordinary story, woven around a severe persecution that killed or displaced some half a million of their number. It began in 1685, when Louis XIV decided to impose a single religion on France—the Catholic faith. More than 2,000 Protestant churches were burned, entire villages massacred, possessions plundered and people killed, tortured, or sent to the galleys if they did not convert. It reached a peak in the Cévennes in 1703, with 466 hamlets destroyed and the people exiled. The Camisards eventually revolted, and there was ongoing conflict from about 1700 to 1710.

In the midst of all this, the Camisards worshipped in caves and houses in the mountains. Without preachers, Bibles or other resources, they turned to inspired prophetic spiritual gifts of prophecy and tongues for spiritual encouragement.

A French book published in 1707 (the title translates to: *The Sacred Theatre of Cévennes, or Tale of Various Wonders*) provides a number of accounts of these times. Coming from pious, firsthand witnesses, they are likely to be authentic. Here are some extracts.[144]

The first is from Jean Vernet, in 1707. (Note that the word "ecstasy" used here does not carry the meaning we apply today. It refers to a person being under the influence of the Holy Spirit.)

> I left Montpellier around May 1702. The first people I saw in inspiration were my mother, my brother, my two sisters and a cousin, Germaine. It has now been 13 years at least since my mother received her gifts (prophecy or tongues or both); she always had them since that time until my departure, and I learned from the various people who had seen her not long ago, she is still in the same state. She has been detained in prison for 11 years now.

> My sisters received the gift some time after my mother had received it; one at the age of 19, the other 11. *They died in my absence.* My mother's greatest agitations were of the chest, which made her produce great tears. She spoke nothing but French during the inspiration; which gave me a great surprise the first time I heard her; *because she had never tried to say a word in this language, nor has ever done since, at least to my recollection;...* [145] (Emphasis in original)

The following is related by a Jean Cabanel who attended a secret meeting in the woods. Note that these also are Camisards and Occitan speakers.

> I believe I saw at least 15 people of one and the other sex speaking at different times under the inspiration. They were all speaking French and I am quite sure that some of these that I specifically knew, *that did not know how to read*, would not have had the ability to express themselves in such good French being outside of ecstasy. [146] (Emphasis in original)

And this from a Jacque Dubois.

> I have seen *many* people of one and the other sex who in ecstasy were pronouncing certain words that the assistants believed to be a foreign language. Afterwards, they that were speaking explained several times the meaning of those sayings which they had been uttered. [147] (Emphasis in original)

It seems remarkable that these people, who must have despised the language of their French tormentors, spoke in French under the inspiration of the Spirit. One benefit of that twist was that some Camisards apparently understood the French language and were able to confirm the miracle and see it as encouragement from God.

THE TRANSITION

As we enter the mid- to late-1700s, two significant events impact the church, setting the scene for the emergence of the Pentecostal church a century later. The first: the increasing desire for spiritual holiness, sparked by the Wesleyan revival, and the second the French Revolution. We will look briefly at these and then walk through several fascinating outpourings during the 1800s.[148]

The Wesleyan Revival and Holiness

Since the Reformation 200 years before, Protestants had rejected the Catholic doctrine of a Holy Spirit blessing (received at confirmation) *subsequent* to salvation. John Wesley's ideas would change that and significantly open the door for the Spirit baptism.

In about 1725, while in his early twenties, Wesley began seeking a life of total holiness (or sanctification) and consecration to God. This commitment laid a foundation for the Methodist idea of Christian perfection which would follow later. Wesley related sanctification to love, saying:

> Entire sanctification, or Christian perfection, is neither more nor less than pure love—expelling sin and governing both the heart and life of the child of God.[149]

It is not easy to nail down Wesley's doctrines. He did not leave any systematic studies of theology, rather a random collection of 60 years of sermons and letters. However, British preacher, W. E. Sangster, an authority on this subject, sifted through them and made this observation:

> Wesley believed that the infusion of love into the soul of the believer, and the consequent expulsion of sin, was a gift of God in answer to faith, and happened in a moment. This infusion of love, he said, was not the fruit of effort and was not received through works of righteousness. It was a work of God, mightily performed by God in a truly believing heart.[150]

NOTE WELL: *"a gift of God, and happened in a moment"*. This was new ground for Protestants. As we have seen, Catholics believed something similar—that the Holy Spirit was received at Confirmation by laying on of hands—essentially also a gift of God that happened in a moment. Protestants had mostly abandoned that, and adopted a once only experience of salvation which included the simultaneous receiving of the Holy Spirit.

Wesley shifted from that position and, when he died, his successor, John Fletcher took it further.

Fletcher was more of a mystic than Wesley, and drew more heavily on the Book of Acts—to which Wesley rarely referred. Fletcher moved from the idea of a "second blessing" towards a "baptism in the Holy Spirit", though the focus was still primarily on holiness. But that new idea, of a second experience, was taught to Methodist leaders and taken up enthusiastically, especially in America. There, in the fast-expanding, pioneering west, the search for sanctification took on a meaning of its own, and people began to seek this special, tangible, experiential "blessing", received "in a moment". Those who received the gift were said to be "sanctified", and churches were established where this experience was a core belief. They became known as "Holiness Churches".

The second event which opened the door for the Pentecostal movement was:

The French Revolution

A renewed interest in Bible prophecy, the Spirit baptism and the gifts of the Spirit, was sparked by the tumultuous events of the French Revolution of 1789–1799. Protestants came to believe that the downfall of the French Catholic church was prophesied in the Book of Revelation. They decided the Millennium was fast approaching and they should expect another Last Days outpouring of the Holy Spirit as prophesied in Joel. Of great interest in this, of course, was the baptism in the Holy Spirit and the supernatural gifts of the Spirit. So, while incidents of tongues among Catholic saints seemed to dry up, over the next century, we find a large number of Holy Spirit outpourings among Protestants, accompanied by speaking in tongues. We will look at these now.

OUTPOURINGS AFTER WESLEY AND IN THE 1800s

Thomas Walsh, one of Wesley's preachers, in 1750 recorded in his diary, "This morning, the Lord gave me a language that I knew not of, raising my soul to him in a wonderful manner."[151]

Edward Irving (1792–1834 AD) Irving was a pioneer in the gifts of the Spirit. But his efforts to introduce these innovations would bring him controversy and, in the end, rejection.

A popular London Presbyterian pastor and theologian, Irving became interested in prophecy and the supernatural gifts of the Spirit, at a time of increasing interest in these subjects. Like Wesley, Irving believed the gifts of the Spirit lay dormant simply because of the absence of faith. When, in 1830, he heard about people speaking in tongues in Port Glasgow, Scotland, an area where he had previously preached on spiritual gifts, he immediately went to investigate. There he met a woman named Mary Campbell who spoke in tongues. Two of her friends, twin brothers, both spoke in tongues and interpreted their messages. People flocked to the Campbell's home for meetings where gifts of the Spirit were exercised freely. By 1831, a number of Irving's churches were exercising the spiritual gifts–all accompanied by intense controversy in the staid Presbyterian Church.

Though Irving did not speak in tongues himself, he came to believe tongues were the "outward and visible sign of that inward and invisible grace which the baptism in the Holy Spirit confereth".[152] As far as I can see, Irving was the first to make this connection between tongues and the Spirit baptism.

Irving's teaching on the subject caused great controversy throughout England. His church, which numbered some 1,500 to 2,000, eventually dismissed him—ostensibly not because of tongues, but because he allowed unauthorised people (including women) to speak, and he held what was seen as a heretical view of Christology. So, Irving and several others formed the Catholic Apostolic Church, where the gifts of the Spirit were taught and practised. But he was removed from leadership not long after. He eventually died of tuberculosis, and the movement petered out by about 1900, unaware that the Pentecostal church they had pre-empted by 70 years was about to begin its meteoric rise.

USA Camp Meetings, early 1800s. These had a tremendous effect on the strengthening and expansion of Christianity in the USA. What happened in these vast gatherings was mind boggling: extraordinary outpourings of the Holy Spirit, heart-rending conviction of sin, deep repentance and powerful conversions. One observer wrote: "They swooned away and lay for hours in the straw prepared for those 'smitten by the Lord'... or they shouted and talked in unknown tongues".[153]

Charles Finney—miraculous reading in the mid-1800s. We have read of the miraculous reading ability given to medieval Christians, but nothing since. Here is an example from Finney. A new convert, whom Finney described as a "tall, dignified-looking woman", had never learned to read and was "greatly distressed that she could not read God's word". But she thought "that Jesus could teach me to read, and I asked him if he would not please to teach me to read his word". Taking a New Testament belonging to her children, she attempted to read and thought she could. Being uncertain, however, she "went over to the school ma'am, and asked her if I *did* read right; and she said I did". Finney reported that the woman "seemed to be quite in earnest and quite intelligent", but quizzed her neighbours about it. They said she was of excellent character and "all affirmed she had been notorious that she had not been able to read a syllable until after she was converted". Finney concluded, "There is no use in theorising about it. Such, I think, are the undoubted facts".[154]

The 1859 Irish Revival. More than 100,000 people were soundly converted in this little-known outpouring. Hardened sinners were transformed, drunkenness and ribaldry gave way to prayer and praise. The annual Protestant Boyne Celebration—which always included a provocative march of Protestants through Catholic areas, with frequent rioting and bloodshed—did not happen. For an inspiring 16-page read about the event, see *The Ulster Revival of 1859,* by William H Harding.[155]

Most of the records about the revival are focused on the conversions. But a couple of brief extracts describe manifestations of the Holy Spirit, similar to those experienced in the Great Awakenings in America, the early days of the Salvation Army and other outpourings:

> The manifestations appeared at the beginning of the revival in Ahogill and continued throughout the course of the movement...After one outdoor meeting in county Antrim, an observer noted that, "the lawn was literally strewed like a battlefield with those that were stricken down in this mysterious manner".

> The emotional intensity of the revival meetings led in some cases to so called "physical manifestations"—prostrations, exaggerated movements, convulsions, uncontrollable utterances and trances, with those affected often claiming special gifts of the spirit, including gifts of "tongues", prophecy and visions.[156]

Portland, Australia 1870s:

> In 1870, a farmer named Joseph Marshall, formerly of Yorkshire...was conducting cottage meetings in the area. As far as is known, these were the first Pentecostal meetings held in Australia and among the first conducted anywhere in the world...He had also come to believe that the infilling of the Holy Spirit was accompanied by speaking in tongues with the result that several people experienced glossolalia.[157]

One of the participants, Richard Beauglehole, wrote:

> After three weeks' seeking, we were all on our knees praying when God took a wonderful hold of me. It was like being in an electrical machine. Although I was kneeling on the ground with my elbows on a stretcher, my knees knocked

together, and my belly trembled and I saw a light shining round me brighter than the noonday sun, and One in that light. It overcame me and my breath was leaving me, but I said, 'Here goes, Lord; sink, live or die, I must have the Holy Spirit'. And, glory to God, he did answer me. For a time, I was lost to everything and when I came to myself, my lips were trembling...and I heard the Spirit's voice, for he had taken possession of my throat and tongue and was speaking through me in other tongues. My mate got through the next morning at nine o'clock. And, oh, the heights and depths of the glory of God![158]

Sunderland, UK, with DL Moody. As we have seen, Moody was a dynamic American evangelist and 'mover and shaker' who impacted both the USA and England. Here again is the reference to a Moody campaign in Sunderland, UK (about 1875):

When I got to the rooms of the YMCA, I found the meeting on fire. The young men were speaking in tongues and prophesying. What on earth did it mean? Only that Moody had been addressing them that afternoon.[159]

The Schearer Schoolhouse Revival (1896) and Benjamin Hardin Irwin (of the "Fire-Baptised Holiness Church"), Camp Creek, North Carolina. In 1892, RG Spurling Jnr, a preacher and church pioneer, and William F Bryant, a Baptist lay preacher, joined forces with their churches and gave themselves to prayer and fasting for the people in their area. The revival began when an itinerant preacher, Benjamin Irwin, came to their area. Originally a lawyer, Irwin was converted in a Baptist church and became a preacher. Transferring later to the Wesleyan Methodists, he became a travelling holiness preacher. In 1895, he experienced what he called a "baptism of fire" and began to preach a *third* blessing, which created considerable controversy. His work spread rapidly, and churches he planted were called the Fire-Baptised Holiness Association. His meetings became known for extreme manifestations, and in this revival in the Schearer Schoolhouse, a number of people spoke in tongues. The people were fiercely persecuted—a log building they built was pulled down and burned by a mob. Much has been made of this event as a prelude to the Azusa Street outpouring.

An imposing marble monument now marks the spot, and boldly tells the story:

> **HOLY GHOST**
> "and the Holy Ghost descended in a bodily shape
> like a dove upon him (Jesus)..." Luke 3:22
> "I will pour out my Spirit upon all flesh..." Acts 2:17
>
> On or near this spot, in a log church house and in the Schearer Schoolhouse some few yards away, a great outpouring of the Holy Ghost occurred in the latter part of the nineteenth century, beginning in 1896. About one hundred persons received the baptism of the Holy Ghost and spoke in other tongues as the Spirit gave the utterance, according to Acts 2:4. Several of these became members of the church which sprang from a historic meeting on June 13, 1903, in Fields of the Wood (a Christian theme park) ...
>
> ..."For the promise is unto you, and to your children, and to all that are afar off, even as many as the Lord our God shall call." Acts 2:39
>
> Erected by the Church of God of Prophecy, Bible Place, Cleveland, Tenn. 1963 AD

Shiloh Community, Frank Sandford and Jenny Glassey: Frank Sandford was a controversial but magnetic leader. In the 1890s, he established a large (about 600 strong) Christian community called Shiloh, in Durham, Maine, USA. A woman named Jenny Glassy was said to have received the miraculous ability to speak and sing in unknown tongues. Sandford wrote:

> Had the joy tonight of hearing Brother Black and Sister Black and Sister Glassey sing a part of the ninth Psalm in an African tongue. Sister Glassey has, at different times,

spoken while in the Spirit, in Greek, French, Latin, German, Hebrew, Italian, Japanese, Chinese and several African dialects, words and sentences given her by the Holy Ghost. She has also written many letters of the Greek and Hebrew alphabet. Words in as many as six of these languages have been recognised as such by one who has studied classics, thus proving the genuineness of God's gifts to our sister. He who said, "They shall speak with new tongues" is proving his words true, thus enabling one like Sister Glassey to preach the "everlasting gospel" to any soul on this globe, with the necessary language at her disposal.[160]

Note that Sandford believed that tongues could be used to preach the gospel to other language groups. This idea would influence Pentecostals, as we shall see shortly.

Unfortunately, Frank Sandford, while sincere and fruitful in his ministry, introduced some unwise and cultish practices, bringing reproach and harm to his community.

India, 1897

In 1908, Thomas Barratt was invited to India to speak to missionaries resting in the hill stations during the summer months. In a place called Coonoor, he met an old Indian Christian who had spoken in tongues since about 1897. He was criticised for this by other Christians but nevertheless practised it in private. He said, "When I am very happy in the Lord and pray to Him, then it comes quite naturally".[161]

PULLING THAT TOGETHER

Church Fathers Chrysostom, Augustine and Aquinas believed God had switched off the supernatural gifts of the Spirit (including tongues). But we have just read many, many stories which tell a different story. Wesley's explanation seems to be the most plausible: any absence of these gifts could be blamed on faith "waxed cold".

For we read of tongues in the lives of Justin Martyr, Irenaeus, the Montanists, through famous saints such as Dominic, Francis of Assisi, Xavier, Hildegard and others, Fox and the Quakers, Thomas Walsh the Wesleyan preacher, the Camisards, the Irvingites, American Camp Meetings, the Irish Revival, Portland Australia, the Schearer Revival in North Carolina, and others who spoke in tongues "as the Spirit enabled them" (Acts 2:4).

Finer details of the earliest incidents are scarce. But through the Middle Ages and the medieval period there was obviously a predominance of gifts that overcame language barriers—in preaching, counselling, fellowship or reading. A few of those same people also used their gift for private devotions in singing praise to God.

Throughout that time, no clear theology of the Spirit baptism, or the gifts of the Spirit, emerged. But Wesley had sown a seed: holiness, he suggested, was a gift of God that could be received in an instant, after salvation. That idea was nurtured by Fletcher, and would evolve and flourish in the 1800s to form a doctrinal foundation for the Pentecostal outpouring in the twentieth century.

From Sanctification to Baptism in the Holy Spirit

During the first half of the 1800s, before the American Civil War, the "gift" of sanctification became highly prized. But, as time went on, expectations shifted from sanctification to an infilling of the Holy Spirit, not as a gift of holiness, but as an empowerment for service.

That shift was epitomised in two versions of a book entitled *Scripture Doctrine of Christian Perfection,* by Asa Mahan, president of Oberlin College, Oberlin, Ohio. His first version, published in 1839, was a defence of the Wesleyan theology of the second blessing (entire sanctification). His key scriptures covered issues such as sin, cleansing, the new heart, Christ in us, perfection, etc. Thirty-one years later, he revised the book and gave it a new title—*The Baptism in the Holy Ghost.* This time, his key verses related to the outpouring of the Holy Spirit, prophesied in Joel and fulfilled in Acts 2, together with many other passages related to the Holy Spirit. He also featured second blessing stories of people like the Wesleys, Madam Guyon (a French mystic, 1648–1717) and Finney, identifying these as the "baptism in the Holy Spirit".[162]

That was a dramatic shift.

Another author, William Arthur, added more fuel to the fire in 1856 with a pivotal book, *The Tongue of Fire*. Arthur dismissed the cessation view and encouraged faith in a resurgence of the spiritual gifts. He said:

> We feel satisfied that he who does expect the gift of healing and the gift of tongues or any other miraculous manifestation of the Holy Spirit... has ten times more scriptural ground on which to base his expectation, than have they for their unbelief who do not expect supernatural sanctifying strength for the believer.[163]

The idea of spiritual gifts of the early church and power for today was steadily emerging.

As the holiness movement expanded in the USA, a similar group arose in England in 1875 called the **Keswick Movement**. Inspired by a book by William Boardman, *The Higher Christian Life*, the Keswick Movement believed in a second work of grace to enable Christians to overcome sin. They rejected the idea of "sinless perfection" preached by some American holiness preachers, but "retained the emphasis that a normative Christian life is characterised by 'fullness of the Spirit.' It is this, they argued, that gives power for living a consistent Christian life".[164] This teaching created fertile ground for the emerging idea of a baptism in the Holy Spirit, whose purpose was not for holiness, but power for witnessing.

The Keswick teachings were also taken up by other key leaders of the time: **DL Moody** (already mentioned), **RA Torrey**, **AB Simpson** and others. Keswick also had an emphasis on the second coming of Christ (the pre-millennial view), healing and the gifts of the Spirit.

DL Moody, the most influential evangelist of his day, ran Keswick Higher Life conferences in Massachusetts each year, attracting thousands of Christians seeking a "personal Pentecost".

In 1855, renowned preacher, **Charles H Spurgeon** added his voice in a sermon entitled, *The Power of the Holy Ghost*, saying:

> Another great work of the Holy Spirit which is not accomplished is *the bringing on of the latter-day glory*. In a few more years—I know not when, I know not how—the Holy Spirit will be poured out in far different style from the present... My heart exalts and my eyes flash with the thought that very likely I shall live to see the outpouring of the Spirit; when "the sons and the daughters of God shall prophesy, and the young men shall see visions, and the old men shall dream dreams".[165]

Spurgeon died in 1892. The glories he dreamed of, in a "far different style", would follow a decade later. Whether he would have recognised them is a moot point.

And so, the understanding of the Holy Spirit was gradually transformed. **RA Torrey** (1856-1928), the first president of the Moody Bible Institute, summed up the new idea:

> The baptism with the Holy Spirit is an operation of the Holy Spirit distinct from and subsequent from his regenerating work, an impartation of power for service... not merely for the apostles, not merely for those of the apostolic age, but for "all that are afar off; even as many as the Lord our God shall call"... It is for every believer, in every age of the church's history.[166]

The interest in the Holy Spirit became so strong at the end of the nineteenth century, that C I Scofield, whose 1909 Reference Bible would become the staple diet of evangelical Christians, claimed that there were more books written about the Holy Spirit in the last decade of the 1800s, than in all preceding Christian history.

And it is worth reflecting again here on the insights of Augustus H Strong, and his pondering the possibility that "the doctrine of the Holy Spirit... may be the work of our age (the twentieth century)"[167]

Catholics

We have already seen significant activity of the Holy Spirit in the Catholic Church over earlier centuries, after which it seemed to decline amidst the bitter conflicts of the Reformation.

In the late 1800s, there was a renewed interest in the Holy Spirit among theologians in the Catholic Church. In 1897, the Pope issued a letter calling for a "novena", special prayers for the Holy Spirit over nine consecutive days, to be conducted each year between Easter and Pentecost throughout the Catholic Church. This was a significant shift, and all the more so in that it coincided with Protestant movement in the same direction.

Finally

The scene is set. The Holy Spirit is front and centre stage, waiting for the curtain to rise. God's hand, poised over the levers, would move into action on the first day of the 20th century–1 January 1901. True to form, however, his methods would be unorthodox, and unexpected. As a result, many saints would be caught unawares, and some would miss out altogether.

We are about to witness the birth of a movement which, we have seen, would be embraced by some 600 million people in a little more than a century. It would require two leaders, immune to entrenched traditions and denominational dogma, and resilient enough to withstand the criticisms and persecutions their ideas would spark.

The first was Charles F Parham, an immensely capable maverick, with controversial doctrines but a powerful and magnetic ministry of the Holy Spirit. The other was William J Seymour, a gentle, humble African-American, the son of former slaves, blind in one eye, his face scarred by smallpox.

They entered the scene at literally the dawn of the twentieth century, ushering in an unprecedented spiritual revolution, the greatest influence on the Christian church since the Reformation.

First of all, Charles Parham.

Discovery consists of seeing what everybody has seen and thinking what nobody has thought.

ALBERT SZENT-GYORGYI (1893–1986)

You have enemies? Good. That means you've stood up for something, sometime in your life.

WINSTON CHURCHILL

A person with a new idea is a crank until the idea succeeds.

MARK TWAIN

CHAPTER 10
THE AZUSA STREET REVIVAL: CATALYST CHARLES PARHAM

CHARLES F PARHAM 1873–1929

In late December 1900, Charles F Parham set a special assignment for his Bible School students, the results of which would shake the Christian world. The idea that emerged was radical and unprecedented, so much so that many would reject it out of hand. Parham, who walked his own path, bowed to no one, and trusted God implicitly, was well-suited to the task of spreading the news. But his stubborn nature also made him a target for criticism and persecution. Some of that persecution he was lucky to survive, and some might have been justifiable. To make things worse for him, he was a holiness preacher, and rebuking all kinds of sin added fuel to the fire. Today, critics of the Pentecostal view are quick to focus on Parham's controversies and weaknesses, real or perceived, to discredit him. We will touch on those controversies later in the chapter. In the meantime, here is his story.

Parham's mother passed away when he was nine. Her words, "Charlie be good", left him with an unshakable determination to meet her again one day in heaven. Along with that experience, a recurring scripture would haunt him, "Woe is me if I preach not the gospel", and he resolved to dedicate his life to that purpose.[168]

At the age of 13, Parham became assured of salvation as he walked home from an evangelistic meeting. He said, "There flashed from the heavens a light above the brightness of the sun, like a stroke of lightning it penetrated, thrilling every fibre of my being".[169]

In those days, out on the prairie, there was no one to prepare him for ministry. So, he trained himself by studying books from his parents' library:

> The letters from hell, a natural history, a few antiquated schoolbooks, a dictionary, a history of all nations, recording facts from early historic times until 1878; and last, but not least the Bible... almost a constant companion... Thus, with no preconceived ideas, with no knowledge of what creeds and doctrines meant, not having any traditional spectacles upon the eyes to see through, I scarcely knew anything about church and Sunday School. These facts are stated to show that any early scriptures were entirely unbiased. I became thoroughly familiar with it, reading it just as it says.[170]

Thus, unburdened by any traditions and denominationalism his peers might have known, Parham was not overly concerned about teaching anything that might 'go against the flow'.

He began preaching at 15, and entered college at 16, but became discouraged about his plans for a future ministry when he became aware of a worldly disrespect for ministers and the poverty they suffered. So he abandoned his call, and set out to be a doctor. Soon after, he contracted rheumatic fever which left him bedridden for months, and near death. After a lengthy battle with God, he reached the conclusion it was God's will to heal, and his lungs and whole body were miraculously and totally restored. Making a recommitment to ministry, he began to evangelise at 18 and, at 19, was asked to pastor a Methodist church—that fact giving us a hint of Parham's capabilities. His church flourished, but the leaders eventually opposed him when he sent some converts to other denominations. He later said:

> Finding the confines of a pastorate, and feeling the narrowness of sectarian churchism, I was often in conflict with

the higher authorities, which eventually resulted in open rupture; and I left denominationalism forever, though suffering bitter persecution at the hands of the church... Oh, the narrowness of many who call themselves the Lord's own![171]

Parham's unorthodox preaching raised eyebrows—on several issues. Firstly, he came to believe in the ultimate annihilation of the wicked. He also embraced British Israelism, another controversial subject, which relates to the "lost" ten tribes of Israel. When the 12-tribed Jews were carried into Assyrian and Babylonian captivity (about 500–700 BC) two southern tribes eventually returned to their homeland, but the other ten northern tribes did not, and were "lost" from history. British Israelism teaches that this group drifted to England (and consequently America), and an alliance of those countries (and others from the same mould) would, in the last days, unite with Israel in the final battle of Armageddon. Parham preached this message using elaborate props from Palestine, and was a zealous supporter of Israel.

He also embraced the contentious ministry of divine healing (more on that shortly). Most contentious of all though, as we shall see, was the Spirit baptism with speaking in tongues. Parham also created many enemies by consistently rebuking the social evils of the day.

His fame spread and he preached to crowds of up to 7,000. Most Christians 'turned a blind eye' to his unconventional doctrines and eccentricities because of the abundant healing miracles and the many lives transformed. Others, though, severely persecuted him and his team.

For example, when Parham first visited Zion City (which had been established by Dowie—who opposed the emergence of Pentecostalism), slanderous posters were placed around the city, warning people to avoid him. In Baxter Springs, Kansas, his tent ropes were cut. In Galveston, after suffering stomach pains, a chemist confirmed that the glass of water in his pulpit was poisoned. Claiming protection from Mark 16:18 (believers would "drink deadly poison, it will not hurt them at all"), he recovered. In Texas, he was controversially arrested on a charge of sodomy. The city attorney dismissed the case, concluding it was lodged because of spite. In Bartley, Nebraska, during WWI, it was rumoured Parham was a German spy. Eggs were thrown at him, and a 50-pound can of water, hurled from an upstairs window, narrowly missed him. In Wichita, Kansas, a group of ruffians with pitchforks and clubs lay in wait as he walked home. A big burly man, however, sympathetic towards Parham, escorted him home by another route.

From the time he began itinerant ministry, Parham trusted God completely for his support. He refused to take a church salary, believing his income should come from faithful giving of Christians, and not raised by "suppers and worldly entertainment". He married and began a family but contracted a heart disease for which medicine was no help. Their baby also became sick with a high fever that defied diagnosis. After further wrestling with God, both were healed through prayer and, from that point, Parham decided to trust only God, and not the doctors, for his and his family's healing—adding one more item to his list of contentious beliefs.

Not long after, two of his closest friends died. Overcome with grief he said:

> As I knelt between the graves of my two loved friends, who might have lived if I had but told them of the power of Christ to heal, I made a vow that 'live or die', I would preach this gospel of healing.[172]

So, he did, witnessing many remarkable miracles, including a blind lady receiving sight. At that time, few understood healing through prayer, and he was further criticised, and the miracles attributed to the devil. But, shutting himself away, he searched the Bible, returning even more convinced he was on the right track. So much so, that he set up a healing home in Topeka, Kansas, which he named Bethel.

In this tranquil place, prayer and counselling for healing were continually available. Classes were run for ministers and evangelists, assistance given to find work, orphans cared for, and a bi-weekly newsletter of testimonies and sermons published. Trusting God completely for finance, his work flourished.

In spite of his successes, Parham was still spiritually dissatisfied and, in 1900, took time to visit ministries in other cities. This included Alexander

Dowie in Zion City, and evangelist Frank Sandford, already mentioned. Of that trip he said:

> I returned home fully convinced that, while many had obtained real experience in sanctification and the anointing that abideth, there still remained a great outpouring of power for the Christians who were to close this age.[173]

It was not long to come. But, before that, one more test of faith lay before him. Prior to leaving on his trip, he had welcomed to his church some Holiness preachers from the east. Consistent with his gracious non-denominational, open-door policy, he was happy to leave his church in their care while he was gone. It didn't go well. He wrote:

> Through underhand scheming and falsehoods, the ministers I left in charge of my work had not only taken my building but most of my congregation. My friends urged me to claim my own, but the Word says, "resist not evil... but if any man will sue thee at the law, and take away thy coat, let him have thy cloak as well".[174] (Quoting from Matthew 5:38–40)

So, he fasted and prayed to seek God's will. Many friends had previously asked him to start a Bible School, and he decided to do that. He described what happened:

> By a series of wonderful miracles, we were enabled to secure what was then known as "Stone's Folly". A great mansion... in Topeka Kansas...
>
> How marvellously God made all things work together for good when we wholly committed our ways unto him and left our case in his hands. Instead of taking up the work that we had (i.e., his church), God had a greater, and grander work for us to do... If we had not fully obeyed the scriptures to "resist not evil", and showed a Christian spirit, I am afraid we would not have received the baptism of the Holy Spirit.

God had taught us that we were not only to preach the Word but to practice it and have it wrought out in our lives if we were to have his best.[175]

A gracious response to a trying incident that had cost him dearly.

Their new facility, "Stone's Folly", was named after its builder, who ran out of money before completion. In the "prayer tower", students were rostered to pray three-hour shifts, day and night, every day, women during the day, men at night. It was here that the fire would fall.

Parham continues with his story.

> We opened the Bible School at Topeka, Kansas, in October 1900. To which we invited all ministers and Christians who were willing to forsake all, sell what they had, give it away, and enter the school for study and prayer, where all of us together might trust God for food, fuel, rent and clothing. The purpose of this school was to fit men and women to go to the ends of the earth to preach "This Gospel of the Kingdom" Matt. 24, as a witness to all the world before the end of the age.
>
> Our purpose in this Bible School was not to learn these things in our heads only, but have each thing in the scriptures wrought in our hearts. And that every command that Jesus Christ gave should be literally obeyed.[176]

One of the students described the approach:

> The method of study was to take a subject, learn the references on that subject, also where each quotation was found, and present to the class in recitation as though they were seekers, praying for the anointing of the Holy Spirit be upon the message in such a way as to bring conviction.[177]

Parham continues:

> No one paid board or tuition, the poor were fed, the sick were entertained and healed and, from day to day, week to week and month to month, with no sect or mission or known source of income back of us, God supplied our every need, and he was our all sufficiency in all things.
>
> In December of 1900, we had had our examinations upon the subject of repentance, conversion, consecration, sanctification, healing and the soon coming of the Lord. We had reached in our studies a problem. What about the 2nd Chapter of Acts? I had felt for years that any missionary going to the foreign field should preach in the language of the natives. That, if God had ever equipped his ministers in that way, he could do it today. That, if Balaam's mule could stop in the middle of the road and give the first preacher that went out for money a "bawling out" in Arabic, that anybody today ought to be able to preach in any language of the world if they had horse-sense enough to let God use their tongue and throat. But still I believed our experience should tally exactly with the Bible, and neither sanctification nor the anointing that abideth taught by Stephen Merritt[178] and others tallied with the 2nd Chapter of Acts. Having heard so many different religious bodies claim different proofs as the evidence of the baptism of the Holy Ghost, that we might go before the world with something that was indisputable because it tallied absolutely with the Word.

So that was Parham's situation: The mystery of Acts 2, the "the evidence of the baptism of the Holy Ghost", speaking in tongues, and how that gift could be used. He knew it was an issue of paramount importance, and desperately wanted to know the answer. But a multitude of diverse views surrounded him.

CM Robeck, in *The Azusa Street Mission and Revival*, compiled important background to this story. Parham had recently spent six weeks with Frank Sandford at his Shiloh Community in Maine. Robeck describes the effect this had on him:

Like Parham, Sandford had embraced the holiness position, taught the Anglo-Israelite theory, was an advocate of divine healing and, as a result of Dwight L Moody's summer conferences in Northfield, Massachusetts, committed to world evangelism. In 1892, following a trip around the world, Sandford came to believe that all current missionary and evangelistic methods were inadequate and ineffective. He decided that God wanted him to work along "apostolic lines", in which "signs, wonders and mighty deeds" would empower those working towards world evangelisation. This shift would require the restoration of New Testament power and would include such things as the restoration of the gift of tongues, that is, the recovery of an ability to speak languages of the world without prior study, under the direct inspiration of the Holy Spirit, for the ultimate evangelisation of the world.

Parham's visit to Shiloh had a profound effect on him. He concluded that the baptism in the Holy Spirit was available to all believers who lived a holy life and sought to attain it. He believed in the restoration of the gifts of the Holy Spirit listed in 1 Corinthians 12–14. He came to believe, like Sandford, that the gift of tongues meant the ability to speak different foreign languages of the world without prior knowledge or study. This would become the ultimate evangelistic tool, for the person with this gift would be able to proclaim the gospel in a foreign setting in complete reliance upon and under the direct inspiration of the Holy Spirit.[179]

As a result of these views, a number of early Pentecostals went to the mission field expecting to preach through the gift of tongues, without learning the local language. But they were all unsuccessful. Unlike the medieval saints we have seen (of whom they were probably unaware), these early Pentecostal pioneers were unable to make themselves understood, and either returned home disappointed, or learned the language like everyone else. What went wrong? This issue is worth investigating, and we will do that at the end of the chapter.

In spite of that setback, and while that understanding of tongues needed refining, the underlying principle lay intact: the Holy Spirit baptism provided supernatural power for witnessing, and was a gift that should be pursued. And they did that passionately.

So, when Parham returned to Topeka, he decided to set the problem as a student assignment. He was due to take a three-day preaching trip, so he told students to complete the task by his return on New Year's Eve.

One of his students, (his sister-in-law Miss Lilian Thistlethwaite), recalled Parham's instruction to them:

> Students, as I have studied the teachings in the various Bible Schools and full gospel movements, conviction, conversion, healing and sanctification are taught virtually the same, but on the baptism (in the Spirit) there is a difference among them. Some accept Steven Merritt's teaching of baptism at sanctification, while others say this is only the anointing and there is a baptism received through the "laying on of hands" or the gift of the Holy Ghost, yet they agree on no definite evidence. Some claim this fulfilment of promise "by faith" without any special witness, while others, because of wonderful blessings or demonstrations, such as shouting or jumping. Though I honour the Holy Ghost in anointing power both in conversion and in sanctification, yet I believe there is a greater revelation of his power. The gifts are in the Holy Spirit and with the baptism of the Holy Spirit the gifts, as well as the graces, should be manifested. Now students, while I am gone, see if there is not some evidence given of the baptism so there may be no doubt on the subject.[180]

Back again to Parham:

> Leaving the school for three days at this task, I went to Kansas City for three days of services. I returned to the school on the morning preceding Watch Night[181] services in the year 1900.

At about ten o'clock in the morning, I rang the bell calling all the students into the Chapel to get their report on the matter in hand. To my astonishment, they all had the same story, that while there were different things occurred when the Pentecostal blessings fell, that the indisputable proof on each occasion was, that they spake with other tongues.

This was, of course, radical new ground. In the centuries prior, as we have seen, there had been many outpourings of the Holy Spirit, and from time to time, people had spoken in tongues. But few had persuasively drawn the conclusion: **the baptism in the Holy Spirit comes with speaking in tongues, and speaking in tongues is the evidence and confirmation of the experience**.

Parham continues his story:

> About 75 people, beside the school which consisted of 40 students, had gathered for the watch night service. A mighty spiritual power filled the entire school.
>
> Sister Agnes N Ozman (now Laberge) asked that hands might be laid upon her to receive the Holy Spirit as she hoped to go to foreign fields. At first I refused, not having the experience myself. Then being further pressed to do it humbly in the name of Jesus, I laid my hand upon her head and prayed. I had scarcely repeated three dozen sentences when a glory fell upon her, a halo seemed to surround her head and face, and she began speaking in the Chinese language, and was unable to speak English for three days. When she tried to write in English to tell us of her experience she wrote the Chinese, copies of which we still have in newspapers printed at that time.[182]

Hear from Ozman in her own words:

> Like some others, I thought that I had received the baptism of the Holy Ghost at consecration but, when I learned that

the Holy Ghost was yet to be poured out in greater fullness, my heart became hungry for the promised Comforter, and I began to cry out for an enduement with power from on high. At times, I longed more for the Holy Spirit to come in than for my necessary food. At night, I had a greater desire for him than for sleep...

On watch night, we had a blessed service, praying that God's blessing might rest upon us as the New Year came in. During the first day of 1901, the presence of the Lord was with us in a marked way, stilling our hearts to wait upon him for greater things. The spirit of prayer was upon us in the evening. It was nearly seven o'clock on this first of January that it came into my heart to ask Brother Parham to lay his hands upon me that I might receive the gift of the Holy Spirit. It was as his hands were laid upon my head that the Holy Spirit fell upon me, and I began to speak in tongues, glorifying God. I talked several languages, and it was clearly manifest when a new dialect was spoken. I had the added joy and glory my heart longed for and a depth of the presence of the Lord within that I had never known before. It was as if rivers of living waters were proceeding from my innermost being.

The following morning, I was accosted with questions about my experience of the night before. As I tried to answer, I was so full of glory that I pointed out to them the Bible references, showing that I had received the baptism according to Acts 2:4 and 19:1–6. I was the first one to speak in tongues in the Bible School and it seemed to me that the rest were wanting to speak in tongues too. But I told them not to seek for tongues but to seek for the Holy Ghost. I did not know at that time that anyone else would speak in tongues. I did not expect the Holy Spirit to manifest himself to others as he did to me...[183]

Following this event, the school cleared a dormitory on an upper floor and waited on God for two nights and three days. Parham continues:

> Those three days of tarrying were wonderful days of blessings. We all got past any begging or pleading, we knew the blessing was ours with ever swelling tides of praise and thanksgiving and worship, interspersed with singing, we waited for the coming of the Holy Spirit.
>
> On the night of 3rd January, I preached at the Free Methodist Church in the City of Topeka, telling them what had already happened, and that I expected upon returning the entire school to be baptised in the Holy Spirit. On returning to the school with one of the students, we ascended to the second floor, and passing down along the corridor in the upper room, heard the most wonderful sounds. The door was slightly ajar, the room was lit with only coal oil lamps. As I pushed open the door, I found the room was filled with a sheen of white light above the brightness of the lamps.
>
> Twelve ministers, who were in the school of different denominations, were filled with the Holy Spirit and spoke with other tongues. Some were sitting, some still kneeling, others standing with hands upraised. There was no violent physical manifestation, though some trembled under the power of the glory that filled them.
>
> Sister Stanley, an elderly lady, came across the room as I entered, telling me that, just before I entered, tongues of fire were sitting above their heads.
>
> When I beheld the evidence of the restoration of Pentecostal power, my heart was melted in gratitude to God for what my eyes had seen. For years, I had suffered terrible persecutions for preaching holiness and healing and the soon coming of the Lord. I fell to my knees behind a table, unnoticed by those upon whom the power of Pentecost had fallen, to pour out my heart in thanksgiving. All at once,

they began to sing, "Jesus Lover of my Soul", in at least six different languages, carrying the different parts but with a more angelic voice than I had ever listened to in all my life.

After praising God for some time, I asked him for the same blessing. He distinctly made it clear to me that he raised me up and trained me to declare this mighty truth to the world, and if I was willing to stand for it, with all the persecutions, hardships, trials, slander and scandal that it would entail, he would give me the blessing. And I said, "Lord I will, if you will just give me this blessing". Right then, there came a slight twist in my throat, a glory came over me and I began to worship God in the Swedish tongue which later changed to other languages and continued so until the morning.

Just a word: after preaching this for all these years with all the persecutions I have been permitted to go through, with misunderstanding and the treatment of false brethren, yet knowing all that this blessing would bring to me, if I had that time and was back there again, I'd take the same way.[184]

A wide cross-section of denominations was involved in that event. As we have seen, there were ministers from twelve denominations, and Parham's sister-in-law also commented:

> I do not know to what denomination all belonged, who received the baptism at Bethel Bible School, but some were Methodists, others Friends, and some Holiness, while many belonged to no denomination. There were only white persons present at the first Pentecostal shower. No coloured people were ever in the school.[185]

When news of the speaking in tongues leaked out, it caused a tremendous stir. Sarah Parham wrote, "No sooner was this miraculous restoration of Pentecostal power noised abroad, than we were besieged with reporters from Topeka papers, Kansas City, St Louis and many other cities sent reporters."[186]

Much was made of the fact that some of the tongues were recognised. Agnes Ozman wrote about it:

> On 2 January, some of us went down to Topeka to a mission. As we worshipped the Lord, I offered prayer in English and then prayed in another language in tongues. A [Czechoslovakian] who was present said that he understood what I said. Some months later, at a schoolhouse with others, in a meeting, I spoke in tongues in the power of the spirit and another Bohemian understood me. Since then, others have understood other languages I have spoken.[187]

Eventually Stone's Folly was sold, and everyone had to leave, so Parham began preaching tours again. In 1903, he had an immensely successful campaign in Galena, Kansas. A 2,000 seat tent became far too small for the huge crowds. There were many miracles and gifts of the Holy Spirit—one newspaper reported that many of the most prominent people in the town "were healed of blindness, cancer, rheumatism and other diseases".[188] Sarah Parham wrote much of the events, quoting several other reports from local papers. For example, from the Cincinnati Enquirer and Joplin News Herald, 27 January, 1904:

> Over three months have elapsed since this man came to Galena, and during that time, he has healed over a thousand people and converted over 800... Mr Parham is the possessor of such a wonderful personality that some have accused him of hypnotising his followers.
>
> Others go so far as to call him a fanatic, but one and all, regardless of sect or prejudices, agree that he has brought about conditions that were never witnessed in this section. Evening after evening, the large room is packed with people, many of whom 'have gone to scoff but remained to pray'.[189]

Accusations against Parham

As I mentioned at the start, Parham had his critics—and still has today. They raise a number of issues, including heresy, the charge of sodomy, and racism, arguing these are symptomatic of a flawed character and consequently cast doubt on his doctrines. For example, John MacArthur writes, "... the personal character of Charles Parham calls into question whether the Holy Spirit would spark a worldwide revival through Parham's ministry".[190] A number of things can be said in response.

Firstly, many eminent past leaders had quite serious faults. For example, it is not widely known that Martin Luther was extremely anti-Semitic. He urged Christians to burn Jewish synagogues and schools, raze their houses, confiscate their writings, take their silver and gold, and more. However, those things, as terrible as they are, do not invalidate the rest of Luther's teachings. They stand or fall on correct understanding of scripture, not the sins or virtues of the teacher. That same principle applies to everyone, including Parham.

Luther's story reminds us that God is happy to employ flawed human vessels, and likely to choose "the foolish things of the world..." (1 Corinthians 1:27). We would love for Christian forbears to have all led exemplary lives. The reality is that is rarely the case.

Secondly, addressing the issues of heresy, sodomy charges and racism:

The heresy accusation refers mainly to his doctrines of destiny of the wicked (annihilation), the British Israel theory (essentially a view of Bible prophecy), divine healing (his rejection of doctors did not help), and the holiness doctrine (which taught sanctification as a separate experience after the salvation). Given Parham's lack of Bible training, it is not surprising that he would deviate, rightly or wrongly, on some issues. Nevertheless, as we have seen, Parham did teach his students important fundamentals: repentance, conversion and consecration, and he carefully prepared them for evangelism (in which, as we have seen, he was very successful). On these core issues, Parham is very solid.

The charge of homosexuality was not proven. It could have been fabricated–many of his persecutors were malicious in their attacks. Or he may have suffered a besetting sin which he was unable to overcome–a problem not uncommon in prominent leaders due to their isolation. (More on this issue in Appendix D: The Fruit of the Spirit–overlooked and concealed faults in prominent leaders.)

Again, if the charge against him is true, his doctrines stand or fall on how they measure up to scripture, and not on his sins or virtues.

Was Parham racist? Based on today's expectations (not always a reasonable measure), Parham would probably be considered racist as he allowed whites only in his Bible college. But we know that Jim Crow laws forbade mixed Bible colleges at that time and those laws would not be easy to defy. However, there was evidence that he supported integrated meetings. For example, at a gathering in Baxter Springs, an observer noted that white people, coloured people and Indians all took part in the meeting and were made to feel at home. Parham famously quipped, "We had the gospel in black, white and red all over".[191]

Parham's sister-in-law gave some insight into Parham's personal life which, allowing for any natural bias, contributes to this discussion. She writes:

> As Mrs Parham's sister, it has been my privilege to be in their home or in touch with their work continually... His family was dear to him. He enjoyed doing the little things about the home, caring for the children and giving the love service, which makes life worth living... He rejoiced in the opportunity to "overcome evil with good". He also practised the command to "Give to every man that asketh of thee, and to him that would borrow of thee, turn not away", and God rewarded a hundredfold. Many times, he gave the last cent he had, or clothes and food that would be needed the following day... A marked characteristic of his work was his ability to reach all classes, the rich and the cultured, the poor and the outcast of society, with the same touch of understanding that makes of one common brotherhood all God's creatures.[192]

One more insight. When Parham died in 1929, at the age of 56, a remarkable 2,500 mourners attended his funeral—in the snow.

The *Daily Commercial*, a local paper from Three Rivers, Michigan, summed him up this way, "He is one of the most loved, and at the same time, one of the most hated, men in the United States".[193]

We will finish with one more criticism of Parham, regarding a doctrine that didn't work out as he expected.

What happened to xenoglossia—preaching in tongues?

As we have seen, Parham believed Christians should be able to speak in the tongues of other nations without learning them. He was criticised for that, then and today. Cessationist, John MacArthur, is forceful:

> (Parham and his students) were convinced speaking in tongues entailed the miraculous ability to speak in authentic foreign languages, just as the apostles did... The gift they received, however, consisted of nothing more than nonsensical gibberish. This reality became painfully obvious when Parham insisted that Pentecostal missionaries could go to foreign lands without first going to language schools.[194]

And that, says MacArthur, "calls the legitimacy of Parham's claims (about the baptism in the Holy Spirit) into serious question".[195]

In response, it firstly needs to be said that Parham was not alone with this creative but unconventional idea.

About ten years prior, AB Simpson (founder of the Christian Missionary Alliance), wrote on this subject. In 1889, one of his missionaries, the famous C T Studd, and seven others, went to the Chinese mission field believing God would empower them to preach in Chinese without them learning the language. But they were unsuccessful. Studd later wrote of the Chinese reaction: "They did not understand us at all at first at Hanchung—thought us idle fanatics".[196] They then learned the language in the normal way.

Others too, entertained the same idea, and Simpson addressed that in a sermon. He said:

> In our own day, there is the same strained and extravagant attempt to unduly exaggerate the gift of tongues, and some have even proposed that we should send our missionaries to the foreign field under a sort of moral obligation to claim this gift, and to despise the ordinary methods of acquiring a language. Such a movement would end in fanaticism and bring discredit upon the truth itself. We know of more than one instance where our beloved missionaries have been saved from this error and led to prosecute their studies in foreign languages with fidelity and diligence, and their efforts have been rewarded by supernatural help in acquiring languages in a remarkably short time, but not in despair of proper industry and the use of their own faculties under God's direction in acquiring these languages.[197]

So, even though Parham's idea failed, he was in good company. Remember, he was fumbling in the dark, trying to understand something new and untried. Kudos to him for stepping out.

Now, while a number of Parham's missionaries had tried this plan unsuccessfully, a decade or so later another Pentecostal ventured into this world, but in a slightly different way.

In 1922, American Assemblies of God missionaries, Henry and Ruth Garlock, went to Liberia in West Africa to evangelise the hostile and cannibalistic Pahn tribe. On one occasion, one of their Liberian helpers, captured by the Pahns, was about to be killed and eaten. So Garlock concocted a brave rescue plan. Trusting God for protection, he walked boldly into the village, straight between two startled guards, and into the hut where the badly beaten man was prisoner. The guards, however, raised the alarm, and the hut was quickly surrounded by the tribe, its chief and the witchdoctor. The trapped missionary, seated on an elephant skull outside the hut, and unable to understand the language, was then berated for a long time by the witchdoctor. When that finally ended, the witchdoctor threw his wand before the missionary, obviously demanding his response. Garlock began to shake, the words of Mark 13:11 coming to his mind: "Whenever you are arrested and brought to trial, do not worry beforehand about what to say. Just say whatever is given you at the time, for it is not you speaking, but the Holy Spirit". Then, impressed by the Holy Spirit, he addressed them all in tongues, in words he obviously did not understand. A silence then followed, after which the witch-doctor took a rooster, broke its neck, and sprinkled its blood on Garlock, the prisoner, the chief and himself. The chief and the elders, communicating by sign language and a few words they knew, pleaded, "Please do not harm us. We see that your God has power and fights for you. What can we do to atone for mistreating you?" Garlock and the prisoner were then freed, and assisted out of the area.[198]

In this extraordinary event, Garlock unwittingly achieved what Parham attempted; he spoke a message from God in tongues, and the people recognised it. What was different this time? We will look at that in a moment, but first, think about this. Although Parham's and Studd's efforts failed, the medieval Christians we have already seen and the Occitan-speaking Camisards, communicated supernaturally with others of different languages. Now here, in 1922, we have missionary Garlock doing the same. More recent examples can be found too—not plentiful, but more than enough to make the point. Here are a few I have gathered from pastor and missionary friends.

Pastor Roger Rice told me that, as he ministered to an Indonesian lady, he felt compelled to pray in tongues. She told him afterwards he had prayed in her language—for her country, and also for her four children. The odd thing was she had three children, not four, but had suffered an earlier miscarriage. It was significant to her that Roger's prayer embraced all four. She was greatly encouraged. Roger, of course, had no idea what he was saying.[199]

At a New Year's Eve prayer meeting, Pastor Rob Bailey sat down, hands lifted, eyes closed, praying quietly in tongues. Suddenly, he became aware that the man beside him had twisted in his seat, and was looking up into his face. The man told Rob he was speaking his own language—Maltese. The man was defensive when Rob asked what he had been saying, but, several months later, he apologised. He said, "I was so shocked at what you were saying, that I lied to you when you asked me what you had said. Actually, God had been talking to me about going back to Malta and setting some things right with someone there. I had been resisting doing that, but your words reminded me I needed to do this".[200]

Pastor Darryl Stott gave me this:

> A new follower of Jesus asked me to come and pray for his son who suffered from attention deficit and hyperactivity disorder quite severely. They had tried medical and psychological treatments to no avail. He was unfamiliar with tongues, so I asked his permission before I spoke out loudly in tongues before ministering to the boy. When I spoke, I realised it was not my usual tongue but a strong guttural sound. The father leaped out of his chair, shaking and stammering. "You spoke ancient Croatian that my grandfather speaks, which I understand but cannot speak fluently! You said 'Demon. Leave this house!'" He wanted more of the Holy Spirit for himself. He received the baptism in the Holy Spirit with his wife, and saw his child have a breakthrough.[201]

Here is another from a different source: Kevin Zadai's book, *Praying from the Heavenly Realms*. After a prolonged period of prayer and fasting, Zadai felt prompted to worship God by singing *Amazing Grace*—in tongues. He was a resident student in a Bible college, and another student in a room nearby, overhearing his song was astonished to recognise his own language—of the Mexican Yucatan Peninsula. It was an enormous encouragement to this student, who was going through a period of difficulty. For several days after that, Zadai would speak to his new friend in tongues, and his friend would tell him what he had just said. Through this means they both received remarkable, accurate, supernatural guidance. The fact that Zadai had been praying and fasting for 21 days beforehand, is probably significant.[202]

What made the difference? Why did all of these succeed, and C T Studd and Parham fail? We can only surmise, but here are a few questions we could ask.

Were C T Studd and Parham presumptuous? In all the recent stories above, no one was expecting God to act this way. They were the orchestra,

God was the conductor. They spoke in tongues, they were willing vessels, but God took the initiative. Perhaps that aspect was lacking in the others. That sounds plausible but, on the other hand, it seems the medieval believers were intentional in their use of the gift.

Was there a need for persevering in prayer? Several of these miracle stories emerged from prolonged prayer: from three hours (Pachomius), to 13 days (Margery Kempe), to 21 days (Kevin Zadai). Prayer is fundamental in the working of miracles. Perhaps that was a key.

Whatever the reason, an exciting picture emerges. This remarkable gift—communicating in an unknown language—is a tool in God's toolbox, to help in preaching the gospel. But how do we do that? One more story might help.

Mike Hicks was employed selling heavy machinery throughout Australia. He was also a charismatic, personal evangelist, and brought many people to Christ—detailed in his inspiring book, *I Dare You God*. On one occasion, prompted by God, he stopped to speak to a boy leaning over a school fence. Unfortunately the boy, newly arrived from Vietnam, could speak no English. Mike, however, had a Gideon Bible which presented John 3:16 in several different languages, and he showed the boy the Vietnamese version. He wrote:

> I shall never forget the look of incredulous joy that swept over his face, and he broke into a torrent of words, not one of which was intelligible to me. At the same time, he pointed to the verse, pointed skywards and then to himself. It was fairly clear that the truth of the words had been made clear to him by the Holy Spirit, yet I was totally powerless to speak with him, or to help him.
>
> A wave of compassion flooded over me, yet I was saddened, because there was no way that I could explain any further the gospel of Jesus. I turned away, choked up with a lump in my throat, "God help me", I cried, "forgive me, it's more than I can handle".
>
> I turned to the boy and opened my mouth to say cheerio and out of my mouth came fluent Vietnamese! He understood me and I understood him, and for maybe 20 minutes

we talked, and I explained the gospel. I was able to read it myself in English from the Bible and, in the instant, speak it out in Vietnamese.

This may sound like an odd statement, but at the time there seemed to be nothing unusual about it. It was only afterwards I realised how strange these events were.[203]

Oddly, on a return visit, when the boy and his English-speaking Vietnamese friend met again with Mike, the gift no longer functioned, and Mike used his friend as an interpreter. He commented afterwards, "I have never needed the gift since then, but I am trusting God for the same miracle, should the need arise in the future".[204].

Clearly, this is a wonderful gift of God, like the gift of prophecy, and operates in much the same way. There seems to be no reason why we should not, by faith, expect it when the need arises.

The essential point from our story: Parham's bold attempt, though unsuccessful on the mission field at that time, was not foolish after all. And his followers were not speaking "nonsensical gibberish". Parham broke new ground, but others had to refine it—which is often the way of new discoveries.

To conclude Parham's story: in 1905 he set up another Bible School in Houston, Texas. From this base, he evangelised throughout Texas and the Southwest. It was in Houston that he met African-American William Seymour, the next milestone in our journey. As mentioned above, strict laws of the time forbade blacks and whites from attending a Bible School together, but Parham, impressed by Seymour's humility and hunger for God, allowed him to take part—albeit from the corridor outside the classroom. It was William Seymour who took Parham's teaching and spread it worldwide, so we will move now to his story.

Reformation in the church has never emerged from the tranquillity of an ivory tower.

ANON

...when Pontius Pilate was governor of Judea, Herod tetrarch of Galilee, his brother Philip tetrarch of Iturea and Traconitis, and Lysanias tetrarch of Abilene—during the high-priesthood of Annas and Caiaphas, the word of God came to...a NOBODY, from NOWHERE!

(APOLOGIES TO LUKE 3:1–2)

CHAPTER 11
THE AZUSA STREET REVIVAL: WILLIAM SEYMOUR

William J Seymour 1870–1922

Born to parents only two years freed from slavery, William Seymour well understood the prejudice against coloured people in the United States of America. In spite of that, while working on a plantation, and using a Bible to teach himself to read, he developed a secure faith in God. Eventually, he moved out of the rural South to Indianapolis, Indiana, and then Cincinnati, Ohio, seeking fellowship with Christians untainted by segregation.

In one of these churches, Seymour felt a call to ministry. However, as he was wrestling with that decision, he contracted smallpox, leaving him blind in one eye and face scarred. Believing this was the consequence of rejecting God's call, he yielded, and was ordained by his church as an itinerant evangelist. Seymour's passion for God ran deeply—he told a fellow evangelist that, "for two and a half years, he had been praying for five hours a day because he had such a hunger for God".[205] Eventually his ministry took him to Houston, Texas where, while working as a waiter, he planned to set up a base.

It was there in Houston that he met Charles Parham who had established a Bible School similar to the one in Topeka.

Mrs Parham described that meeting:

> One coloured man, W J Seymour, became a regular attendant each day for the Bible lessons. In Texas, you know, the coloured people are not allowed to mix with the white people as they do in some other states; but he was so humble and so deeply interested in the study of the Word that Mr Parham could not refuse him. So, he was given a place in the class and eagerly drank in the truths which were so new to him and food for his hungry soul.[206]

Seymour embraced Parham's new beliefs about the Spirit baptism and speaking in tongues though he did not experience it for himself at the time. He quietly shelved Parham's views about annihilation of the wicked and British Israelism but enthusiastically embraced his other more-orthodox teachings.

In 1906, Seymour unexpectedly received a request to lead a small church in Los Angeles. He accepted, Parham paid his fare, and he arrived on 22 February. He said:

> It was the divine call that brought me from Houston, Texas, to Los Angeles. The Lord put it on the heart of one of the saints in Los Angeles to write me that she felt the Lord would have me come there, and I felt it was the leading of the Lord. The Lord provided the means and I came to take charge of a mission on Santa Fe Street.[207]

At that time, Los Angeles was a city of 238,000 people, growing rapidly, and culturally diverse. The biggest non-white groups were African-American and Mexican. There were about 200 churches, mostly Protestant, and 90% of the people attended church.

Many of those Christians were agog with news of the Welsh Revival, which commenced late 1904 under the leadership of Evan Roberts, and lasted for about a year. More than 100,000 people came to faith in Wales in that time. In June 1905, Frank Bartleman, who would become a key figure in the coming Los Angeles revival, distributed 5,000 pamphlets to churches. They were entitled, "The Revival in Wales" and, he said, the pamphlets had a "wonderful quickening influence". He corresponded three times with Evan Roberts in Wales, asking him to pray for Los Angeles, and Roberts graciously responded each time. For example, on 14 November 1905, in his third response he wrote: "... May the Lord bless you with a mighty downpouring... I pray God to hear your prayer, to keep your faith strong, and to save California." [208]

Seymour's Church

Seymour's new church was African-American, a Nazarene group that had broken away from the Holiness movement. So, they were not likely to embrace a *third* work of grace, and certainly not speaking in tongues. However, Seymour was soon preaching from Acts 2:4, telling the people they were not baptised in the Holy Spirit if they had not spoken in tongues. He preached this, despite willingly admitting he himself had not yet done so. After a fierce backlash, he was locked out of the church and, with nowhere to go, was taken in by a sympathetic church family. There he stayed in his room, praying and fasting. Before long, his hosts joined him in prayer, then others too, until there were about 15 African-Americans, including children, who embraced Seymour's new teaching. On about 15 March, they moved to a larger home which would accommodate them all. It belonged to Richard and Ruth Asberry, at 214 North Bonnie Brae Street. There Seymour, the Asberrys, and others would pray for hours, seeking the Holy Spirit.

Seymour then invited a lady from Houston to come and assist. She was specially gifted in teaching people about the Spirit baptism. When she arrived, Seymour declared a ten-day fast for the purpose of receiving the Holy Spirit. During that time, they would study Acts 2:1–4 and pray each evening until they received.

On the third day, Monday, 9 April 1906, the Holy Spirit fell. Earlier that day, one of the men had spoken in tongues at home, and he told the gathering about it. As soon as he finished, someone else spoke out in tongues and then, "The whole company was immediately swept to its knees as by some mighty power".[209] The result was dramatic. Many spoke in tongues. Some rushed into the street, praying in tongues, shouting and preaching. Jennie Evans Moore, who would become Seymour's wife, went to the piano and began singing in tongues, interpreting what she sang. It was a powerful outpouring of the Spirit on this African-American gathering. Seymour would receive his Spirit baptism and speaking in tongues three days later. Journalist Frank Bartleman joined the group six days later.

So the meetings began, and continued day after day. Crowds increased and began to fill the street. The veranda collapsed under their weight. Moving to a derelict, two-storey building on Azusa Street, the revival exploded. After just three months, hundreds were attending.

The unstructured multicultural services would run for ten to twelve hours or even more, with people sitting on planks supported by nail kegs. People would just turn up, someone might lead in a song, another might give a testimony, reports would be read from other churches where the revival had spread, someone might preach (always spontaneously), and there was continuous prayer. Sometimes it was noisy, sometimes there were holy silences. Sometimes people could not even stand, and would remain lying down for hours under the power of the Spirit. Any little direction was provided by Seymour, but mostly he was famously on his knees behind the pulpit, his head in one of the two wooden boxes from which it was constructed. It was an extraordinary time, and people were awestruck.

News spread—by word of mouth, religious publications and a mocking press—sometimes fed by hostile ministers. One minister told his congregation:

> They come with the blare of trumpets out of tune and harmony, but lustily blown with all the power of human or inhuman lungs; they shine with phosphorescent gleam, strangely like that of brimstone, and with odour more or less tainted; they distract the affrighted atmosphere with a bewildering jargon of babbling tongues of all grades—dried, boiled and smoked; they rant and dance and roll in a disgusting amalgamation of African voodoo superstition and Caucasian insanity, and will pass away like the hysterical nightmares that they are.[210]

The pot was being stirred. Newspaper headlines declared, "Religious Fanaticism Creates Wild Scenes", "Holy Kickers Carry On Mad Orgies", "Women with Men Embrace", "Whites and Blacks Mix in a Religious Frenzy", and "Crazed Girls in the Arms of Black Men".

It should be noted that, while some church leaders were fiercely critical of Azusa, there were others who, while rejecting the Spirit baptism and tongues, recognised the evangelical zeal and its fruit. So much so, that Los Angeles Church Federation ministers decided to combine for regular street meetings, using the Azusa model. They organised prayer bands, divided the city into regions for their work, and cooperated in follow-up with a city-wide evangelistic campaign.

The criticism and bad press, of course, simply made people go and see for themselves. And many of those were won over. So, by mid-July, according to press reports, some 500–700 were attending regularly. Trainloads of people came—as many as 1,500 would attend on a given Sunday.

As they became somewhat more organised, services were conducted at 10 am, 3 pm and 7.30 pm, EVERY DAY. Sometimes they went longer, and ran together. And this continued for THREE AND A HALF YEARS![211]

There were many conversions. Baptismal services were held on beaches at nearby San Pedro and Terminal Island. Hundreds would make their way there on trains and streetcars, where as many as 150 to 250 people would be baptised.

The Earthquake

On Wednesday, 18 April 1906, nine days after the Holy Spirit fell in Los Angeles at Bonnie Brae Street, San Francisco was struck by a massive earthquake of estimated magnitude 7.9. Aftershocks were felt in Los Angeles the following day. Up to 3,000 people died—the greatest loss of life from a natural disaster in California's history. More than 80% of the city was destroyed—most of the destruction the result of fires, triggered by the earthquake, that raged for four days. People were in turmoil.

For those at Azusa Street, the timing was significant. On the morning of the earthquake, a front page story in the Los Angeles Times reported this:

> Another speaker (at Azusa) had a vision in which he saw the people of Los Angeles flocking in a mighty stream to perdition. He prophesied awful destruction to this city unless its citizens are brought to a belief in the tenets of the new faith.[212]

Bartleman believed unequivocally that the earthquake was a judgment of God on the wickedness of San Francisco, and he proclaimed it forcefully in the face of fierce criticism—much of this from pulpits. He wrote:

> I found the earthquake had opened many hearts...Nearly every pulpit in the land was working overtime to prove that God had nothing to do with earthquakes and thus allay the fears of the people. The Spirit was striving to knock at hearts with conviction, through this judgment. I felt indignation that the preachers should be used of Satan to drown out his voice...[213]

He published a tract containing verses linking earthquakes to the judgments of God and distributed 75,000 around Los Angeles and 50,000 in the Bay Cities around San Francisco. Many people were enraged, many others convicted. Whatever the case, people traumatised by the disaster that filled their papers were open to Bartleman's message and the attention it drew to the outpouring at Azusa.

The Newspaper

In September 1906, Seymour launched a publication called *The Apostolic Faith*. Within months the mailing list grew to more than 20,000, and double that a year later. It was a major vehicle for spreading the news of Azusa, and the Spirit baptism, not only throughout America, but around the world.

The paper was packed with teachings, happenings and many testimonies. Here are a few of those testimonies from the first edition. Names were never given—the plan was for God alone to receive the glory.

A little girl who walked with crutches and had tuberculosis of the bones, as the doctors declared, was healed and dropped her crutches and began to skip about the yard.

A sister was healed of [tuberculosis] when she had but a part of a lung left. She lay in a trance for three days, and saw heaven and hell and unutterable things. She received the Pentecost and gift of tongues and feels called to a foreign land.

A drunkard got under conviction in a street meeting and raised his hand to be prayed for. They prayed for the devil of drink to be cast out and the appetite was gone. He came to the meeting and was saved, sanctified and baptised with the Holy Ghost and, in three days from the time he was drunk, he was speaking in a new tongue and praising God for Pentecost. He hardly knows himself.

A [Muslim], a Sudanese by birth, a man who is an interpreter and speaks 16 languages, came into the meetings at Azusa Street and the Lord gave him messages which none but himself could understand. He identified, interpreted and wrote a number of the languages.

A brother who had been a spiritualist medium, and who was so possessed with demons that he had no rest and was on the point of committing suicide, was instantly delivered of demon power. He then sought God for the pardon of his sins and sanctification, and is now filled with a different spirit.[214]

In that first year, several other congregations were established around Los Angeles. About 20 evangelists preached up and down the west coast of America and many other states, and at least 13 missionaries—nine of them African-American—were sent to Africa where churches were established. The following year, missionaries were sent to many more countries including Europe, Asia, the Middle East and northern Russia. The simple Azusa Street mission had exploded into a world-changing event.

Segregation and women preachers

In the light of the Jim Crow laws that forbade coloured people from mixing with whites, it was remarkable that segregation was set aside in the revival. The leader was black, and so were all of the original congregation, but eventually whites outnumbered blacks. As mentioned earlier, it was said the "'colour line' was washed away in the blood".[215] That integration was criticised by many, and explains headlines like "Whites and Blacks Mix in a Religious Frenzy".

Not only were meetings racially mixed, they also welcomed rich and poor, educated and illiterate. Azusa was a wonderful leveller.

Seymour's leadership team (about a dozen people) was mixed from the beginning, with men and women of all nations and colours. At that time, most other churches were racially segregated, and women were to be "silent in the church". Robeck made the observation that, historically, Protestants and others were reluctant to embrace the ministry of women—and did that only because of criticism from feminists. Azusa, however, did so on the basis of Joel 2:28–32, God's promise to pour out his Spirit on men and women alike.[216]

The Meetings: spirit, heart, love, power, singing

People who attended the meetings were profoundly impacted by a pervading Spirit of holiness. Frank Bartleman wrote:

> Great emphasis was placed on the "blood" for cleansing, etc. A high standard was held up for a clean life... Divine love was wonderfully manifested in the meetings. They would not even allow an unkind word said against their opposers, or the churches. The message was the love of God. It was a sort of "first love" of the early church returned. The "baptism" as we received it in the beginning, did not allow us to think, speak or hear evil of any man. The Spirit was very sensitive, tender as a dove... We seemed to live in a sea of pure divine love... The false was sifted out from the real by the

Spirit of God. The Word of God itself decided absolutely all issues. The hearts of the people, both in act and motive, were searched to the very bottom. It was no joke to become one of that company. No man "[dared] join himself to them" (Acts 5:13) except he meant business, to go through. It meant a dying out (sic) and cleaning up process in those days, to receive the "baptism"...Only honest seekers sought it, those who meant business with God.[217]

Testimonies were endless, and the presence of God tangible. Bartleman wrote again:

> We had real testimonies, from fresh heart-experience... A dozen might be on their feet at one time, trembling under the mighty power of God. Someone might be speaking. Suddenly the Spirit would fall on the congregation. God himself would give the altar call. Men would fall all over the house like the slain in a battle, or rush for the altar en masse to seek God. The scene often resembled a forest of fallen trees. Such a scene cannot be imitated...I have stopped more than once within two blocks of the place and prayed for strength before I dared go on. The presence of the Lord was so real.[218]

People were entranced by the singing and singing in tongues.

> ...a young lady of refinement was on the floor for hours, while at times the most heavenly singing would issue from her lips. It would swell away up to the throne, and then die away in an almost unearthly melody. She sang "Praise God! Praise God!" All over the house men and women were weeping. A preacher was flat on his face on the floor, dying out. [sic] "Pentecost" has fully come.[219]

The most popular hymn, sung repeatedly without hymn books, was *The Comforter has Come*, by Thomas Bottome. The chorus is as follows:

> The Comforter has come, the Comforter has come!
> The Holy Ghost from Heav'n, the Father's promise giv'n;
> Oh, spread the tidings 'round, wherever man is found,
> The Comforter has come!

Many church leaders received the Holy Spirit. Bartleman wrote:

> A Free Methodist preacher's wife came through to a mighty "baptism", speaking something like Chinese. All who received the "baptism" spoke in tongues. There were at least six Holiness preachers, some of them grey-headed, honoured and trusted for fruitful service for years, seeking the "baptism" most earnestly.[220]

A Baptist minister, who later went to Egypt as a missionary, spoke of his experience:

> As suddenly as on the Day of Pentecost, while I was sitting some 12 feet right in front of the speaker, the Holy Spirit fell on me and filled me literally. I seemed to be lifted up, for I was in the air in an instant, shouting "Praise God", and instantly I began to speak in another language. I could not have been more surprised if at the same moment someone had handed me a million dollars.[221]

Apparently, while some required extended time waiting and praying to receive the Spirit, others were surprised by a sudden and unexpected outpouring such as that.

Experienced leaders, drawn to Azusa Street, added maturity to the new and fragile work. Bartleman wrote:

> One reason for the depth of the work at "Azusa" was the fact that the workers were not novices. They were largely

called and prepared for years, from the Holiness ranks, and from the mission field etc. They had been burned out, tried and proven. They were largely seasoned veterans. They had walked with God and learned deeply of his Spirit. These were pioneers, "shock troops", the Gideon's three hundred, to spread the fire around the world. Just as the disciples had been prepared by Jesus.[222]

Cecil M Robeck, possibly the leading authority on the Azusa revival, said he was aware of about 500 people who had visited Azusa between 1906 and 1909, and more than a third of these were pastors and evangelists.[223]

The chaos and concern

People who tried to preach without the anointing of the Holy Spirit were discouraged—often by groans or cold stares. Problem people were prayed away. Nevertheless, meetings were often marked by a chaotic mix of unusual spiritual, demonic, and fleshly manifestations. Seymour was slow to intervene, believing God should have his way. As a result, there were sometimes extremes and confusion. Concerned people wrote to Parham, by far the more experienced leader, requesting he come and help sort it out. Seymour was similarly concerned, and he too wrote to Parham, asking him to come and help "discern between that which was real and that which was false, and weed out that which was not of God".[224] Unfortunately, when Parham eventually did come, the two developed strong differences, and Seymour ended the arrangement.

Parham later wrote harshly about Azusa's methods of praying for people to receive the Holy Spirit and the way manifestations were managed. He was later criticised for that harshness and even accused of racism. However, he did concede the following:

> There are many in Los Angeles who sing, pray and talk wonderfully in other tongues, as the Spirit gives utterance, and there is jabbering here that is not tongues at all... let us guard

carefully against every form of fanaticism, and stand firm and true, helping one another and reasoning together.[225]

Seymour, as always, was gracious in response. He wrote in *The Apostle of Faith*:

> We thought of having [Parham] as our leader, and so stated in our paper, before waiting on the Lord. We can be rather hasty, especially when we are very young in the power of the Holy Spirit. We are just like a baby—full of love—and were willing to accept anyone that had the baptism with the Holy Spirit as our leader. But the Lord commenced settling us down, and we saw that the Lord should be our leader. So, we honour Jesus as the great shepherd of the sheep. He is our model.[226]

Criticisms of Azusa were often directed at its humble circumstance and Seymour's poor education. The indignant Bartleman was quick to defend, comparing the life of Luther. He wrote:

> Many high dignitaries of the Roman church in Luther's time were convinced of the need for a reformation, and that he was on the right track. But they declared, in so many words, that they could never consent that this new doctrine should issue from "such a corner". That it should be a monk, a poor monk, who presumes to reform us all, said they, is what we cannot tolerate. "Can any good thing come out of Nazareth?"[227]

There are plenty of other precedents Bartleman could have mentioned. Jesus was born in a stable, not a palace. His herald was John the Baptist, out in the wilderness, eating locusts and honey—not an eminent leader. Jesus praised the Father because he had "hidden these things from the wise and learned, and revealed them to little children" (Luke 10:21). An uneducated black man with one eye, preaching in a derelict building from a packing case pulpit is, in fact, quite consistent with God's ways. You might even say that God is so committed to such methodology, that if Azusa had been birthed with pomp and ceremony by a distinguished bishop, or a theologian with multiple degrees, we might well doubt it.

The manifestations

The unusual manifestations were unsettling for some observers. The supernatural and the natural were all jumbled together, and people had to learn to discern.

The fact is, such a sorting out process is a hallmark of many spiritual awakenings. For example, even one of the most respected, conservative and scholarly religious leaders, Jonathan Edwards, faced the same problems. Following a remarkable revival known as the Great Awakening which swept many American colonies between 1730 and 1745, he wrote of:

> "...conviction and conversion of sinners, and great revivings, quickenings and comforts of [believers], and for extraordinary external effects of such things. It was a very frequent thing to see a houseful of outcries, faintings, convulsions and suchlike, both with distress and also with admiration and joy... there were some that were so affected, and their bodies so overcome, that they could not go home, but were obliged to stay all night at the house where they were.[228]

> There were some instances of people lying in a sort of trance, remaining perhaps for 24 hours motionless, and with their senses locked up; but in the meantime, under strong imaginations, as though they went to heaven and had there, visions of glorious and delightful objects.[229]

We don't expect words like "outcries, faintings, and convulsions" from a person like Edwards, a conservative intellectual and theologian. In spite of Edward's best efforts to calm the waters, the church divided into "Old Lights" (those who rejected the new activities) and the "New Lights" (those who embraced them). So unusual manifestations at Azusa Street were by no means a new thing.

Part of the problem at Azusa was the lack of a scriptural framework for their new experiences. Eventually, teachers emerged who taught and wrote books on these subjects and, with that, Pentecostal churches settled down to become a steady force.

But Seymour lacked those years of hindsight and biblical understanding we enjoy today, and he inevitably let a few excesses and imprudent actions slip past.

What was Seymour like?

From the beginning, Seymour was the unquestioned leader at Azusa. His special message was the Spirit baptism and speaking in tongues. He was the one who introduced the idea, and he was the one who guided it throughout. Numerous observers have written about Seymour, consistently recognizing humility as his standout quality. Adolphus S Worrell, a Baptist preacher, known for his translation of a study version of the New Testament in 1904, visited Azusa in 1906 and said:

> The writer has not a single doubt, but that brother Seymour has more power with God, and more power from God, than all his critics both in and out of the city. His strength is in his conscious weakness and lowliness before God; and so long as he maintains this attitude, the power of God will, no doubt, continue to flow through him.[230]

Chicago pastor, William H Durham, who came to Azusa in 1907 seeking the Holy Spirit, said:

> [Seymour] walks and talks with God. His power is in his weakness. He seems to maintain a helpless dependence on God and is as simple-hearted as a little child, and at the same time, is so filled with God that you feel the love and power every time you get near him.[231]

Robeck observed that Seymour's demeanour was unusual for a holiness preacher of that time—others "seemed to thrive on conflict and confrontation".[232] It was not that Seymour was weak or indecisive. He fully believed everyone was equal, and provided a place where they could make their contribution, even if he disagreed with them. There was no fear of recrimination.

One evangelist, critical of Azusa, came with a determination to set them right. He took to the open pulpit and began berating the people. Seymour simply looked on smiling—as was his custom. But the further the man went, the more convicted he became of his own faults. Eventually giving up, he fell on his knees and asked for forgiveness and prayer, that he could receive the Holy Spirit like everyone else.[233]

When Seymour faced a problem, he would turn to the Bible for solutions. For example, a few people, newly baptised in the Holy Spirit and speaking in tongues, experimented by writing down their languages. The congregation was fascinated. It became an issue, so Seymour searched his Bible for an answer. Finding nothing there on the subject, he wrote, "We do not read anything in the Word about writing in unknown languages, so we do not encourage that in our meetings".[234] That gentle but firm pronouncement settled it, and they moved on. On another occasion, he made this statement to the people:

> I need to say something important. We got too many folk comin' in here a-seeking the tongues. When you go down to the shoe store, you don't say to the clerk, "I want to buy a pair o' tongues". You just buy the shoes and the tongues come with 'em. Folks just need to be seekin' the Holy Ghost. The tongues part will take care of itself.[235]

Seymour was in a unique position. He was a black man leading whites, at a time when that was not only highly unconventional, but sometimes dangerous. You could be beaten up or even killed for involvement in mixed gatherings. What's more, Seymour had a tiger by the tail—the baptism in the Holy Spirit with speaking in tongues. He had to be cautious as he crept along, careful not to quench anything the Holy Spirit might be doing. Step by step, he took what he had learned from Parham and applied it humbly and persistently. He prayed and fasted many, many hours, searching his Bible diligently, and gently guiding the outpouring as it exploded around the world.

A classic description

What was Azusa really like? Sometimes cynics can bring a unique and helpful perspective. They don't embellish facts, and can shine light into dark corners. Here is an extract from the Los Angeles Herald, which does just that in one pithy story.

> A lanky, black wench took the centre of the stage. The most noticeable things about her were her neck and mouth. Her neck was remarkable for its length and her mouth for its width. When she opened that mouth, there was nothing to do but dodge or be engulfed by the undertow. She was the orator of the evening, and "felt de han' of Gawd laid on heh hea't to preach to de shepa'ds".
>
> "Ah read fum de thuty-foth chapte' of Zekel."
>
> She read from the "thuty-foth chapte' of Zekel" for about an hour and a half. She would read one line and expound it until she had told all she could think of, and then read another line. She concluded her oration to the shepherds...
>
> "An' you shepa'ds, you pasto's, you'd bettah feed youh flock on de Holy Ghost o' they won't feed you. If you all don't git right wid Gawd you won't have no mo' congregation and you'll have to go out to wuk."[236]

In a few succinct lines, this nameless journalist captured the unique elements of the Azusa outpouring: mixed races, lay ministry, women ministry (many lowly and uneducated), protracted services, Holy Spirit focus and provocative preaching. All flourishing in the face of endless criticism and mockery.

Incredibly, on this particular day, those "shepa'ds" listening to this

90-minute message, were submitting themselves to not just a woman, but an uneducated black woman, absorbing her exhortations about "de Holy Ghost", humbly embracing them, taking them home, and proclaiming them to their worlds.

Such was the extraordinary Azusa Street outpouring.

How did it end?

A number of factors contributed to its demise. The harmonious relationships between whites and other races deteriorated, as did the open and egalitarian nature of the meetings. Some were unhappy that Seymour married. Two white women, who managed the 50,000 mail listing, moved to Portland, taking the list with them. Seymour painted the name *Apostolic Faith Gospel Mission* on the building, making some feel it was no longer non-denominational. And, regarding the once free-flowing meetings, Frank Bartleman said:

> ... in the beginning, platforms and pulpits were as far as possible moved out of the way... Priest class and ecclesiastical abuse were entirely swept away. [God] might speak through whom he would... As the movement began to apostatise, platforms were built higher, coat tails were worn longer, choirs were organised, and string bands came in to "jazz" the people... We were no longer "brethren". Then the divisions multiplied etc. While brother Seymour kept his head inside the old empty box in "Azusa", all was well. They later built for him a throne also. Now we have, not one hierarchy, but many... Every meeting was now programmed from start to finish. Disaster was bound to follow, and it did.[237]

There were two peaks in the outpouring, the first in 1906–8, the second in 1911–12.[238] As the church declined, Seymour continued to pastor what eventually became a small, African-American congregation, until he died of a heart attack in 1922. His wife continued to lead it until poor health ended her involvement.

Azusa had run its course. But the fiery baton which once burned so bright and clear in that remarkable old building had certainly not been extinguished. A multitude of fervent believers, from all walks of life, had taken it up and were now running the race, eyes fixed on the prize before them.

WHERE DID IT GO FROM THERE?

The Azusa Street message—which became the Pentecostal and charismatic message—spread via literally thousands of avenues around the globe. To cover them all would require many large books. We will look at just a few: Europe, England, the USA, and Australia, for a small taste of what happened next.

EUROPE

In 1905, Methodist pastor, Thomas Barratt, left Norway to go to New York, to raise funds for a hall to be built in Oslo. His fundraising was a dismal failure—people were caught up with San Francisco's devastating earthquake—and he became deeply discouraged. But he heard about Azusa Street and, while he never went there, he wrote to them. They encouraged him to seek the blessing of the Holy Spirit, which he did with a passion, sometimes praying as much as 12 hours at a time. One Sunday, following the morning service, he went to his room, locked the door and stayed there fasting and praying. Then:

> Shortly before 5 pm, "the fire fell". He had to hide his face in a towel so as not to disturb his neighbours, as he shouted aloud his praises. "I was seized by the Holy Power of God throughout my whole being..." was how he afterwards described it. Next day, he wrote in his diary, "I am the happiest man in the world, everything has become new, I am filled with peace and joy and love to God and man". Someone told him he looked ten years younger.[239]

However, he did not speak in tongues and he had not been expecting that. But, on the encouragement of his new Los Angeles friends, he allowed some people to pray for him. One of them later described seeing a crown of fire over his head, and tongues of fire in front of that. He was immediately (in his own words), "Filled with an indescribable power, and began to speak in a foreign language as loudly as I could... I am sure that I spoke seven or eight different languages— they were clear and plain". He also began to sing in the Spirit, and so continued until about 4 o'clock in the morning. He spoke too, of "waves of God's love sweeping over him..."[240]

Barratt returned to Norway, but not everyone accepted his enthusiastic message. In 1916, he and a number of others reluctantly left the Methodist church and formed the Filadelfia Pentecostal Church in Oslo. In 1926, Barratt commented that it was not possible to hold the Pentecostal belief and remain in another denomination. His experience of the Holy Spirit had given him an overwhelming burden for world evangelism, and he had a significant pioneering influence in the new Pentecostal movement. Authoring more than 60 books and pamphlets, he became known as the apostle of the Pentecostal movement in Europe.

One of those baptised in the Holy Spirit as a result of Barratt's ministry was 22-year-old Swedish Baptist pastor, Lewi Pethrus. After reading Barratt's story in a Stockholm paper, he told a friend, "I'm going to Oslo tomorrow... and not coming back unless the Lord baptises me in the Holy Spirit".[241] He became firm friends with Barratt and, eventually, one of the greatest Pentecostal leaders. More conservative in his approach, Pethrus once wrote, "I joined entirely in the revival, but I considered it to be my task, for the blessing of God's work, to subdue its often fierce manifestations".[242]

Pethrus, like Barratt, was forced to leave his denomination. His church became the largest Pentecostal church in the world at that time, and held that place until the 1970s. A prolific writer, his books were translated into many languages and had a significant stabilising influence on the Pentecostal movement worldwide.

ENGLAND

The message reached the shores of England through the ministry of the Reverend Alexander Boddy, vicar of All Saints, Sunderland from 1886 until

1922. His interests were colourful and diverse: previously a solicitor and author of travel books, Fellow of the Royal Geographical Society, keen supporter of the Keswick Movement, and author of *The Laying on of Hands*. He had also visited the Welsh Revival, and met its leader, Evan Roberts.

In March 1907, hearing about Thomas Barratt, he travelled to Oslo and was deeply impacted. He wrote in several English newspapers, "My four days in Oslo can never be forgotten. I stood with Evan Roberts in Tonypandy (the Welsh Revival) but have never witnessed such scenes as those in Norway".[243]

However, back in England, he received a cool reception. Eventually, he asked Barratt to make a short visit to his church. That visit stretched into a seven-week stint during which time many were baptised in the Holy Spirit and meetings gained attention in the media. One headline read, "Strange Revivalist Scenes—Vicar's Child Talks Chinese", others reported, "staid, unemotional matrons taken home to bed o' night 'drunk' with ecstatic joy".[244] Many came to see what was happening and to seek the Holy Spirit. Sunderland became to England what Azusa Street was to America—a Holy Spirit oasis. Among those who came to drink from that were George Jeffreys and Smith Wigglesworth. It was Mrs Boddy who introduced healing evangelist, Smith Wigglesworth, to the baptism in the Holy Spirit. In spite of those many blessings, there was also much scepticism and criticism from the inherently conservative British church. Nevertheless, from those beginnings, the message spread across the United Kingdom.

UNITED STATES OF AMERICA—
Divisions and new denominations

When the new Pentecostals exploded across America, not everything ran smoothly and there were a number of divisions, two of which stand out.

Firstly, the conflicting ideas on sanctification, which had simmered for so long, led to a division into what were called "Holiness" churches (who believed, as we have seen, that sanctification was a second work of grace), and "finished work" churches, (who believed the "finished work of the cross" provided both salvation and sanctification to all believers at conversion).

Secondly, in a 1913 camp meeting, a speaker made an issue over the words spoken over baptism candidates—whether they should be baptised "in the name of Jesus Christ" (as the apostles had done), or in the name of the Father, Son and Holy Spirit (as in Matthew 28:19). Another preacher fuelled this fire with a non-Trinitarian idea, and a new movement emerged, known as "oneness" or "Jesus Name" Pentecostals. They baptised only in the name of Jesus, and taught there was only one personality in the Godhead (Jesus Christ), and that the terms "Father" and "Holy Spirit" were titles designating different aspects of Christ. All this was firmly rejected by the newly-formed Assemblies of God, forcing a number of churches to withdraw.

The origin of the AG, and the Church of God in Christ (COGIC), is of particular interest.

The Church of God in Christ is a predominately black Pentecostal Holiness church with around five million members and 12,000 churches in the USA and many more worldwide. It is rated the fifth-largest denomination in the USA.

It began with two men, Charles Harrison Mason and Charles Price Jones.

Mason, the son of former slaves, felt the call to preach as a young man and entered Arkansas Baptist College to prepare for the ministry. But, after just three months, he left because of liberal teaching—possibly the so-called "higher criticism" that was prevalent at that time.

In 1895, on a visit to Jackson, Mississippi, Mason met Jones who was pastor of Mt Helms Baptist Church in Jackson. Jones was well known as author of popular hymns (many still sung today, including "Deeper, deeper, in the love of Jesus").

They began to teach together in Baptist churches but were eventually asked to leave because they were teaching holiness doctrine.

In 1896, they established an independent church in Lexington. Then, in 1897, they established a legally-chartered incorporated body in Memphis, which became the headquarters of the church. Their work expanded rapidly so that, by 1906, there were nearly 100 churches in three states.

In 1906, the men heard about Azusa Street. Jones was cautious, but Mason—who had from time to time experienced visions and dreams—was enthusiastic. So, Mason and two other leaders were sent to Los Angeles to investigate. Mason was the only denominational leader to visit Azusa Street and he stayed for a month. He was persuaded by what he saw and he and one of the others received the Spirit baptism and spoke in tongues. But, on their return, Jones, the general overseer and presiding elder, was unconvinced. This eventually, in 1907, led to a parting of ways, from which two separate groups emerged, one led by Jones, the other by Mason.

Jones' group adopted the name Church of Christ (Holiness) USA. They maintained his stance in rejecting the Azusa Street teaching. Today, their website states: "We believe that the receiving of the Holy Spirit is an integral part of conversion".[245] They accept the reality of tongues, but not as evidence of receiving the Holy Spirit.

Mason's group kept the COGIC name, and about half the ministers and laity joined him. So, in 1907, and with ten congregations, the Church of God in Christ became the first legally-chartered Pentecostal body incorporated in the United States.

Incorporation was highly valued at that time because it enabled the formal ordination of ministers, and provided government recognition and entitlements such as railroad permits and exemption from the army draft. (The denomination held pacifist views and, in fact, Mason was briefly jailed in 1918 for forbidding his followers to join the armed forces.) Because of that incorporation, hundreds of white pastors took membership with COGIC, and the denomination eventually became the most integrated in the USA.

The movement grew quickly. They had many successful programmes meeting the needs of poor and disenfranchised blacks in both rural and urban situations and, by the end of WW2, had spread to every state. Their headquarters was in Memphis, Tennessee, where Mason built a 10,000 seat auditorium. It was here in 1968 that Martin Luther King preached his famous sermon, "I have been to the mountaintop". When Mason died in 1961, there were 400,000 members in the USA

However, back in 1914, there was a move by a number of white COGIC pastors to establish an independent body for the ordination of white pastors. As we have already seen, Azusa Street was unique in its success with integration, with whites happily working under Seymour's leadership. Efforts had always been made to remain integrated but, because of violent racial unrest in many cities and strong competition for jobs and housing, it was difficult to maintain that revolutionary stance. Mason was gracious through this process and did not oppose the change. A powerful preacher with a charismatic personality, he was loved by the people and, at the first gathering of the new organisation in Hot Springs Arkansas in 1914, he was one of the speakers. That new, largely-white body, was called the Assemblies of God, and quickly became the powerful force that it is today.

Three different groups, the same origin. After a century of activity, how have they fared? Here are the statistics as best as I can find. Up-to-date figures are hard to obtain, so I have specified the year they were provided.

DENOMINATION	WORLDWIDE NUMBERS	USA NUMBERS
ASSEMBLIES OF GOD	69.2 million (in 2018)	3.2 million (in 2018)
CHURCH OF GOD IN CHRIST (COGIC)	8.8 million (in 2020)	5 million (in 2020)
CHURCH OF CHRIST (HOLINESS) USA (Non-Pentecostal)	"Missions sponsored in three countries."[246] (No stats given.)	12,960 (in 2012)

Obviously the AG has had explosive growth around the globe.

It is interesting to compare the other two movements, knowing their different views of the Holy Spirit. COGIC had remarkable success under the long leadership of Mason, and is now the largest Pentecostal church in America. Jones' Church of Christ (Holiness) USA has obviously not fared as well. What made the difference? Two possibilities come to mind. One is leadership—the capabilities of the two men. The other is the different view of the Holy Spirit. Exactly what effect either of these had, we can only guess. But it is certainly consistent with what we have already seen to conclude that the Spirit baptism, provided by God for proclaiming the gospel with power, was the significant factor. And that probably understates it.

AUSTRALIA

The background of Australian Pentecostalism differs from that of America. The holiness movement is non-existent, and the same black Christian culture is also absent. Early Pentecostals were middle class, not poor or disenfranchised. In the 1930s, for example, the percentage of Pentecostal professionals was about double that of the rest of the population, and Pentecostal labourers about half. In addition, the first Pentecostal churches were predominantly in the country, not the cities. By the 1930s, 23 of the first 34 churches were in regional areas.[247]

And women played a big role. By the 1930s, more than half the churches were led by women. In fact, the origin of the movement can be traced to one woman, a humble, former Methodist and mother of seven. Her name was Sarah Jane (Jeannie) Lancaster (1858–1934). Few Pentecostals have even heard of her. (More of her shortly.)

A number of spiritual factors had prepared the ground for the new movement.

The first was Methodism, a booming evangelical denomination at the time. In 1861, Methodists made up 6.7% of the population, by 1901, that had increased to 10.2%.[248] Methodist emphasis on Christian perfection, together with the idea of a second blessing (which morphed into the baptism in the Holy Spirit) provided fertile ground for the emerging Pentecostal church.

Secondly, controversial preacher and evangelist, John Alexander Dowie, stirred the waters. He spent his first sixteen years of ministry in Australia, before moving to the United States and setting up Zion City. Many Australians who imbibed his radical teaching on commitment, faith and spiritual healing, moved easily into the Pentecostal movement.

And then there was the influence of the evangelical movement. The Keswick Movement, having commenced in England in the 1870s, found its way to Australia a few years later, to become a vital and influential force. It was best known for its annual conventions in Geelong and Belgrave Heights.

In the same spirit as the Keswick Movement was the highly successful ministry tour in 1901 of the famous American evangelist/writer, Reuben Torrey. Hundreds of churches, and thousands of volunteers were involved in the campaign, resulting in some 20,000 conversions. Torrey had embraced the idea of the baptism in the Spirit as a discrete experience after salvation, and described such an event in his own life:

> One day, as I sat in my study, something fell on me, and I literally fell to the floor, and I just lay there and shouted. I had never shouted before... but I lay there shouting, "Glory to God! Glory to God! Glory to God!"... The Spirit had put something in me that was not there before.[249]

He preached on this subject and, though he did not mention speaking in tongues and didn't identify with the later teachings of Azusa Street, his ministry in Australia would have left a hunger for the message the Pentecostal movement would bring.

So into this scene came the little-known, determined and godly, Jeannie Lancaster. Dr Barry Chant writes:

> Wherever we look in the first 20 years of Pentecostal history, the imprint of [Jeannie Lancaster] can be found... she was involved in evangelism, church planting, preaching and prayer... She conducted meetings in halls and houses... She edited a magazine. She published thousands of tracts. She engaged with welfare work for the poor. She prayed for the sick. She encouraged people to be filled with the Spirit. She eschewed the things of the world for the things of God. Perhaps most significant of all, she was a woman of integrity, prizing love, sacrifice, unity and honesty above all else. Australian Pentecostalism is her enduring legacy.[250]

What was her story? An active Methodist, in 1902, at the age of 44, Mrs Lancaster was challenged by a sick old man who complained, "I have been lying here for 20 years waiting for [the elders of the church] to come and raise me up!"[251] Unable to find elders who would do that, she searched the scriptures, became convinced of the truth of divine healing, and began to minister to the sick. Her own broken and disfigured arm was totally restored and, in spite of opposition to her new belief, a number of people were healed.

Then, in October 1906, six months after the Azusa Street outpouring, she acquired from England some books and a pamphlet entitled *Back to Pentecost*.

Whether or not it was linked to Azusa we are not told. But she became convinced of the Pentecostal message. Dr Chant describes her experience.

> She began to pray earnestly to be filled with the Spirit... [and] "God deepened her consecration even unto death" and she experienced some manifestations of the Spirit she did not understand. [Two years later]... she went through what she described as a "Gethsemane". Still on her knees at 2 am, she was baptised in the Spirit. She "thought that the valves of her heart were giving way" and felt as though "electric shocks went through her frame". But then the Holy Spirit came. "Strange and unwonted notes burst from her mouth, cleaving the air like living creatures." She spoke four different languages and she burst into songs of praise to the Lord.[252]

In 1909, she purchased a building, naming it Good News Hall, where she proclaimed the message of salvation, the Spirit baptism, healing, and the imminent return of Christ. Outreach was at the fore and, in 1910, she visited each of the seven states of Australia. By 1925, there were about 11 congregations across the country, and numerous home meetings. In 1910, she also launched a magazine called *Good News*. Its circulation reached 3,000, a remarkable achievement for such a paper at that time. For 25 years, it was enthusiastically received by eager Christians around Australia and in many other countries. Featuring articles by Mrs Lancaster and her assistants, together with extracts from overseas Pentecostal magazines, it had a significant influence on the spread of the Pentecostal message.

Many people received miraculous healings and *Good News* reported amazing recoveries from conditions such as deformed fingers, kidney stones, pneumonia, deafness, a heart condition, appendicitis and a broken arm.[253]

With Pentecostal doctrine very much a work in progress, a few theological errors crept into early teachings. Doctors were avoided, all trust was placed in God for healing. As a result, some died, who otherwise might have lived. Mrs Lancaster also believed in the ultimate annihilation of the wicked, and her understanding of the Trinity was confused. She believed that, while God the Father and the Holy Spirit were one, Jesus, as God's son held a different place. Consequently, a number of prominent ministries distanced themselves from Good News Hall, which contributed to the decline of the movement in later years. It also led to a disastrous visiting ministry tour, as follows.

In 1922, Good News Hall had conducted a highly successful campaign with healing evangelist, Smith Wigglesworth. It was a massive venture, Wigglesworth's fare from England alone was 250 Australian pounds, about six months' wages for an average Australian. Soon after that, they arranged a visit with renowned American evangelist, Aimee Semple-McPherson. But, after arriving and learning about Mrs Lancaster's unorthodox views, the evangelist withdrew from the arrangement. A non-Pentecostal group agreed to run her campaign on the condition she remain silent on the issue of tongues, which she did.[254] The visit was still an enormous success in mainline and evangelical churches, but a severe disappointment to Good News Hall. Mrs Lancaster, characteristically gracious in her response, said, "we must take it as one of the 'all things' that are working together for good to those who love God..."[255]

An outstanding feature of Good News Hall was ministry to the poor. From the beginning, they provided food and clothing to the needy and, during the crippling Depression of 1929–1933, spent large sums of money and even went into debt, providing for desperate people. For example, in 1931, 700 free lunches were provided each week and 140 to 180 unemployed men received assistance at the centre.

Today, Jeannie Lancaster lies in an unmarked grave in the Fawkner Cemetery, Melbourne, typical of her unassuming life. Her work, while almost completely unknown and unrecognised, lives on in the form of a number of Australian Pentecostal denominations which have risen in her wake. The largest of these is Australian Christian Churches, affiliated with the World AG Movement. Others are CRC Churches International, the C3 Movement (originally Christian City Churches), and COC churches (Christian Outreach Centres).

More on Azusa

For more on Azusa Street, there are several YouTube clips under the title, *The Azusa Street Revival Documentary*. Another features an interview with the two last known witnesses of the revival, now deceased. Both experienced healings during that time, one from tuberculosis, the other from total deafness. That link is https://www.youtube.com/watch?v=Q8Kjc6Qdtko. Recommended books are *The Century of the Holy Spirit* by Vinson Synan, *The Azusa Street Mission and Revival* by Cecil M Robeck Jr. and Frank Bartleman, *The Azusa Street Revival, Eyewitness account*.

A phenomenal event, the Azusa Street revival sent shock waves around the world that echo, even louder today.

Now we need to put all that together.

PART FOUR
THE CONCLUSIONS

At the beginning of Chapter Nine, I wrote this:

> After the death of the apostles, and in the ensuing centuries, formal ecclesiastical structures stifled spiritual gifts. Occasionally, however, pious individuals received Holy Spirit infillings and experienced tongues and other gifts. Many such stories emerged throughout history. However, with no developed theology of the Holy Spirit, these people could not pass on their experience, and it went with them to the grave, until someone else stumbled on the same thing, and the cycle repeated. Eventually, though, a new idea emerged: the baptism of the Spirit was a powerful, discrete experience, to equip the believer in his service to God. That discovery process was slow, but eventually culminated in a powerful Pentecostal event at the beginning of the century. There, a theology of the Holy Spirit baptism was formulated, which, when explained to others, could be replicated. With that tool, plus a band of committed people and a remarkable outpouring of the Holy Spirit, the Pentecostal movement exploded.

That "powerful Pentecostal event" was, as we saw, Azusa, and the newly formulated "theology of the Holy Spirit" was the belief that the Spirit baptism is a discrete experience, accompanied by speaking in tongues. After some 1,800 years of Holy Spirit wilderness, the different elements were eventually encapsulated into one clear doctrine, and it exploded throughout the world.

It is time to revise all the components that preceded that history, and draw to a conclusion.

*We have it in our power to begin
the world over again.*

THOMAS PAINE, 1776

*Life can only be understood backwards.
But it must be lived forwards.*

SOREN KIERKEGAARD

CHAPTER 12
BRINGING IT ALL TOGETHER

Here are the major points we covered, and the lessons learned.

Growth rates

The purpose of the Spirit baptism is summed up in Jesus' words, "... you will receive *power* when the Holy Spirit comes on you; and you will be my *witnesses...*" (Acts 1:8). However, Holy Spirit theology is disputed. As I have argued, if Pentecostals and charismatics have accessed this power, and others have not, then results should reflect that. Do they? In our analysis, we found:

- In less than one-third the time, Pentecostals outnumbered the others more than three to one.
- Pentecostals grew more than four times faster.
- If Pentecostals had grown at the same rate as the others their number would be only 127,000 instead of 279 million.
- Charismatics numbered 200 million after 59 years—a growth rate of 22.4% (and Catholic charismatics 160 million after 52 years—a rate of 26%).

In spite of assumptions used in these calculations, the picture is clear. Groups which embrace the Spirit baptism and speaking in tongues significantly outperform all others. Their distinctive theology of the baptism in the Holy Spirit is the stand-out reason.

Church Survey

The National Church Life Survey has investigated "what vital and healthy churches look like" in Australia since 1991. Commissioned by mainline and evangelical denominations, the survey, while not intended for comparing denominations, sheds light on our subject. Does the Spirit baptism make a difference in normal Christian and church life? What did we find?

- Pentecostals scored highest in 30 of the 33 issues analysed in the survey
- Pentecostals scored 47.5% higher than mainline Protestants
- And Pentecostals scored 31.5% higher than Other Protestants.

An outstanding result. What caused it? Again, one issue draws our attention: the view of the baptism in the Holy Spirit.

The Holy Spirit in Music

The Holy Spirit is linked to music. Paul said, "... be filled with the Spirit, speaking to one another with psalms, hymns, and songs from the Spirit" (Ephesians 5:19).

For centuries, people have written wonderful, godly songs, obviously under the inspiration of the Holy Spirit. However, a unique phenomenon has emerged in recent decades as churches switched from hymns to contemporary songs. From Baptists to Lutherans, from Salvation Army to Presbyterians, from Pentecostals to Anglicans, from charismatics to traditionalists, churches everywhere have embraced contemporary songs, drawn by their freshness, familiar contemporary sound, intimate lyrics, and flexibility in worship.

The remarkable thing is that the most loved songs are almost invariably birthed in churches embracing the Spirit baptism and speaking in tongues.

The rest are missing in action. No special promotion or trickery drives this little-known phenomenon. The playing field is level. It boils down to the fact that some songs have a unique spiritual "X-factor", recognised by Christians of all persuasions.

What is this X-factor? Again, the distinctive view of the Spirit baptism is the stand-out reason.

Signs, Wonders and Miracles

Miracles are interwoven with the promised Holy Spirit and the gospel. Paul told the Romans, "... by the power of signs and wonders, through the power of the Spirit of God... I have fully proclaimed the gospel of Christ" (Romans 15:19). But many people are sceptical of miracles, a legacy of the atheistic Enlightenment.

In this chapter, we walked with healing evangelists who encountered the power of the Holy Spirit, and ministered like Philip of old. Wigglesworth was one of them. Late in life, he had already achieved much, including wonderful healing miracles, but his dramatic Spirit baptism multiplied that a thousandfold.

But such ministries invariably emerge from churches embracing the Spirit baptism and speaking in tongues, a significant endorsement of their distinctive doctrine.

Born of the Spirit and baptised in the Spirit

These are two different things. That is evident right through the Bible: first God puts his people right, then he powerfully equips them for service.

In the New Testament, God brought a refinement to this plan. Whereas in the Old Testament, the Holy Spirit fell on SOME people, in our dispensation, that promise is now available for ALL who ask. A critical verse is Joel 2:28: "In the last days, I will pour out my Spirit on ALL people".

The Spirit baptism, given AFTER salvation, provides convicting power for the gospel message, together with miracles, signs and wonders to confirm it.

The Holy Spirit and the Renowned Revivalists

George Fox, the Wesleys, Finney, Moody, the Booths—remarkable ministries, each with a Holy Spirit story to tell.

The ministry of George Fox, in the transforming power of the Holy Spirit and signs and wonders and miracles, was truly outstanding, particularly for that time. It was evident in many wonderful miracles. Remember the poor possessed woman who would "make such a noise in roaring, and sometimes lying along upon her belly upon the ground with her spirit and roaring and voice..." Priests were unable to help. Who could adequately describe her joy when set free after 32 years of that torment?

John Wesley's heart was "strangely warmed" at Aldersgate but it was seven months later, after a "Pentecost season" at 3 am, that the Wesley's ministry exploded.

Finney had a mighty baptism of the Holy Ghost, bellowing out the "unutterable gushings of his heart". What a mighty ministry he then had.

Moody's work, after many quite fruitful years, exploded after the Holy Spirit came on him. When it happened, he "had to ask God to withhold his hand, lest he die on the spot for very joy".

The Booths set the Holy Spirit above all else in soul winning. Their meetings were powerhouses.

Dynamic Holy Spirit activity in the lives of revered forebears.

But none of them had a developed theology of the Holy Spirit and, in spite of any passion they may have had to pass on their experience to others, they did not achieve that in any significant way.

Tongues and Two Thousand Years— what happened during that time?

A few church fathers believed the supernatural gifts of the Holy Spirit— including tongues—had ended. Wesley disagreed. He declared emphatically: it was because love had waxed cold—nothing else. And so, we read of tongues from the stories of Justin Martyr, Irenaus, the Montanists, saints such as Dominic, Francis of Assisi, Xavier, Dominic, Hildegard and others, Fox and the Quakers, Thomas Walsh the Wesleyan preacher, the Camisards, the Irvingites, American Camp Meetings, the Irish Revival, Portland Australia, the Schearer Revival in North Carolina and others who spoke in tongues "as the Spirit enabled them". Supernatural speech has been alive and well. All it needed was a theological framework and a launching pad, to reach the world.

The 1800s saw interest in the Holy Spirit soaring, seeded by Wesley's belief in a second blessing, setting the stage for Azusa Street, on day one of the twentieth century.

And eminent theologian, Augustus H Strong, after observing the centuries-long theological journey to develop the doctrine of Christ, expressed his optimistic hope that "the doctrine of the Holy Spirit... may well be the work of our age (the twentieth century)".

The Azusa Street Revival—where it started

Charles Parham, self-taught and uncluttered by preconceived ideas about the Holy Spirit, earned his place in history with uncompromising faith and perseverance amid trials of many kinds. His forty Bible School students searched and came to the same conclusion: the evidence of receiving the Spirit baptism was speaking in tongues. They tested it and, to their amazement, it happened. The die was cast.

Parham's 40 Students—what did they find?

How did Parham's students reach their conclusion? What did they find in the Bible?

Whenever God poured out his Spirit, right through the Bible, there is EVIDENCE. The Holy Spirit has POWER, and does powerful things. In the Old Testament, when that power was not expressed in things like Samson killing a lion, or Bezalel creating artistic temple design, it was marked by *prophecy*. At Pentecost, that prophecy morphed into *tongues*. We looked at these examples:

WHO	EVIDENCE
70 elders	Prophecy
2 others	Prophecy
Saul	Prophecy
Saul's men	Prophecy
Saul again	Prophecy
Joel, all people	Prophecy
Elizabeth	Prophecy
Zechariah	Prophecy
Simeon	Prophecy
The Pentecost 120	Tongues, wind, fire,
Cornelius	Tongues and praise
Ephesians	Tongues, prophecy
Samaritans	Tongues probably
Paul	Tongues plausible

That *audible* response to the Holy Spirit is consistent with many life experiences—we laugh at things funny, we cry at things sad, we overflow in inspired languages when filled with the Holy Spirit. The unique aspect of tongues is that they are a mystery to us, the supernatural stamp of their supernatural author.

We conclude, along with Parham's students, that the effect of the Spirit baptism is such that the recipient responds with Spirit-inspired speech.

The Azusa Street Revival—William Seymour

The revival of the Spirit baptism with speaking in tongues exploded from a derelict building in a poor part of Los Angeles, amidst unusual spiritual manifestations, criticism and controversy. Interwoven with that extraordinary mix, we saw undeniable Holy Spirit power, Christian love that broke racial barriers, humble leadership, wonderfully transformed lives, and miracles of healing and restoration.

An unconventional white man and his Bible School birthed the new doctrine.

An uneducated black man gave it to the world.

Parham and Seymour. An unlikely pair to launch the biggest transformation in the Christian church since the Reformation.

This was how Azusa Street unfolded and, as strange and imperfect as it might have been, it bore the unmistakable stamp of God. Today, a century later, when we gaze around us as we have done in these chapters, we are faced with a mountain of fruit of all kinds, the fruit we ought to expect when millions of people discover the reality and fullness of the third person of the Trinity in their lives.

From Facts to Feelings

So, there we have it. Factual and biblical evidence demonstrating that the baptism in the Holy Spirit is a discrete experience, different from salvation, is accompanied by speaking in tongues, and empowers the church to spread the gospel. A plethora of evidence, culminating in a mighty event at Azusa Street, which exploded around the world.

Evidence to persuade the mind. We will now finish off with stories to persuade the heart.

I've learned that, whenever I decide something with an open heart, I usually make the right decision.

MAYA ANGELOU

CHAPTER 13
STORIES FROM THE HEART; RECEIVING THE HOLY SPIRIT

A key figure in the charismatic renewal was South African-born pastor David du Plessis. His influence was so great he was dubbed "Mr Pentecost". In 1936, Smith Wigglesworth had prophesied that God would pour out his Spirit over the historic churches, and that du Plessis would play a key role in it. And so he did. On one occasion, a Jesuit priest came to du Plessis, enquiring about the Holy Spirit. Aware of the man's fine intellect, du Plessis prepared himself with the best scriptural and academic case he could muster, but was disappointed when the Jesuit was not convinced. That night, he felt impressed by God that next day he should simply share his own experience of the Holy Spirit. He did, and the priest was persuaded, commenting that, while the first day had informed his mind, the second day had swayed his heart.

So here are a few Holy Spirit stories from my own world which, hopefully, might sway the hearts of readers who might be still unsure. Over the years, I have prayed for several hundred people to receive the Holy Spirit, with many unusual results. And I have witnessed many other fascinating Holy Spirit incidents. Not all were as remarkable as those I share here. Others were more restrained, or less spectacular, but precious nevertheless to those who received them, and who went on to nurture their new gift from God.

Of course, in sharing these stories, I claim no special ability or holiness.

Far from it. Any Pentecostal or charismatic minister of the gospel could relate incidents like these which God, by his grace, had wrought around them. But I share these because I know them. They happened in my world.

The Chicken Farmer

As I drove to one of our worship seminars in a regional city, I asked God if he had any special words for the gathering. In my mind came the words "chicken farmer", and, with it, a picture of an athlete, launching out at the beginning of a race. My attention was drawn to the athlete's power, and I became aware that this power was important, as he was beginning a long-distance event.

Not being strongly prophetic by nature, I was apprehensive as I faced the hundred or so worship leaders and others. Nevertheless I girded my loins and began by asking was there a chicken farmer in the gathering. Mercifully, a tall wiry man raised his hand, so I shared what I had seen, telling him I believed God had given him power, but he needed to know this power was for a long-distance event, not a sprint. He nodded, so I turned back to the intrigued congregation and began my message about worship. The church was evangelical, and the pastor had been cautiously trying to introduce charismatic elements.

During the break, the pastor told me the chicken farmer had recently been baptised in the Holy Spirit. That was apparently the power part. In addition, would you believe, he was an athlete—a long-distance runner. People had come straight to the pastor after my message, asking if he (the pastor) had informed me of these things. Of course, he hadn't. The incident was what Paul described in 1 Corinthians 14:24–25: "But if an unbeliever or an inquirer comes in while everyone is prophesying, they are convicted... as the secrets of their hearts are laid bare. So, they will fall down and worship God, exclaiming, 'God is really among you!'"

The Crusty Bricklayer

In my wife's old Methodist church circuit, a crusty bricklayer named Cecil Lark was well known for his bold faith and his unbridled passion to protect the pulpit from the modernism of some Bible colleges. He loved to tell how

God would speak to him, directing him to certain places to pray for sick people. If ever there was a Spirit-filled Methodist it was Cec Lark. One day he dropped in, and Nolene's brother, Ray grabbed him (and me), telling Cec he was a man running on half a tank of fuel and he needed the other half filled too—with the Holy Spirit of course. Cec bristled, but we got to pray together and, as we did, he launched into an odd mixture of prayer and conversation, telling God he already had the Spirit and didn't need any more. But we persevered, and eventually Cec agreed to ask for the Spirit baptism. Kneeling on the hard wooden floor, we placed our hands on him and, shortly, to our astonishment, he threw his head back and burst out with loud singing in tongues, the sound echoing gloriously around the bare walls. When he eventually stopped, Cec was astonished. This fervent Christian man, long familiar with the hand of God on his life, told us he had never had an experience like that before. More than that I can't tell you—our paths separated and that was the last time I saw him.

More than all of them

A man in our church liked a joke. His previous church was actively evangelical but firmly non-charismatic and, during his time there, he was baptised in the Holy Spirit and spoke in tongues. When word got around, a meeting was called so that the pastor could explain the church's beliefs on this subject (and, I am sure, hopefully put him right!). My friend was the only one in the group who spoke in tongues and everyone knew that. Seated in a circle, they began with each reading in turn a verse from 1 Corinthians 14—a chapter explaining speaking in tongues and prophecy. When my friend's turn came, his was verse 18: "I thank God I speak in tongues more than all of you".

The Nun-kisser

At the height of the charismatic movement, the unthinkable happened. Catholic priests and nuns were visiting Pentecostal services (and vice versa). It was the strangest sight: nuns, dressed in their unmistakable black-and-white habits, sitting happily in a building packed with enthusiastic Protestant

Pentecostals. After all those centuries, ever since the Reformation, an invincible gulf had separated Catholics and Protestants. What could bridge that gulf? The Holy Spirit baptism! There was a huge buzz as it all came to pass and the wife of my pastor visited a large church where it was all happening. A very reserved and conservative lady, when she returned, I had never seen her so animated, bursting out, "I've been in Adelaide kissing nuns!"

The Lay Catholic

A number of years ago, I was part of a committee which ran an annual charismatic, cross-denominational event in Melbourne, Australia. The group was led by a capable lay Catholic charismatic man, Alan Panozza, who was the head of the Australian Catholic Charismatics. For some reason, while the Catholic hierarchy has embraced charismatics in their denomination, they are led by lay people, not priests.

I came to know Alan well. We met several times a year, planning this charismatic event. Eventually, I learned Alan had become the world leader of the Catholic charismatics. In his lounge, above the mantelpiece, was a photo of him, standing beside a smiling Pope. I asked him how many Catholic charismatics were in the world and he told me an independent audit they commissioned provided a figure of 120 million. He was their leader!

Sometime after that, I was involved in another cross-denominational committee of pastors and leaders. They were responding to an upcoming Global Atheist Convention in our city of Melbourne. At one of the meetings, Alan walked in—the only Catholic. (And I was the only one who knew anything about him.) During the friendly introductions, he explained what he did, then someone asked how many people he was responsible for. I enjoyed the silence as he told them. While each of them were responsible for groups of a couple of hundred at the most, Alan, the Catholic, looked over 120 million.

The Intoxicated Schoolteacher

An itinerant evangelist preached at my church and, after one of the meetings, several of our leaders and others came back to my home for coffee. One had brought a friend, a schoolteacher, who sat in the middle of the room in a bean bag. He wanted to receive the baptism in the Holy Spirit, so we gathered round, laid hands on him and prayed. Soon, he was overcome by the presence of the Holy Spirit and began speaking in tongues. After a while, we left him alone to enjoy the experience. He was quite overcome, sprawled out backwards, arms wide, eyes closed, oblivious to the noise around him. He was still there, motionless, at the end of the evening when most had gone. Efforts to arouse him were fruitless—he was completely intoxicated by the Spirit. It was modern-day Acts 2:13, "These people have had too much wine". His friends were amused as this was totally out of character. Two strong men had to half drag him, one under each arm, out to the street and into a car. I hoped the neighbours wouldn't see. This situation happens occasionally. We can understand Paul's analogy, "Do not get drunk on wine, which leads to debauchery. Instead, be filled with the Spirit..." (Ephesians 5:18)

The Forgiven Businessman

This final story came from a work incident of a lady in my church: Robyn Kyte. She tells the story.

> The first thing my new, temporary boss, Mr Gray, said to me was, "Miss Kyte, you are the seventh secretary I have had in six months. Do you—or do you not—intend to stay?" I was taken aback by his aggressive manner but assured him I would stay. However, within two days I decided to leave— the man was so bad-tempered—but someone persuaded me to stay a little longer.
>
> On the second day, during my lunch break, I took my sandwiches and a Bible over to a comfortable chair. Mr Gray came over to ask a question, but didn't leave. He seemed taken by the Bible on my lap. He began to pace up and down in front of me, making me nervous. Then he swung around and barked, "You know you're saved by grace and not by works lest any man should boast, DON'T YOU!" (He was

quoting a Bible verse: Ephesians 2:8–9.) I was frightened by his forcefulness, but squeaked out, yes, I did know.

Mr Gray said nothing more to me which would make me think he had any religious inclinations, and certainly his behaviour didn't show it. His bad temper was at the surface all the time.

My Christian inclination was to bring people to know Jesus; to do that I would invite them to church. I found out that Mr Gray lived close to my church so, on the first Friday afternoon, I nervously approached him and asked if he would like to come with me on Sunday. Of course, I expected him to refuse, and be his usual disagreeable self in doing so, but he agreed! He had no transport and asked how he would get there, so I told him I would pick him up.

He sat through the service, and we continued sitting there after everyone had filed out. I felt sure Mr Gray would not have liked it. He was a pompous, reserved Englishman who spoke in a refined accent, dressed in finely-cut suits, and wore bowler hats. The free-flowing, "happy-clappy" Pentecostal meeting he had just visited would have been very different from the stilted services he might have attended in England. But Mr Gray gave no hint as to his reaction. He merely said, "Hmm, very interesting."

The following week, he said nothing to me about the church service, or God, or anything about religion, and continued to be excessively bad-tempered. On Friday afternoon, I asked him if he would like to come to church again. He queried, "You'll be organising transport, Miss Kyte?" I said I would, and so he came.

Next week, once again, he said nothing about church or religion. Despite him being so cross all the time, I had managed to persevere with the job. On the Friday afternoon, I said, "Mr Gray, if you're planning on going to church this Sunday, I won't be able to take you, as I have to go somewhere else". He fired back at me, "Then organise alternative transport for me, Miss Kyte!" So, I did.

The next Monday, I came into work and Mr Gray was working at his desk. Without looking up, he spoke, "Miss Kyte, this baptism in the Holy Spirit. I want it. Organise it for me!" I laughed and said, "Mr Gray, you can't organise the baptism in the Holy Spirit". "Just do it!" he retorted. So I rang my pastor, and he spoke to Mr Gray and arranged for him to come to his house on Saturday afternoon to receive the baptism in the Holy Spirit he was seeking.

The Sunday morning after this appointment, I was driving to Mr Gray's house to pick him up. Not far from his house, I was stopped at traffic lights when I noticed him walking towards me. Usually he walked stiff and erect, carrying an umbrella. This time he was swinging the umbrella around and around and singing at the top of his voice! *Mr Gray singing!* I pulled up beside him, and he got into the car. "Robyn!" he said, (using my Christian name for the first time), "I have been forgiven!"

I had no idea what he was talking about but, during the following week, I came to understand as Mr Gray revealed to me the story of his life. He had made and lost an immense fortune on two occasions. The first was from the illicit timber industry in Africa; the second was from running Asian opium dens. He had done every bad thing it was possible to do, with one exception—he had never killed anyone, although he had paid people to kill on his behalf. One incident that haunted him was seeing someone, whom he had paid to be killed, burn to death.

It was at his mother's funeral that he realised how wrong it was to live such a life. His mother had prayed for him all his life, and so too his sister who was a missionary. At the funeral, he came to believe that his mother had died from a broken heart because of his sinful life. He went to France and admitted himself into a monastery. He left after two years because he could not believe God could forgive him for what he had done. When he departed, the senior monk told him that their monastery–and its sister monastery in England–would pray for him every day until they heard that he had come to believe God could forgive him. Eight years had gone by and, although he read the scriptures diligently, he still had no understanding of God's forgiveness.

Until he spent that afternoon with my pastor.

Mr Gray and I worked together for just another ten days before he moved on to New Zealand. His manner changed completely, he became kind and friendly, even fatherly. During this time, he was baptised. I will never forget his face as he came up from the water. He shone with joy as he revelled in the knowledge of sins washed completely away.

From New Zealand, he wrote several times. One letter began, "The stars cannot tell, the moon cannot say, the change in me since Jesus came into my life." He went on to speak to many influential people around the world, telling them about Jesus.

I was the pastor in that story. Robyn has been a member of our church for decades. I had no idea of Mr Gray's background when he came to me, and he told me nothing about it. Our meeting was quick and businesslike, his stiff British reserve dominating the mood. I began by explaining to him Jesus' great exchange—taking our sin on himself and giving us, in return, his own righteousness, making us eligible for heaven. I asked had he made such a transaction—either knowingly or intuitively—to which he mumbled "intuitively". I wasn't encouraged by his subdued response but nevertheless went on to explain the baptism in the Holy Spirit. I then placed my hand on his shoulder, and prayed for him to receive. That time was unspectacular when I think of the hundreds I have prayed for like this, though I did hear him speak a few quiet words in another language. But one thing startled me. When we finished praying, he raised his head and locked his eyes on mine.

I was completely taken aback to see astonishment etched on every muscle of his face. I waited for him to explain but, to my surprise, that expression slowly changed, and took on once again his British reserve. Politely thanking me, he left. Only when Robyn got back to me later did I learn what had happened.

I often think of the two fruitless years Mr Gray spent in that monastery, trying to lay hold of God's forgiveness. And the eight years of prayer that followed. The final key to his miracle was a 2,000-year-old, simple, biblical, God-ordained gift—the baptism in the Holy Spirit, with speaking in tongues. If only the monks had known about it! If only *the world* knew about it! How many other Mr Grays are out there, fumbling in the dark, waiting for a Spirit-filled saint to bring them the miraculous, life transforming power of the Holy Spirit?

CONTENDING FOR THE HOLY SPIRIT

You know, if a new idea emerges among God's people and, if half a billion people embrace it in just a century or so, and if it breaks all spiritual records on the way, there has to be merit in that new idea. In the words of Ezra, it has to be the "hand of the Lord our God" upon us (Ezra 7:28). And that being the case, we ought to grasp it, and run with it, with every fibre of our being.

How do you receive the Holy Spirit?

Here are two key verses:

> If you then, though you are evil, know how to give good gifts to your children, how much more will your Father in heaven give the Holy Spirit *to those who ask him*! (Luke 11:13)

> Did you receive the Spirit by the works of the law, or by *believing what you heard*? (Galatians 3:2)

Their message is simple:

ASK:

Firstly, the Holy Spirit is given to those who *ask*. Some might say, "If God wants me to receive the Holy Spirit, that's OK, I will let him". That will not happen. He tells us to *ask*. *Then* we can receive.

BELIEVE:

Secondly, we ask, *believing*. We ask, convinced by the scriptures we have studied and absorbed that the Spirit baptism is real, valid, and *for us personally*.

PERSEVERE:

We become so convinced that we will *not give up* until we have received. When Jesus taught about the Holy Spirit in Luke 11 (above), he was answering the disciples' question about how to pray. He used the story of a friend coming at midnight seeking food for a visitor. His point: fervently persist. "Shameless audacity" is how the NIV translates it. So be prepared to take time, pray into the night, fast, in fact do whatever is necessary, being convinced your loving heavenly Father will lavish upon you this incomparable gift he has promised.

In addition to those three keys, remember to do this:

DEPEND ON GOD:

When praying, empty yourself of all that has any hint of self-sufficiency. In many other aspects of Christian life, we can draw on our natural ability to get the job done. Not now. We depend totally on God.

PRAISE AND WALK ON WATER:

Begin praying with heartfelt gratitude and praise for what God has already done in your life. The Holy Spirit responds to praise. Let that overflow from your heart. Speak it out, audibly. Persist in that. Take as much time as you need. Eventually, when you sense the moment is right, ask God for the gift of the Holy Spirit, believing it will happen. With that expectation, by faith, begin to speak words you don't know. God responds to faith like that. But how can you begin to speak in tongues when you have never done that? Remember, when Peter walked on water he had never done that before either. He just did.

YIELD TO GOD:

You are alone with God. Grant him access to every part of your life, listen for the still small voice and, most of all, enjoy him.

APPENDIX

Without a doubt, the explosion of Holy Spirit activity has been the outstanding event of the Christian church in the twentieth century, and continues to be so. Much has happened and many questions need to be answered. The following Appendix fills in a number of gaps remaining, and answers questions like the following:

APPENDIX A: Can we compile an **overview** of Holy Spirit New Testament action, as a guide for what we should expect in the church today?

APPENDIX B: Didn't Church Creeds and Systematic theology books explain the doctrine of the Holy Spirit prior to Azusa Street? How did Bible teachers justify the idea that spiritual gifts ceased with the Apostles?

APPENDIX C: Did the early church believe the Spirit baptism was a discrete experience? If so, why did this belief disappear? What did Catholics and the early reformers teach on the subject? Is it OK to develop Holy Spirit doctrine from *historical* New Testament writings (Like Acts), or should *theological* writings, like Paul's letters, be the source? What key passages set out the difference between salvation and the Spirit baptism?

APPENDIX D: If love is the first fruit of the Spirit, should Pentecostals demonstrate more? Do they? What about moral failures of prominent evangelists?

APPENDIX E: Why is Speaking in tongues so controversial? What are the arguments against, and how are they answered?

APPENDIX F: Does the baptism in the Spirit lead to neglect of our love for Jesus? Are tongues authentic languages? Are tongues linked to the occult? What is the "prosperity gospel"? Is the Spirit baptism divisive? Did any church fathers believe in cessationism?

APPENDIX G: Can we update the Apostle's Creed to include a Holy Spirit statement?

APPENDIX H: A more detailed look at the National Church Life Survey statistics.

*No man ever believes that the Bible means
what it says. He is always convinced
that it says what he means.*

GEORGE BERNARD SHAW

*"I beseech you, in the bowels of Christ,
think it possible you may be mistaken."*

OLIVER CROMWELL, TO THE
DOUR SCOTTISH PRESBYTERS

*I know that most men, including those at ease
with problems of the greatest complexity, can
seldom accept even the simplest and most obvious
truth if it be such as would oblige them to admit
the falsity of conclusions which they have proudly
taught to others, and which they have woven,
thread by thread, into the fabric of their lives.*

LEO TOLSTOY

APPENDIX A

THE HOLY SPIRIT: WHERE HE OUGHT TO BE

The following is a very simple analysis, achieved by gathering Bible verses about the Holy Spirit and discovering what they tell us. You can do this yourself. Just open BibleGateway.com, enter "Holy Spirit" in the search tool, and compile the results. This is roughly what you will find.

THE ROLE OF THE HOLY SPIRIT

Jesus' omnipresent substitute

When Jesus departed this earth, he sent the Holy Spirit **in his place** to be our **Helper**. The disciples were appalled by the idea. They didn't want to lose their extraordinary leader. But the plan was a winner. Jesus had been confined to one place at one time, the Holy Spirit would be anywhere—all the time. This was for their good, he told them: "... you are filled with grief ... But very truly I tell you, it is **for your good** that I am going away. Unless I go away, the **Advocate** will not come to you; **but if I go, I will send him to you**" (John 16:5–7).

So, the Holy Spirit would swap places with Jesus. Two things would be different. The Holy Spirit would be invisible and omnipresent. Being omnipresent in the lives of multitudes of believers, his contribution would be infinitely multiplied. Jesus said, "Very truly I tell you, whoever believes in me **will do the works I have been doing, and they will do even greater things than these, because I am going to the Father**". (John 14:12) An extraordinary promise. Try to think about that.

Now here are a number of verses relating to various aspects of the work of the Holy Spirit, and how it was expressed in the New Testament church.

Truth about sin (Jesus speaking):

(John 16:8) When [the **Holy Spirit**] comes, he will prove the world to be in the wrong about sin and righteousness and judgment.

Prophesied centuries before (Peter, quoting from Joel):

(Acts 2:17–18) In the last days, God says, I will pour out my **Spirit** on all people. Your sons and daughters will prophesy, your young men will see visions, your old men will dream dreams. Even on my servants, both men and women, I will pour out my **Spirit** in those days, and they will prophesy.

Power

(Acts 1:8) But you will receive power when the **Holy Spirit** comes on you; and you will be my witnesses...

(Romans 15:19)... by the power of signs and wonders, through the power of the **Spirit of God**. So, from Jerusalem all the way around to Illyricum, I have fully proclaimed the gospel of Christ.

(1 Corinthians 2:4) My message and my preaching were not with wise and persuasive words, but with a demonstration

of the **Spirit's** power, so that your faith might not rest on human wisdom, but on God's power.

(Acts 14:3) So Paul and Barnabas spent considerable time there, speaking boldly for the Lord who confirmed the message of his grace by **enabling them to perform signs and wonders**.

(Romans 1:11) I long to see you so that I may impart to you some **spiritual gift** to make you strong.

(2 Timothy 3:1–5) There will be terrible times in the last days. People will... [have] a form of godliness but denying its **power**...

The dramatic Day of Pentecost

(Acts 2:1–4) When the Day of Pentecost came, they were all together in one place. Suddenly a sound like the blowing of a violent wind came from heaven and filled the whole house where they were sitting. They saw what seemed to be tongues of fire that separated and came to rest on each of them. All of them were filled with the **Holy Spirit** and began to speak in other tongues as the **Spirit** enabled them.

The Holy Spirit outpouring in Samaria

The evangelist, Philip preached in Samaria, with many converts and wonderful miracles of healing. The apostles heard about it and came down. Then:

(Acts 8:18–19) Peter and John placed their hands on [the new converts], and they received the **Holy Spirit**. When Simon the magician saw that the **Spirit** was given at the laying on of the apostles' hands, he offered them money and said, "Give me also this ability so that everyone on whom I lay my hands may receive the **Holy Spirit**".

Outpouring on Gentiles (non-Jews)

By a remarkable set of events, God directed Peter to preach to the marginalised Gentiles.

> (Acts 10:44–46) And, while Peter was still speaking these words, the **Holy Spirit** came on all (the Gentiles) who heard the message. The circumcised believers [Jews] who had come with Peter were astonished that the gift of the **Holy Spirit** had been poured out even on Gentiles. For they heard them speaking in tongues and praising God.

Outpouring in Ephesus (Paul, addressing 12 disciples)

> (Acts 19:2–6) 'Did you receive the **Holy Spirit** when you believed?'... When Paul placed his hands on them, the **Holy Spirit** came on them, and they spoke in tongues and prophesied.

Spiritual life

> (Galatians 5:18)... if you are led by the **Spirit**, you are not under the law.

> (Galatians 5:25) Since we live by the **Spirit**, let us keep in step with the **Spirit**.

> (2 Timothy 1:6) For this reason, I remind you (Timothy) to fan into flame the **gift of God**, which is in you through the laying on of my hands.

Guidance and prophetic insight

(Acts 8:29) The **Spirit** told Philip, "Go to that chariot and stay near it."

(Acts 8:39) When they came up out of the water, the **Spirit of the Lord** suddenly took Philip away, and the eunuch did not see him again, but went on his way rejoicing.

(Acts 10:19) While Peter was still thinking about the vision, the **Spirit said to him**, "Simon, three men are looking for you".

(Acts 11:28) One of [the prophets], named Agabus, stood up and, through the **Spirit,** predicted that a severe famine would spread over the entire Roman world. (This happened during the reign of Claudius.)

(Acts 13:2–4) While they were worshipping the Lord and fasting, the **Holy Spirit** said, "Set apart for me Barnabas and Saul for the work to which I have called them". So, after they had fasted and prayed, they placed their hands on them and sent them off. The two of them, sent on their way by the **Holy Spirit**, went down to Seleucia and sailed from there to Cyprus.

(Acts 13:9–11) Then Saul...filled with the **Holy Spirit**, looked straight at Elymas and said, "You are a child of the devil and an enemy of everything that is right!... Now the hand of the Lord is against you. You are going to be blind for a time, not even able to see the light of the sun."

(Acts 21:4b) Through the **Spirit** [the Christians at Tyre] urged Paul not to go on to Jerusalem.

> (Acts 21:11) [The prophet Agabus] took Paul's belt, tied his own hands and feet with it and said, "The **Holy Spirit** says, 'In this way the Jewish leaders in Jerusalem will bind the owner of this belt and will hand him over to the Gentiles.'"

> (Acts 15:28) It seemed good to the **Holy Spirit** and to us not to burden you with anything beyond the following requirements...

The nine supernatural gifts of the Holy Spirit

Paul devotes three chapters to the use of the nine gifts of the Holy Spirit: wisdom, knowledge, faith, healing, miracles, prophecy, distinguishing spirits, tongues and interpretation of tongues (in 1 Corinthians 12, 13 and 14). He focuses particularly on speaking in tongues and prophecy. The following verse also speaks of the gifts:

> (Hebrews 2:3–4) This salvation, which was first announced by the Lord, was confirmed to us by those who heard him. God also testified to it by signs, wonders and various miracles, and by gifts of the Holy Spirit distributed according to his will.

Worship, singing and praying with the Holy Spirit

Several passages link worship, singing and the Holy Spirit:

> (John 4: 23–24)... a time is coming and has now come when the true worshippers will **worship the Father in the Spirit** and in truth, for they are the kind of worshippers the Father seeks. God is spirit, and his worshippers must worship in the Spirit and in truth.

> (Ephesians 5:18–20)... be **filled with the Spirit**, speaking to one another with psalms, **hymns, and songs from the Spirit**. Sing and make music from your heart to the Lord...

(Ephesians 6:18) And pray in the **Spirit** on all occasions with all kinds of prayers and requests.

(Romans 8:26–27) In the same way, the **Spirit** helps us in our weakness. We do not know what we ought to pray for, but the **Spirit** himself intercedes for us through wordless groans. And he who searches our hearts knows the mind of the **Spirit**, because the **Spirit** intercedes for God's people in accordance with the will of God.

(1 Corinthians 14:14–15) For, if I pray in a tongue, my spirit prays but my mind is unfruitful. So, what shall I do? **I will pray with my spirit** but I will also pray with my understanding; **I will sing with my spirit,** but I will also sing with my understanding.

Note in this last passage, "pray with my spirit" means praying in a tongue, and "pray with my understanding" means praying in English (or the vernacular).

Neglecting the Holy Spirit

(Ephesians 4:30) And do not grieve the **Holy Spirit** of God, with whom you were sealed for the day of redemption.

(Acts 7:51) You stiff-necked people! Your hearts and ears are still uncircumcised. You are just like your ancestors: You always resist the **Holy Spirit**!

(1 Thessalonians 5:19) Do not quench the **Spirit**.

(Hebrews 10:29) How much more severely do you think someone deserves to be punished who has... insulted the **Spirit of grace**?

(Jude 1:19) These are the people who divide you, who follow mere natural instincts and do not have the **Spirit**.

(Mark 3:29)... but whoever blasphemes against the **Holy Spirit** will never be forgiven; they are guilty of an eternal sin.

Summarising:

The above collection of scriptures paints a clear picture of the remarkable activities of the early church: working with the promised helper and his power, signs, wonders and miracles, duplicating the works of Jesus, guidance from the Spirit, supernatural insight, prophecy, speaking in tongues. All these were normal fare for Christians back then. If the Holy Spirit is the same today as he was then—*and he is*—then the entire Christian church should be comfortable and familiar with all these things.

But in many places that is just not the case. Why not? The next chapter looks at that issue, and the reasons behind it.

Two wise men, faith and hope, two stooges, two musketeers, two little pigs, two bears, two blind mice, two Amigos, Huey and Dewey, Snap and Crackle, Newton's two laws of motion, scones and jam, learning your ABs, Father and Son. Something is missing.

ANON

APPENDIX B

THE NEGLECT, AND WHY IT HAPPENED

HOLY SPIRIT IN THE CREEDS

At several points in church history, creeds were formulated to encapsulate important beliefs, to bring consistency, and combat heretical ideas. Let us see how much they tell us about the big three—Father, Son and Holy Spirit. Look, in particular, for references to the Holy Spirit.

Nicene Creed (325 AD)

This creed was established to settle a dispute about the relationship between God, the Father, and God, the Son. It has a lot to say about Jesus–133 words.

God, the Father is allotted 16 words, and the Holy Spirit is acknowledged with the following 31 words:
We believe in the Holy Spirit, the Lord, the giver of life, who proceeds from the Father and the Son. With the Father and the Son, he is worshipped and glorified. He has spoken through the Prophets.

So, the Holy Spirit is given a place here as an important part of the three, but there is no mention of his wide-ranging work as our helper, as we have seen in the Book of Acts.

Apostles' Creed (390 AD or earlier)—an early statement of Christian belief.

I believe in...

> GOD: the Father Almighty, creator of heaven and earth; (eight words describing God)

and in..

> JESUS CHRIST: his only Son, our Lord; who was conceived by the Holy Spirit, born of the Virgin Mary, suffered under Pontius Pilate, was crucified, died and was buried. He descended into hell; on the third day he arose again from the dead. He ascended into heaven, and sits at the right hand of God, the Father Almighty; from thence he shall come to judge the living and the dead. (67 words describing Jesus)

I believe in the

> HOLY SPIRIT,
> ..the Holy Catholic Church, the communion of saints, the forgiveness of sins, the resurrection of the body and life everlasting. Amen.

How many words are allocated to the Holy Spirit?...**NONE.**

Chalcedonian Creed (451 AD)

Like the Nicene Creed, this was also formulated in response to heretical views about Jesus. It also tells us nothing of the Holy Spirit. To be fair, that is not unexpected when you consider the purpose of the creed. Nevertheless, we still have no formal acknowledgement of his work, and what he does.

Athanasian Creed (500 AD)

This creed focuses on the Trinity and on Jesus. It was formulated to combat the error of Arianism which held heretical views about the Trinity. Apart from his mention as an equal member of the Trinity, the Holy Spirit and his work is not mentioned either.

So, we find no definitive statements in the creeds to teach us the role of the Holy Spirit on earth. In the face of other issues, he was 'given a back seat'.

Another place we can look for the Holy Spirit is in:

BOOKS OF SYSTEMATIC THEOLOGY

Compiled by the most-gifted academics and theologians, these massive tomes expound in minute detail the major Bible teachings about God, and how he relates to us. The various ideas of the author are supported by views from a wide range of eminent scholars. These books are not light reading but students of theology and pastors find in them a wealth of information. I bought two different versions years ago to help prepare a mini Bible School for my church. When I opened them for the first time, I looked with interest to see what they had to say about the Holy Spirit. Here is what I found.

Systematic Theology by Augustus H Strong: First printed 1907; 1056 pages
    Pages devoted to God: 323
    Pages devoted to Jesus: 107
    Pages devoted to the Holy Spirit: NONE[256]

Systematic Theology by L Berkhof: Published 1939; 784 pages
    Pages devoted to God: 176
    Pages devoted to Jesus: 105
    Pages devoted to the Holy Spirit: FOUR

I was surprised. Two scholarly books, hundreds of pages devoted to God and Jesus but, apart from a brief analysis of his place in the Trinity, the Holy Spirit is ignored.

Those books were written early in the twentieth century. Here are a few more, from several decades later, and the page count.

Christian Theology by Millard Erickson (1983)	42 pages of 1225 (3.4%)
Moody Handbook of Theology by Paul Enns (1989)	42 pages of 607 (6.9%)
Theology of the New Testament by Udo Schnelle (2007)	17 pages of 747 (2.3%)
Theology of the New Testament by George Eldon Ladd (1957)	12 pages of 720 (1.7%)

So we have the Holy Spirit, an equal member of the Big Three, and commissioned as helper of the church in this dramatic final age, effectively sidelined. We have, it appears, a Trinity in two parts!

Now, to be fair, some more recent books of theology include more thorough information about the Holy Spirit. Perhaps the rise of the Pentecostal church, and its emphasis on the Holy Spirit, has spurred authors to action. But there are enough examples above to convince us that these remarkably gifted and scholarly men have paid little or no attention to the third member of the Trinity, the Holy Spirit.

Of course the number of pages devoted is not always a reliable measure of a subject's importance. It is just a simple way to demonstrate here that the subject of the Holy Spirit has not been addressed as it could be, or that scholars and teachers feel they do not know enough about it. Is it important? Of course it is. You might compare this to writing a book about the workings of a motor car, and ignoring the engine.

How did this happen?

As mentioned earlier, after the death of the apostles, the church slowly became more structured and formalised. Bibles were non-existent, fragmented or rare, and a consistent solid Christian theology and culture was still developing. The church drifted from its initial dynamic spiritual roots, a drift which becomes evident in early Christian writings. We read about specific days set aside for fasting, and rules on how baptisms and services should be conducted. Many of the rules and regulations seem good and noble but they inevitably quenched the spontaneity and unpredictability of the Holy Spirit.

So the supernatural gifts of the Spirit became less common. Eventually, some early church fathers came to believe the gifts had served their purpose (to aid in the establishment of the church, they said) and God removed them. That view (cessationism) has been embraced by many down through the centuries and is still relatively common today. Here is an example, from the doctrinal statement of Dallas Theological Seminary:

> We believe that some gifts of the Holy Spirit such as speaking in tongues and miraculous healings were temporary. We believe that speaking in tongues was never the common or necessary sign of the baptism nor of the filling of the Spirit, and that the deliverance of the body from sickness or death awaits the consummation of our salvation in the resurrection.[257]

Although this view seems to have lost favour in recent years, it is still, nevertheless, the undergirding belief in many evangelical churches today.

Some Christians believe tongues are still available today but as a lesser gift, not highly desirable, and not definitive evidence of the baptism of the Holy Spirit. Pentecostals disagree—Appendix E explains that.

We need to look at the scriptures that cessationists use to justify their belief. There are two main (but conflicting) arguments, based on two different passages. The first is this:

> Love never fails. But where there are prophecies, they will cease; **where there are tongues, they will be stilled**; where there is knowledge, it will pass away. For we know in part, and we prophesy in part, but when **completeness** comes, what is in part disappears... For now, we see only a reflection as in a mirror; then we shall see face to face. (1 Corinthians 13:8–10).

Clearly, we see, tongues will cease. But what is this "completeness" (or "maturity", or "perfection" in some translations) which will bring it to an end? Cessationists disagree amongst themselves once again here. Some say it means love itself, others the completed New Testament, and still others, the mature church.[258]

But the far more likely meaning of "completeness", which most commentators suggest, is the new and glorious era ushered in when Christ returns. At that time, as Paul said above, "we shall see face to face". Clearly this depicts us in heaven, seeing Jesus, face to face, and nothing in between. God's plan will most certainly be "complete" then.

The second cessationist argument is based on this passage:

> Consequently, you are no longer foreigners and strangers, but fellow citizens with God's people and also members of his household, built on the foundation of the apostles and prophets, with Christ Jesus himself as the chief cornerstone. (Ephesians 2:19–20)

The view is outlined as follows, by prominent cessationist, John MacDonald:

> To determine the point in church history when the miraculous and revelatory gifts would pass away, we must look elsewhere than 1 Corinthians 13:10 ("where there are tongues, they will be stilled") to passages like Ephesians 2:20, where Paul indicated that both the apostolic and prophetic offices were only for the foundational age of the church.[259]

Putting that another way, MacDonald is saying that the apostles and prophets were uniquely and supernaturally gifted for their task of establishing the church and, when that job was done, and they all died, those supernatural gifts died with them. There is obviously a considerable leap between Ephesians 2:20 ("built on the foundation of the apostles and prophets") and that conclusion. There is no scripture which makes the point clearly. It is a belief, an interpretation. In addition, the fact that there is much disagreement (as pointed out above) on other aspects of the cessationist view makes the case very weak. We have every reason to believe tongues have continued unchanged through the ages, albeit on a lesser scale.

And, as we have seen in chapter nine, history has convincingly confirmed that belief, with records of spiritual gifts prevailing multiple times through the ages, till the explosion at Azusa Street in 1901.

A **second issue** that contributed to the stifling of the Holy Spirit was as follows.

Much of the church came to believe that being **born** of the Holy Spirit was the same as being **baptised** in the Holy Spirit. These two concepts which are, in fact, very different, are identified in these verses:

- **Born** of the Holy Spirit, in John 3:5: "No one can enter the kingdom of God unless they are **born** of water and the **Spirit**"
- **Baptised** in the Holy Spirit, in John 1:33: "The man on whom you see the Spirit come down and remain is the one who will **baptise in the Holy Spirit**..."

Much of the church had come to believe **both** occurred at **conversion**. Pentecostals (along with Catholics, Anglicans and Orthodox) disagreed. Why?

Pentecostals believed the **purpose** of the two experiences was different. Yes, being **born** of the Holy Spirit brings regeneration to our dead spirit, as in Titus 3:5: "He saved us through the washing of rebirth and renewal by the Holy Spirit". That is not usually disputed. But scripture tells us the **baptism** of the Holy Spirit has an entirely different purpose. It provides power for witnessing and spreading the gospel. Acts 1:8 spells it out: "you will receive power when the Holy Spirit comes on you, and you will be my witnesses..."

That is the essence of the idea. But the subject is important and needs further analysis in both Old and New Testaments. We will do that in the next chapter. But before we do—a contribution from an unexpected source.

Prophetic insight from Augustus H Strong

When the early church drifted from its roots, the need for establishment of important doctrines became obvious to scholars. So, they searched the scriptures, and gradually wrestled from them, one by one, the truths we hold dear today. The subject of the Holy Spirit, however, remained untouched, with all attention on Christ and our salvation. When that was eventually settled, attention then turned to the Holy Spirit.

Some steps involved in that restoration process have been suggested by Augustus H Strong, in a lengthy footnote in his *Systematic Theology* (mentioned above). In a discussion about the Person of Christ, he says this:

> In the history of doctrine, as we have seen, beliefs held in solution at the beginning [of the Christian church] are only gradually precipitated and crystallised into definite formulas. The first question which Christians naturally asked themselves was, "What think ye of Christ?" (Matthew 22:42); then his relation to the Father; then, in due succession, the nature of sin, of atonement, of justification, of regeneration. Connecting these questions with the names of great leaders who sought respectively to answer them, we have:
>
> 1. The Person of Christ, treated by Gregory Nazianzen (328)
> 2. The Trinity, by Athanasius (325–373)
> 3. Sin, by Augustine (353–430)
> 4. Atonement, by Anselm (1033–1109)
> 5. Justification by Faith, by Luther (1485–1500)
> 6. Regeneration, by John Wesley (1708–1791)
>
> [So, we have] six week-days of theology, LEAVING ONLY A SEVENTH, FOR THE DOCTRINE OF THE HOLY SPIRIT, WHICH MAY BE THE WORK OF OUR AGE.[260] (Emphasis added)

In other words, Strong tells us, the full understanding of Christ took many centuries to fully emerge. Then, obviously recognising that the Holy Spirit was as little understood today as Christ was at the beginning, Strong proposes a glorious hope: that the Holy Spirit may be the work of his age—*the emerging twentieth century.*

Next: So, there are conflicting views on the Holy Spirit. Pentecostals believe being baptised in the Spirit is a discrete experience, different from being born of the Spirit; others believe the two are synonymous. It is time to see what the Bible says. I will lay out the Pentecostal view, and discuss a few objections from the alternative point of view. And I will lay some important Old Testament foundations, which are often not considered in this discussion.

To be accepted as a paradigm, a theory must seem better than its competitors, but it need not, and in fact never does, explain all the facts...

THOMAS S KUHN [261]

APPENDIX C
SALVATION AND SPIRIT BAPTISM-THE DIFFERENCE (EXPANDED VERSION)

First, some background. The early church predominantly believed the Spirit baptism was an experience to be received after salvation. For example, Origen of Alexandria (185-284 AD) had this to say:

> ... the grace and revelation of the Holy Spirit [was] bestowed by the imposition of the apostles' hands after baptism. Our Saviour also, after the resurrection, when old things had already passed away and all things had become new... his apostles having also being renewed by faith in His resurrection, says, "Receive the Holy Spirit".[262]

And Cyprian (195-258 AD), Bishop of Carthage, said:

> One is not born by the imposition of hands when he received the Holy Ghost, but in baptism, that so, being already born, he may receive the Holy Spirit, even as it happened to the first man, Adam. For first God formed him and then breathed into his nostrils the breath of life.[263]

This view prevailed until the Reformation. At that time, the great reformer, Calvin (and other reformers too) emphasised the importance of faith in conversion and the work of the Holy Spirit in this process. Calvin was highly contemptuous of the Catholic theology of confirmation, which taught a second spiritual experience to complete the work of grace at conversion. He said:

> But the Papists are worthy of no pardon, who being not content with the ancient rite, durst thrust in rotten and filthy anointing, that it might not be only a confirmation of baptism, but also a more worthy sacrament, whereby they imagine that the faithful are made perfect who were before only half perfect—whereby those are armed against the battle, who before had their sin only forgiven them. For they have not been afraid to spew out these horrible blasphemes.[264]

Because of his outspoken stance, the Reformed church has ever since firmly believed in a single work of grace. This is in contrast to Catholic, Anglican, some Orthodox, Methodist and Pentecostal denominations. So today we have the church divided on the issue, and we need to study the scriptures for ourselves.

Born of the Spirit and baptised in the Spirit.

What do these expressions mean? They are found only in the New Testament, so you might think that's where we should begin.

However, God poured out his Spirit in the **Old Testament** too, often described in this way: *"The Spirit of the Lord came on..."* Those Old Testament instances laid a foundation we can build on, and the New Testament spells out unique aspects for our unique age.

In a nutshell, the story that unfolds is this:

Consistently, throughout the Bible, God gives his redeemed children specific, noble **assignments.** These assignments are **not achievable by human ability alone. To make them achievable, God provides the supernatural, experiential, power of the Holy Spirit.**

The similarities and differences between Old and New Testament outpourings are illuminating.

The similarities:

In both Old and New Testaments, God provides:

- redemption from sin
- assignments, and
- supernatural power for the assignments

Three differences:

First, the MEANS of REDEMPTION or SALVATION are different:

- In the Old Testament, people were saved from sin by faith in God, trusting him to keep his Covenant promises and redeem his people. They had to obey his laws, and make ongoing animal sacrifices for their sins–a forerunner of Jesus' sacrifice for us.
- In the New Testament, we are saved by placing our faith in the sacrifice and resurrection of Jesus. We are born of the Holy Spirit, our spirits are regenerated by the Holy Spirit, and we are filled with his Holy Spirit.

Second, God's ASSIGNMENTS are different:

- In the Old Testament, God poured out his Spirit for EITHER **one-off assignments,** OR **ongoing general service**.
- In the New Testament, God poured out his Spirit for the **ongoing task of spreading the news about Jesus to the whole world.**

Third, ELIGIBILITY to RECEIVE is different:

- Old Testament outpourings were for people **specially chosen by God.** These people were **not expecting** it.

- New Testament outpourings are for **all believers**. (The **onus**, however, **placed on the believer** to **ask for** the Holy Spirit, and to **expect to receive that gift by faith**.)

Now to build the case.

Let scripture, not experience, be the guide

It goes without saying that scripture must do the talking. Even more so on this subject because the Spirit baptism experience is quite that—an experience. Experiences can vary dramatically from person to person and be open to interpretation.

For example, consider the apostle Paul in Acts 9. As he was travelling around persecuting the church, God stopped him: with a blinding light, an audible voice from heaven and a force that hurled him to the ground. A powerful experience. A person going through that today might well believe they had been baptised in the Holy Spirit. But, as awe-inspiring as it was, that was not the case for Paul. His baptism in the Holy Spirit came three days later when God sent the disciple Ananias to pray for him. So we must anchor ourselves on scripture.

There is another issue.

The idea that the Spirit baptism is not the same as salvation is theologically prickly. Many of the scriptures we use are from the Book of Acts and some theologians baulk at that. Acts is a record of history, they say, and doctrine should be built from books which address theological issues (such as Paul's letters), not books of history. However, other theologians differ. Craig S Keener[265], for example, names three eminent theologians (as well as himself) who disagree with that view. He points out that Paul used historical passages to develop doctrine, giving 1 Corinthians 10:6 as one example (where Paul points out that Old Testament stories such as crossing the Red Sea "occurred as examples to keep us from setting our hearts on evil things as they did"). Keener also quotes 2 Timothy 3:16: "All scripture is... useful for teaching..." He is frank: "While not every (scripture) example is a positive or universal one, examples of God's working that do not fit our paradigms may require us to adjust our paradigms." In simple words, we don't own the right to decree how scripture must always be interpreted.

So, we will run with the historical books where we need to, and let all scripture be our guide.

Now the scriptural case.

Old Testament outpourings and their purpose

There are several examples in the Old Testament where God chose Israelites for a specific task, and equipped them with the Spirit. Here they are:

Bezalel—artistic designs: "I (God) have filled [Bezalel] with the **Spirit of God**, with wisdom, with understanding, with knowledge and with all kinds of skills—to make artistic designs for work in gold, silver and bronze..." (Exodus 31:3)

Othniel—equipped for war: "But when [the Israelites] cried out to the LORD, he raised up for them a deliverer, Othniel son of Kenaz, Caleb's younger brother, who saved them. The **Spirit of the LORD** came on him, so that he became Israel's judge and went to war."(Judges 3:9–11)

Gideon—leadership: "Then the **Spirit of the LORD** came on Gideon, and he blew a trumpet, summoning the Abiezrites to follow him." (Judges 6:34)

David—his task as king: "So Samuel took the horn of oil and anointed him in the presence of his brothers, and from that day on, the **Spirit of the LORD** came powerfully upon David." (1 Samuel 16:13) (This was when God chose David to be king of Israel, to equip him for that role. Note how David cherished this anointing. In Psalm 51:11, the story of his sin against Uriah the Hittite, he repented and begged God: "Do not...take your Holy Spirit from me.")

Samson—to fight: "The **Spirit of the LORD** came powerfully upon him so that he tore the lion apart with his bare hands as he might have torn a young goat." (Judges 14:6)

"Then the **Spirit of the Lord** came powerfully upon him. He went down to Ashkelon, struck down 30 of their men..." (Judges 14:19)

"The **Spirit of the Lord** came powerfully upon him. The ropes on his arms became like charred flax, and the bindings dropped from his hands. Finding a fresh jawbone of a donkey, he grabbed it and struck down a thousand men." (Judges 15:14–15)

Ezekiel—to prophesy: "Then the **Spirit of the Lord** came on me, and he told me to say: ..." (Ezekiel 11:5–9)

Moses' 70 elders—for ongoing leadership: The Lord said to Moses: "Bring me 70 of Israel's elders who are known to you as leaders and officials among the people... I will take some of the **power of the Spirit** that is on you and put it on them. They will share the burden of the people with you so that you will not have to carry it alone." (Numbers 11:16–26)

King Saul—for leadership: (Samuel speaking to Saul) "The **Spirit of the Lord** will come powerfully upon you, and you will prophesy with [the prophets]; and you will be changed into a different person." (1 Samuel 10:5–6)

So, Bezalel, Othniel, Gideon, David, Samson, Ezekiel, Moses' 70 elders and King Saul, were all Israelites, commissioned by God for difficult (if not impossible!) tasks. When the time came, *the **Spirit of the Lord** came on them, and they got the job done.* Note that, in each case when the Spirit fell, the results were *tangible, if not dramatic.* We could expect the same in the New Testament.

Not for salvation

The Old Testament Holy Spirit experience was not for salvation. The Israelites were already "believers", embraced by God and "saved" under the unique arrangements of the Old Testament. All were Israelites, God's chosen sons and daughters, privileged as custodians of the Law, the temple worship and the divine glory. They lived under God's favour on the basis of forgiveness provided by the death of animal substitutes and obedience to God (e.g. Deuteronomy 5:33).

Then, to chosen individuals, God gave his Spirit for special assignments.

That is the Old Testament pattern, and it sets the stage for the New Testament. Remembering that "The law is only a shadow of the good things that are coming…" (Hebrews 10:1), we can expect something similar in the New Testament, but much, much better.

Change prophesied by Joel

Several hundred years before Christ, the prophet, Joel, said this: "And [in the last days], I will pour out My Spirit on ALL people" (Joel 2:28).

In those days, God poured out his Spirit on SOME people. A day was coming, Joel promised, when "SOME" would become "ALL". The gates would be flung wide, so that ALL COULD ENTER and experience this extraordinary and wonderful gift. That promised day, of course, was the Day of Pentecost (full story in Acts 2). When it came, and astonished crowds were asking questions, Peter turned straight to Joel for his answer. And he made it clear there was now a UNIVERSAL PROMISE of the Holy Spirit, saying:

> …you will receive the gift of the Holy Spirit. The promise is **for you and your children and for ALL who are far off— for ALL whom the Lord our God will call**. (Acts 2:38–39)

A great and mighty promise, to all people everywhere.

Next: New Testament distinctives. We will now look at scriptures which identify differences between being born of the Spirit and baptised in the Spirit. Some are not conclusive on their own but I include them as they help build the picture. Others are convincing in their own right. Together, they form our complete case.

BORN OF, AND BAPTISED IN, THE HOLY SPIRIT: NEW TESTAMENT DIFFERENCES

John's declarations:

Salvation: "Look, the Lamb of God, who takes away the sin of the world!" (John 1:29)

Holy Spirit: "...the one who sent me to baptise with water told me, 'The man on whom you see the Spirit come down and remain is the one who will **baptise with the Holy Spirit**.'" (John 1:33)

Jesus' "water" analogies:

Salvation: "...whoever drinks the water I give them will never thirst. Indeed, the water I give them will become in them a spring of water welling up to **eternal life**." (John 4:13–14)

Holy Spirit: "Jesus stood and said in a loud voice, 'Let anyone who is thirsty come to me and drink. Whoever believes in me, as scripture has said, rivers of living water will flow from within them.' By this he meant **the Spirit**, whom those who believed in him were later to receive." (John 7: 37–39)

The disciples (a):

Salvation: Before the Day of Pentecost (when they were baptised in the Holy Spirit), their "names [were] written in heaven". (Luke 10:20) They were: "already clean because of the word I (Jesus) have spoken to you" (John 15:3). Jesus told them they were branches of the vine–himself (John 15:5). They were "not of the world even as I (Jesus) am not of the world" (John 17:14). Jesus "breathed on them and said, 'Receive the Holy Spirit'" (John 20:22).

Holy Spirit: After his resurrection, Jesus promised the disciples: "...in a few days, you will be baptised with the Holy Spirit" (Acts 1:5). Then, on the Day of Pentecost, "All of them were **filled with the Holy Spirit** and began to speak in tongues as the Spirit enabled them" (Acts 2:4).

The disciples (b):

Salvation: Jesus also told the disciples, "… I will ask the Father, and he will give you another advocate to help you and be with you forever—the

Spirit of truth. The world cannot accept him, because it neither sees him nor knows him. But you know him, for he lives with you and..."

Holy Spirit: ..."will be in you." (John 14:16–17)

Philip preached to the Samaritans:

Salvation: "... when they believed Philip as he proclaimed the good news of the kingdom of God and the name of Jesus Christ, they were baptised..." (Acts 8:12). So these believing and baptised Samaritans were now saved, born of the Spirit (John 3:16). Note also Mark 16:16: "Whoever believes and is baptised will be saved".

Holy Spirit: Several days after the Samaritans believed, the apostles travelled from Jerusalem and "... prayed for the new believers there that they might receive the Holy Spirit, because the Holy Spirit had not yet come on any of them; they had simply been baptised in the name of the Lord Jesus. Then Peter and John placed their hands on them, and **they received the Holy Spirit.**" (Acts 8:15–17)

The apostle Paul:

Salvation: Saul yielded on the road to Damascus, calling Jesus, "Lord" (Acts 9:4–6), becoming obedient to the heavenly command (see Acts 22 and Acts 24), and praying (Acts 9:11). Clearly, this was his conversion experience.

Holy Spirit: Three days later, the disciple Ananias was sent to Saul, placing his hands on him, not to secure salvation but "so that you may see again and **be filled with the Holy Spirit**" (Acts 9:17).

The Ephesian disciples:

Salvation: Paul met the Ephesian "disciples" (Acts 19) and asked, "Did you receive the Holy Spirit when you believed?" (Verse 2). Apparently they had not so, after sorting out their baptism doctrine, "they were baptised in the name of the Lord Jesus" (Verse 5). There was no doubt now about their salvation. Then...

Holy Spirit: (Verse 6): "When Paul placed his hands on them, **the Holy Spirit came on them**, and they spoke in tongues and prophesied" (See note below on this verse).

Ephesians 1:13:

Salvation: (NASB) "In Him, you also, **after** listening to the message of truth, the gospel of your salvation—having also believed..."

Holy Spirit: "...you were **sealed in him with the Holy Spirit** of promise..." (See comments below).

COMMENTS ON THE ABOVE:

Jesus' water analogies are compelling: the spring is vigorous and life giving, welling up inside, a fitting portrayal of eternal life, given for our benefit. The baptism in the Holy Spirit, however, provides mighty rivers, of living water, to flow out from the believer for the benefit of others.

The disciples and John 20:22: Jesus *breathed on them and said, 'Receive the Holy Spirit'*. The meaning of this passage is disputed. Some say this is the moment when the disciples were born of the Holy Spirit, or regenerated. Others say it is prophetic, looking forward to Pentecost for fulfilment. The fact that Jesus breathed on them suggests something was happening (i.e., the new birth) as he spoke. There is support for this idea in Adam's story, when God *breathed into his nostrils the breath of life, and the man became a living being* (Genesis 2:7). As God breathed on Adam, something spiritual happened right then. It is likely Jesus was following the same pattern.

Acts 8: The incident in Samaria: This passage (together with Acts 19:1–6), is probably the most compelling of our arguments. Clearly the Samaritans were saved, yet they did not receive the Holy Spirit until the Apostles came down and prayed for them several days later. Theologians challenging the Pentecostal view acknowledge they have a significant problem here but struggle to provide a convincing answer. To respond to their diverse and lengthy theories would take many pages. It is more effective in this book to say no more than this: those who differ disagree among themselves. The Pentecostal view, on the other hand, is simple and reasonable: the Samaritan new converts were saved under Philip's ministry, and received the Holy Spirit days later—a separate and distinct experience after salvation.

Acts 19:2: the Ephesian believers: The question, "Did you receive the Holy Spirit when you believed?" clearly implies it is possible to believe and yet not receive the Holy Spirit. **Otherwise, it does not make sense.** Note too that the Ephesians were already "believers" (a term consistently used in Acts to describe Christians), and also that their receiving the Holy Spirit was distinct from their water baptism, even though close in time. Paul had first baptised them then, after that, laid his hands on them specifically to pray for the Holy Spirit.

Ephesians 1:13: In the NASB and KJV Bibles (quoted above), the word "after" tells us the sealing of the Holy Spirit occurs **after** salvation. Other translations differ. They give us "**when** you believed", suggesting believing and sealing occur at the same time. Which is correct? The eminent conservative evangelical, Dr Martin Lloyd Jones, firmly believes it should be "after". In saying this, the great man controversially deviates from his evangelical peers. In a sermon titled, *Sealed with the Spirit*[266], he cites the following scholars to support his view: Puritan Thomas Goodwin; his contemporary, Oxford theologian John Owen; Princeton theologian Dr Charles Hodge; and prominent Anglican evangelical clergyman, Charles Simeon.

In his sermon, Dr Lloyd Jones says:

> "...the sealing of the Holy Spirit does not always follow immediately when a man believes, but it may not follow, and there may be a great interval, and that it is possible for one to be a believer, and therefore to have the Holy Spirit, and still not know the sealing of the Spirit... I am not sure that this [belief in separate and distinct experiences] is not one of the most vital of all Christian doctrines, as we think of the need of revival and the reawakening of the Christian church...I would even go so far as to suggest that the poverty of spiritual experience today, is very largely to be attributed to the fact that people have not drawn this distinction".

Dr Lloyd Jones did not move in Pentecostal or charismatic circles; for such an eminent scholar to hold so firmly to such a belief against that of his peers is compelling.

NOTE: While there is one, initial baptism in the Spirit, there are many ongoing "fillings" of the Holy Spirit. It seems we "leak" this power, and need to be refilled. In Acts 4:31, Peter and John and others *were all filled with the Holy Spirit* when they prayed for power to preach with boldness. They had previously been baptised with the Spirit at Pentecost. **Ongoing infillings are the norm**. It is our responsibility to seek that, as per Paul's instructions in Ephesians 5:18–19: "Do not get drunk on wine, which leads to debauchery. Instead, be filled with the Spirit, speaking to one another with psalms, hymns, and songs from the Spirit". The Greek verb used here for "be filled" carries the idea of a continual, ongoing filling, not a once-for-all event.

Purpose of the New Testament baptism in the Holy Spirit

Old Testament Holy Spirit outpourings enabled Bezalel to carve exquisite designs, Samson to kill a lion with his bare hands, Moses' elders to lead the people with wisdom, and so on. What then, is the purpose of Joel's promised outpouring in the New Testament?

Jesus was very clear:

> I am going to send you what my Father has promised (i.e. the Holy Spirit); but stay in the city until you have been clothed with **power from on high**. (Luke 24:49)

> ...you will receive **power** when the Holy Spirit comes on you; and **you will be my witnesses** in Jerusalem, and in all Judea and Samaria, and to the ends of the earth. (Acts 1:8)

Being baptised in the Holy Spirit provides supernatural power to **spread the gospel**. It has nothing to do with being **born** of the Holy Spirit or forgiveness of sins. Power and forgiveness are two distinct and different works of the Holy Spirit. Jesus explained being **born** of the Holy Spirit (or new birth) at length in John 3. He concluded with these words:

> For God so loved the world that he gave his one and only Son, that whoever believes in him shall not perish but have **eternal life**. (John 3:16)

Eternal life is the purpose of the new birth. Titus expresses that idea this way:

> He **saved** us through the washing of **rebirth** and renewal by the **Holy Spirit**. (Titus 3:5)

And Paul explained that people **born** of the Holy Spirit are **indwelt** by the Holy Spirit:

> And if anyone does not have the Spirit of Christ, they do not belong to Christ. But if Christ is in you, then even though your body is subject to death because of sin, the Spirit gives life because of righteousness. (Romans 8:9–10)

Spirit baptism: a gift received by specific faith

While the New Testament **promise** of the Spirit baptism is made to **all** people, there is a condition, spelled out in these words of Jesus:

> If you...know how to give good gifts to your children, how much more will your Father in heaven give the Holy Spirit **to those who ask him**!" (Luke 11:13)

God gives the Holy Spirit to intentional, fervent seekers. Here is a prayer that will not work: "God, if you want me to have the baptism in the Spirit, go ahead, it's OK with me". No. God has made an offer. He wants a response. So we must believe his promise, and ask for the gift, fully expecting it will happen.

Notice that Paul asked the Galatian church, "...does God give you his Spirit and work miracles among you by the works of the law, or by your believing what you heard?" (Galatians 3:5). God works **miracles** among us in response to believing prayer. Paul places **receiving the Spirit** in the same basket.

Once again, this differs from the Old Testament pattern. They were sovereign events, provided only at God's discretion. We live in a new, different, and glorious day, with a wonderful promise for everyone the Lord calls.

Conclusion

So, there it is: God's two-step purpose for his lost people.

- He draws us to himself, providing forgiveness for sin, and
- He equips us with the Holy Spirit to spread the gospel.

NEXT:

Now to an issue raised in the National Church Life Survey under the core quality PRACTICAL AND DIVERSE SERVICE. If love is the first fruit of the Holy Spirit, and Pentecostals claim more of the Holy Spirit, shouldn't this be reflected here? Pentecostal scores are OK, but don't stand out as they do in other core qualities. Why not? This is an important issue.

*The actions of men are the best
interpreters of their thoughts.*

JOHN LOCKE

Well done is better than well said.

BENJAMIN FRANKLIN

APPENDIX D
THE FRUIT OF THE SPIRIT: SHOULD PENTECOSTALS AND CHARISMATICS DEMONSTRATE MORE?

Paul's nine elements of the FRUIT of the Spirit are renowned: "...love, joy, peace, forbearance, kindness, goodness, faithfulness, gentleness and self-control" (Galatians 5:22).

Do Pentecostals, with "more" of the Holy Spirit, produce "more" of this fruit?

Some say no, they do not.

We could also ask, if Pentecostal **pastors** experience more of the Holy Spirit, are they more self-controlled, and less likely to fall into moral failure?

Again, some say they are not.

What is the answer?

It is this.

The source of the nine-dimensional fruit of the Spirit is **the indwelling Spirit of the new birth**. **Every** Christian is filled with the Spirit by virtue of this new birth. ("...if anyone does not have the Spirit of Christ, they do not belong to Christ"—Romans 8:9).

The **baptism** in the Holy Spirit has a different purpose—**not linked to spiritual fruit**. It provides supernatural power for witnessing, for signs, wonders and miracles, and the nine supernatural gifts of the Spirit listed in 1 Corinthians 12:7–11.

In other words, as far as producing fruit of the Spirit is concerned, we have a level playing field. All Christians possess the same Spirit, received when we were born again, and we all rely on that same Spirit to help us live holy lives. That being the case, we anticipate no difference in spiritual fruit from believers who claim to have received the discrete Spirit baptism.

Having said that, consider the following.

OTHER ISSUES

There are a couple of "cultural" issues I have noticed, that could impact the fruit of the Spirit in western Pentecostal and non-Pentecostal churches. Consider these:

Sermon themes

I have noticed that non-Pentecostals place much emphasis on loving one another, service and good works—more so than Pentecostals. They are frequently highlighted in sermons, and congregations are continually admonished to do better. Pentecostals, on the other hand, while not ignoring "fruit" issues, focus more on things like redemption, faith, victorious living, Holy Spirit gifts, miracles and evangelism.

I have no doubt that those emphases are reflected in the lives of people. Non-Pentecostals may well achieve better on the love/service side, while Pentecostals bear more fruit in evangelism, church growth, miracles, etc.

Mavericks

In my observation, and especially in earlier days, Pentecostal and charismatic people can lean towards to the "maverick" end of the spectrum. (I use that word affectionately—mavericks have strengths, as well as weaknesses.) That should not surprise us. The Spirit baptism and speaking in tongues is controversial, and conservative people can be reluctant to embrace it. Mavericks will go against the flow, but their independent nature can sometimes be expressed in relaxed attitudes towards rules. Fruit of the Spirit might be a casualty of this. That is no excuse, of course. Holiness is for everybody. But the maverick personality can sometimes be like that, and a disproportionate number of mavericks might skew the results against Pentecostals and charismatics.

Note this, however. Weak spiritual fruit in a Pentecostal believer does not invalidate the Spirit baptism. It does not provide an excuse to say, "The Spirit baptism is invalid—I will have none of it".

(In the same way, weak spiritual fruit in a **non-Pentecostal** doesn't provide an excuse for an **unbeliever** to say, "**Christianity** is invalid—I will have none of it". How many times have we heard, "I am not a Christian because the church is full of hypocrites"?)

Ideally, we should all produce good fruit all the time. But when it doesn't happen, it does not invalidate our experience—of either salvation or Spirit baptism.

Pastors

Next question: how do Pentecostal pastors measure up? Are they more self-controlled, and less prone to moral failure?

From media reports you would think not. Eminent miracle-preaching, Pentecostal TV evangelists are big targets for a sensation-loving media which can easily convince you such men are all charlatans.

Here are some things to remember.

In the fake world of television, temptations of glory, money and sex are multiplied, far beyond those experienced by multitudes of pastors who labour faithfully but unseen, day by day. Comparisons between the two groups are unrealistic.

Secondly, there are eminent **non-Pentecostal** ministries whose work or personality is less attention-grabbing, but who also suffer serious failures from time to time. But because they attract less attention from the media, the public does not hear about them. I recently learned of a Christian leader whose books were renowned in the evangelical world. But he committed serious and systemic offences against female students over a long time. When finally exposed, very few heard about it. Failures of prominent Pentecostal TV evangelists, however, echo endlessly in every corner of the globe.

To give a little perspective, here is a statistic I found, from a USA Pentecostal denomination with 28,980 pastors. (That sample size gives us reasonable confidence of reliability.) In the late twentieth century, 82 of these pastors were disciplined for moral failure in one year. This is 0.28%, or about one in 300, per annum.[267] The author who presented these figures said that, in his discussions with denominational leaders, it seemed the rate of about 0.3% per annum is consistent *across denominational boundaries*. Of course, anything above zero is too much, but this figure might bring some clarity on the issue.

While we are on this subject, we need to consider one more aspect of the fruit of pastors and leaders.

Overlooked and concealed faults in prominent leaders

Few great Christian leaders have lived unblemished lives. Bad choices, or faults great or small, are inevitable. And, from time to time, skeletons are hidden away because everything else in that life was exemplary.

As mentioned earlier, Martin Luther was bitterly anti-Semitic. He even wrote a book on the subject (*On the Jews and their Lies*), copies of which have been flaunted at Nazi rallies. It was a tremendous blot on his life. But so significant was Luther's contribution to Christianity, and so devoted and fruitful was his life in many areas, that the world chooses to overlook this. Luther was not alone. The great reformer John Calvin successfully lobbied for the death penalty for his long-time adversary Michael Servetus, for the crime of heresy. That too has been glossed over, and Calvin's writings are still highly regarded. Charles Wesley persuaded his brother John to break his engagement because his fiancée (who had once worked as a servant) was below his social level. When John realised his mistake it was too late; she had married another. John clashed terribly with Charles as a result, though they later reconciled. John then married a woman who brought him 30 years of terrible grief. The Wesleys' ministry, however, was so gloriously fruitful that people gloss over these issues. King David, the man of God's own heart, arranged for the faithful Uriah to be killed in battle, so that he could have his wife. Paul and Barnabas had a disagreement, so severe they parted ways, but both continued preaching (Acts 15:3). They did reconcile later (e.g., 1 Corinthians 9:6) but their story exposes the frailty of leaders, no matter who they are.

Another little understood aspect of ministry failure relates to *concealed* sins or weaknesses. Here is a scenario, possibly far more common than we realise.

A child or teen is sexually abused, or is complicit in an illicit sexual activity, telling no one. In adulthood, a character flaw develops around that hidden sin, making him vulnerable to temptation. Endless cycles of temptation, sin, repentance, confession and prayer follow. A minister in that situation, who "should have all the answers", has no one to talk to, but struggles on faithfully. That faithfulness leads to success and promotion, but diminishes the number of dependable people they could turn to for help. Compounding this process is the unceasing pressure of ministry: to be a godly example, to raise good children, for the church to grow, and much more. Not to mention the wiles of Satan. Under those pressures the minister succumbs, and has an illicit sexual experience, perhaps homosexual or even paedophilic. The public is shocked and confused, "How could a man of God do that?" And the minister, and any of his achievements, is disgraced.

Here is the point. Fruit of that ministry might well be valid. Books or songs written, ministries established, teaching material, etc., may well be genuine spiritual fruit of a sincere, faithful, servant of God, struggling to overcome a problem. Many great Christian accomplishments have been hammered out on the anvil of affliction and temptation. A failure at some point does not necessarily invalidate all previous work.

This issue is important in some of the lives we will study. We will, in the last section, look at several significant leaders, some of whom may have had "Luther-like" skeletons in their closets, or concealed sins (alleged or real) exposed after successful ministry. Remember to set aside the dross, and draw the gold from their lives.

Summarising

The fruit of the Spirit flows from the Spirit received by Christians when they are born again. All are the same in this respect.

The godliness (or ungodliness) of Pentecostal TV evangelists is not definitive evidence of the validity of the Spirit baptism. A Pentecostal with poor fruit provides no excuse for a non-Pentecostal to dismiss the Spirit baptism, any more than a non-Pentecostal with poor fruit warrants an unbeliever to dismiss Christianity.

The Spirit baptism stands on its scriptural foundation (laid out in the previous chapter), and can be validated by experience. Higher growth rates, prolific song writing, miracles, the NCLS, all contribute significantly to validate the belief.

NEXT:

This is the subject that lights the fires. We can't see the Holy Spirit, how do we **know** when we have received him?

We read about Charles Parham, and the assignment he set his 40 students: "What is the Bible evidence for receiving the baptism in the Holy Spirit?" As we know, three days later they all came up with the same answer: speaking in tongues. How did they get that answer? Where in the Bible did they look?

If only we had those 40 essays! Alas, they are gone. However, we have the same Bible, and we can look for ourselves, and try to walk where they walked. In this next chapter we will tread that path, and uncover some interesting, little-known, aspects of the subject.

APPENDIX E

IS TONGUES THE "EVIDENCE"? (EXPANDED VERSION)

How do we know when a person has received the baptism in the Holy Spirit? His presence is intangible, indefinable, so how do we know if he has come? We are told to *ask* for him to come—how do we know *when it has happened*, so that we can stop asking? When the Spirit fell in the Bible there were dramatic, immediate, visible results. In one case, as we know well, it was so obvious that Simon the magician even offered money for the gift (Acts 8:9–24). Compare that with the common idea that we should simply pray for the Holy Spirit, believe we have received and, if nothing dramatic has happened, we have nevertheless received—just believe it. Would that have persuaded the shrewd Simon? Not likely. This was a dramatic, visible event.

So how *do* we know we have received it? What is the "evidence"?

Once again, our case will be built largely from historical books of the Bible. Some might object to that but, again, we remember that Paul was happy to work that way.

So, our goal is to discover, from biblical outpourings of the Holy Spirit, what evidence there was of that phenomenon.

That is not difficult. We find incidents where the Holy Spirit fell on people, note what happened, compile results, and look for patterns.

What might we expect? We could think of a variety of biblical manifestations: spiritual fire, power that can knock people down, a voice from heaven, invincible evangelism, ecstatic feelings…or perhaps something more peaceful: fruitful service, quiet confident faith, gracious Spirit-filled living.

Is there a clear answer in the Bible?

Here, in a nutshell, is what we will find.

> Holy Spirit outpourings in the Bible fall into two groups: firstly, outpourings for a SPECIFIC, ONE-OFF purpose and, secondly, outpourings for a GENERAL, ONGOING PURPOSE. In both groups, there is always tangible EVIDENCE.
>
> That evidence is not the same for the two groups. However, in the second group, we find that prophecy is the consistent evidence of receiving the Holy Spirit prior to Pentecost, and after Pentecost it is speaking in tongues. Watch this unfold.

OLD TESTAMENT: OUTPOURINGS WITH A SPECIFIC PURPOSE

In the Old Testament, outpourings were often described by the phrase "the Spirit of the Lord came on…" There are a number of incidents where that phrase is used. You might categorise them as follows: artistic design work in the tabernacle, specific leadership tasks, conflict, and prophetic warnings.

Here are the key passages:

PASSAGE	PURPOSE	EVIDENCE
Exodus 31:3	God filled Bezalel with the Spirit to make artistic designs for work in the tabernacle in gold, silver and bronze.	Beautiful work

Judges 3:9–11	**Specific leadership tasks:** The Spirit of the Lord came on Othniel, and he became Israel's judge, went to war, and overpowered their enemies.	Commanding leadership
Judges 6:34	The Spirit of the LORD came on Gideon: he blew a trumpet, and the Abiezrites followed him.	
1 Samuel 16:13	Samuel took a horn of oil and anointed David, and the Spirit of the LORD came powerfully upon him.	
Judges 14:6	**Conflict:** The Spirit of the LORD came powerfully upon Samson so that he tore a lion apart with his bare hands.	Supernatural victory
Judges 14:19	The Spirit of the Lord again came powerfully on Samson, and he struck down 30 men.	
Judges 15:14–15	The Spirit of the Lord came powerfully on Samson and "the ropes on his arms became like charred flax, and the bindings dropped from his hands. Finding a fresh jawbone of a donkey, he grabbed it and struck down a thousand men".	
Ezekiel 11:5–9	**Prophetic warning or judgment** The Spirit of the Lord came on Ezekiel, and he told the people they would be driven out of their city and punished because of their murders. That came to pass.	Accurate prophetic warning

In each case, the outward **evidence** of the outpouring became obvious – beautiful artistic work, commanding leadership, supernatural victory and accurate prophetic warnings.

NOW, WHERE THE RUBBER MEETS THE ROAD

There is another type of outpouring that is different altogether. I call it **general service for God**. This is different because **the immediate outward evidence** is **supernaturally inspired speech**. That inspired speech, we discover, has two formats: Before Pentecost it was **prophecy**. After Pentecost it became **tongues**.

So, we will leave behind artistic design, specific leadership tasks, crises, and prophetic warnings, and concentrate on outpourings for general service to God and their evidence: prophecy and tongues.

Prophecy and Tongues

What is prophecy? What are tongues?

Prophecy is speech inspired by God. While it can include predicting the future, it is much more than that. Paul wrote about the gift in 1 Corinthians 14:

> ...the one who **prophesies edifies** the church. (Verse 4)

> ...if an unbeliever or an inquirer comes in while everyone is **prophesying**, they are **convicted** of sin and are brought under judgment by all, as the **secrets of their hearts are laid bare**. So, they will fall down and worship God, exclaiming, "God is really among you!" (Verses 24–25)

> For you can all **prophesy** in turn so that everyone may be **instructed and encouraged**. (Verse 31)

So, in the church prophecy edifies the congregation, convicts and reveals the heart's secrets, instructs and encourages.

Speaking in tongues is also speech inspired by God. But this is not usually understood by the speaker or the hearer. Paul said:

> "Unless you speak intelligible words with your tongue, how will anyone know what you are saying?

> ...For this reason, the one who speaks in a tongue should pray that they may interpret what they say. For if I pray in a tongue, my spirit prays but my mind is unfruitful." (1 Corinthians 14:9–14)

We are told of just one occasion when tongues were understood. On the Day of Pentecost, the disciples were "...declaring the wonders of God" in tongues recognised by the crowds (Acts 2:11). This was clearly a one-off miracle, intended to reach the diverse crowd gathered from many surrounding countries. All other times when tongues are mentioned there is no record of them being understood, and no need for them to be understood. So, what do tongues do? Paul said speaking in tongues brings praise and thanks to God:

> ...when you are **praising** God in the Spirit (i.e., in tongues), how can someone else, who is now put in the position of an inquirer, say "Amen" to your **thanksgiving**, since they do not know what you are saying? You are **giving thanks** well enough, but no one else is edified. (1 Corinthians 14:16–17)

From these scriptures, we see that tongues are inspired praise and thanksgiving to God, and a declaration of the wonders of God.

The fundamental similarity between prophecy and tongues is that **both are speech inspired by God.**

With that understanding, we can study **all the Bible outpourings, Old Testament and New Testament, associated with prophecy and tongues.** Here they are:

Old Testament

WHO	INCIDENT/PASSAGE	EVIDENCE
Moses and 70 elders **Numbers 11:16–26**	Elders received the same Spirit Moses received: The Lord said to Moses: "I will take some of the **power of the Spirit** that is on you and put it on [the 70 elders]. They will share the burden of the people with you so that you will not have to carry it alone". Then the Lord...took some of the power of the Spirit that was on [Moses] and put it on the 70 elders. When the **Spirit** rested on [the elders], they **prophesied** – but did not do so again.	Prophecy

Same passage	Same incident, Eldad and Medad outside the camp: "However, two men...were listed among the elders, but did not go out to the tent. Yet the **Spirit** also rested on them, and they **prophesied** in the camp." Note that Moses' elders prophesied once, but not again. It seems their experience that day was so overwhelming that they overflowed with these prophetic words. The long-term purpose of the outpouring was to equip them for God's ongoing work, which apparently was not accompanied by more inspired utterance.	Prophecy

King Saul
1 Samuel
10:5–6
	Samuel speaking to Saul: "...you will meet a procession of prophets coming down from the high place...and they will be prophesying. The **Spirit of the Lord** will come powerfully upon you, and you will **prophesy** with them; and you will be changed into a different person".
	
	    Note Samuel's words: "you will be changed into a different person", is the purpose of the Spirit falling on him.
	
	    Samuel's prediction was fulfilled in verse 10: "...a procession of prophets met [Saul]; the **Spirit** of God came powerfully upon him, and he joined in their **prophesying**".
		Prophecy

Saul's men. **1 Samuel** **19:20–23**	"...the **Spirit of God** came on Saul's men, and they also **prophesied**..." It is significant that this happened three times, to each of three different groups of men whom Saul sent to kill David.	Prophecy
Same passage, Saul again	"So, Saul went to Naioth at Ramah. But the **Spirit of God** came even on him, and he walked along **prophesying** until he came to Naioth."	Prophecy

So there we have Moses' elders and Saul and his men, all called by God to weighty, ongoing tasks. The Spirit of God fell on all of them, and all of them prophesied.

THAT IS OUR PATTERN. Will we find it in the New Testament?

A New Era

In the Old Testament, we saw the phrase, "the Spirit of God came on..." In the New Testament we find a number of different expressions for this experience. For example, the "Holy Spirit comes on you" (Acts 1:8); "baptised with the Holy Spirit" (Acts 1:5); "filled with the Holy Spirit" (Acts 2:4); "pour out my Spirit" (Acts 2:18); "receive the gift of the Holy Spirit" (Acts 2:38).

We will look at these New Testament incidents now, and see how they unfolded—can we find our EVIDENCE?

The New Testament: PRE-PENTECOST

WHO	INCIDENT/PASSAGE	EVIDENCE
Elizabeth **Luke 1:41–43**	When Mary found she was pregnant, she visited Elizabeth (Zechariah's wife). "When Elizabeth heard Mary's greeting, the baby leaped in her womb, and Elizabeth was **filled with the Holy Spirit.** In a loud voice she **exclaimed**, 'Blessed are you among women, and blessed is the child you will bear! But why am I so favoured, that the mother of my Lord should come to me?'" Note that Elizabeth's words "blessed are you... blessed is the child you will bear...mother of my Lord" were **prophetic words.** They were inspired, and not from her own experiential knowledge.	Prophecy
Zechariah **Luke 1:67–76**	"...Zechariah was **filled with the Holy Spirit** and **prophesied**, 'Praise be to the Lord, the God of Israel, because he has come to his people and redeemed them...And you my child will...go on before the Lord to prepare the way for him...'"	Prophecy
Simeon **Luke 2:27–35**	"**Moved by the Spirit**, [Simeon] went into the temple courts...took [baby Jesus] in his arms and **praised God, saying**, 'Sovereign Lord...my eyes have seen your salvation...This child is destined to cause the falling and rising of many in Israel, and to be a sign that will be spoken against, so that the thoughts of many hearts will be revealed. And a sword will pierce [Mary's] own soul too.'" Once again, these words were inspired **prophetic** words, beyond Simeon's experiential knowledge.	Prophecy

Obviously these incidents are consistent with those of Moses and Saul. The Holy Spirit fell, and it was marked by prophecy.

Next, and before we look at the Day of Pentecost, there is a pivotal verse in the Book of Joel which sets the pattern for the "last days". This is important. Note it well.

Transition from Old to New Testaments

Centuries before Jesus came to Earth, the prophet Joel prophesied a monumental shift in the way God would deal with men and women. His prophecy was fulfilled in one glorious moment on the Day of Pentecost, 50 days after Jesus' resurrection. Here is the passage and, once again, we look closely for "evidence".

WHO	INCIDENT/PASSAGE	EVIDENCE
ALL PEOPLE Joel 2:28	"And afterward, I will **pour out my Spirit** on **all people.** Your sons and daughters will **prophesy**..."	Prophecy

Again we see *prophecy* linked to this (promised) outpouring. Our case is building.

Next, we look into what happened in this new dispensation, beginning with the Day of Pentecost.

The New Testament: PENTECOST AND BEYOND

WHO	INCIDENT/PASSAGE	EVIDENCE
120 disciples Acts 2:1–33	**Acts 2:2–4:** "Suddenly a sound like the blowing of a violent wind came from heaven and filled the whole house where they were sitting. They saw what seemed to be tongues of fire that separated and came to rest on each of them. All of them were **filled with the Holy Spirit** and began to **speak in other tongues** as the Spirit enabled them..." **Verse 33:** Peter explains to the people: "[Jesus] has received from the Father the promised Holy Spirit and has poured out what you now see and hear (tongues)".	Wind, fire, tongues

Cornelius' household **Acts 10:45-46**	"The [Jews]...were astonished that the gift of the Holy Spirit had been poured out even on Gentiles. For they heard them **speaking in tongues and praising God**." Note: **Firstly, this is a clear example of evidence being used to identify the Spirit baptism. "For"** they heard them speaking in tongues. Secondly, Peter's later explanation of this incident to the other apostles is illuminating: "As I began to speak, the Holy Spirit came on them **as he had come on us** at the beginning." (Acts 11:15) Speaking in tongues was the only observable similarity between the two events.	Tongues and praise
Ephesians **Acts 19:6**	"When Paul placed his hands on them, the **Holy Spirit** came on them, and they **spoke in tongues and prophesied**."	Tongues and prophecy
Samaria **Acts 8:1–24**	"When **Simon saw** that the **Spirit was given** at the laying on of the apostles' hands, he offered them money and said, 'Give me also this ability so that everyone on whom I lay my hands may receive the Holy Spirit.'" As mentioned before, Simon had already witnessed miracles of healing and deliverance, but had not offered money for these abilities. It is likely he witnessed tongues/prophecy, from which he saw prospects of wealth from fortune telling. Many Bible commentators draw this conclusion.	Tongues? Prophecy?
Paul	**Acts 9:17** "Placing his hands on Saul, [Ananias] said, 'Brother Saul, the Lord Jesus—who appeared to you on the road as you were coming here—has sent me so that you may see again and be **filled with the Holy Spirit**.'" We are not told if Paul spoke in tongues when he was filled with the Holy Spirit. But we do know he did speak in tongues–he wrote "I thank God that I speak in **tongues** more than all of you." (1 Corinthians 14:18). If we were told Paul never spoke in tongues, this would negate our argument. But he did, we just don't know when. With our many Old and New Testament scriptures describing a vocal response on receiving the Holy Spirit, we can reasonably conclude Paul's experience was the same.	Tongues?

Now we will condense all that, Old Testament and NT, and let it speak for itself.

Who	Passage	Evidence
	THE COMPLETE PICTURE	
	OLD TESTAMENT	
70 elders	"When the **Spirit** rested on [the elders], they **prophesied**"	Prophecy
2 others	"...the **Spirit** also rested on them, and they **prophesied** in the camp"	Prophecy
Saul	"...**Spirit** of God came powerfully upon him...he joined in...**prophesying**"	Prophecy
Saul's men	"the **Spirit of God** came on Saul's men, and they also **prophesied**"	Prophecy
Saul again	"the **Spirit of God** came even on him, and he walked along **prophesying**"	Prophecy
All people	"...I will **pour out my Spirit** on all people...will **prophesy**"	Prophecy
	NEW TESTAMENT BEFORE PENTECOST	
Elizabeth	"Elizabeth was **filled with the Holy Spirit**...", then spoke **prophetic** words	Prophecy
Zechariah	"...Zechariah was **filled with the Holy Spirit** and **prophesied**..."	Prophecy
Simeon	"**Moved by the Spirit**..." he spoke **prophetic** words	Prophecy
	NEW TESTAMENT: PENTECOST AND BEYOND	
The 120 at Pentecost	"...**filled with the Holy Spirit** and began to **speak in other tongues**"	Tongues, wind, fire
Cornelius	"...the gift of **the Holy Spirit had been poured out** even on Gentiles. For they heard them **speaking in tongues and praising God**"	Tongues and praise
Ephesians	"...the **Holy Spirit** came on them, and they **spoke in tongues and prophesied**"	Tongues, prophecy
Samaritans	"Simon saw that the **Spirit was given** by the laying on of the apostles hands"	Tongues probable
Paul	"...be **filled with the Holy Spirit**...I speak in **tongues** more than all of you"	Tongues probable

So our "evidence", as you can see, is plain:

> Old Testament: Holy Spirit falls, person prophesies.
> New Testament: Holy Spirit falls, person speaks in tongues.

A consistent pattern, but with a new and significant change—from prophecy to tongues.

So we can formulate our doctrine:

> The infilling of the Holy Spirit in the Bible is a dramatic, observable, spiritual experience.
>
> The impact is such that the recipient responds with **Spirit-inspired speech**.
>
> That was the experience of Moses' elders, Saul, Saul's men, Elizabeth, Zechariah, Simeon, the 120 disciples, Cornelius' household, the Ephesians, most likely the Samaritans and Paul, and it was foretold by Joel centuries before Pentecost.
>
> In the **Old Testament** the Spirit-inspired speech was **prophecy**.
>
> In the **New Testament** it became **tongues**.

It should not surprise us that we have a *vocal* response to the Spirit baptism. Think about our reactions to other life experiences. If something is funny, we laugh, if it is sad, we cry, if we are in pain we might moan, if our team wins we cheer. God obviously designed us to respond vocally to life experiences. So, it is quite consistent that the Spirit baptism provokes speaking in tongues. And it is understandable that God would put his unique stamp on those tongues—they are *unlearned and unknown to us*. A supernatural response to a supernatural event, confounding human logic. Note we are completely dependent on God's *supernatural* ability for this, and he, not we, receives the glory.

Receiving the Spirit is not a small thing. The famous 19th century evangelist, Charles Finney, described his experience when the Holy Spirit fell on him, "...I wept aloud with joy and love...I literally bellowed out the unutterable gushings of my heart..." His experience of God was tangible, climactic, glorious, and he responded with love and passion with "unutterable", "gushing" words from his heart.

All that, of course, clearly contradicts the idea that the Spirit baptism is always synonymous with salvation. If that was true, you would expect people at conversion to burst into inspired speech. That is certainly not what we see.

QUESTIONS AND COMMENTS ON THIS CHAPTER

Why not consider the fruit of the Spirit as the evidence for receiving the Spirit?

As we have seen, the fruit of the Spirit relates to the Spirit of Christ in us, received at salvation. The baptism in the Holy Spirit is (usually) received later, providing power for witnessing. So, the fruit of the Spirit is not a confirmation of the Spirit *baptism*.

In addition, notice that every instance of receiving the Holy Spirit in the Book of Acts is sudden and identifiable. When Simon the magician saw the Holy Spirit fall, he wanted to buy it on the spot. He did not wait until he saw love, peace and patience etc., and it is hard to imagine that shady character even being drawn to those things. He needed a shake up to convince him, and he got it.

Why the change—from *prophecy* in the Old Testament to *tongues* in the New?

We are not told. However, Peter's explanation on the Day of Pentecost is illuminating. Look at the passage:

> ...listen carefully to what I say...this is what was spoken by the prophet Joel: 'In the last days, God says, I will pour out my Spirit on all people. Your sons and daughters will prophesy, your young men will see visions, your old men will dream dreams. Even on my servants, both men and women, I will pour out my Spirit in those days, and they

will prophesy.' (Acts 2:14–18) …"Exalted to the right hand of God, (Jesus) has received from the Father the promised Holy Spirit and has poured out what you now see and hear." (Verse 33)

Several things emerge from this passage:

- Joel's promised outpouring would be accompanied by **prophecy.**
- Prophecy is equated to speaking in tongues. Peter said the **tongues** they could hear were the fulfilment of Joel's promise "they shall **prophesy**". Both are **inspired speech**.
- The bewildered crowd came from about 15 surrounding regions (See verses 5–12). Amid the babble of voices and the wind and tongues of fire, all these groups recognised their own language being spoken. For them, the tongues they heard was **prophecy**—they could understand it. So, this pivotal outpouring provided a clear demonstration of the transition from prophecy to tongues.
- Moses' elders prophesied, but only once. The New Testament is different. Tongues is the **initial** evidence of the Holy Spirit baptism, but the ability to speak is **ongoing**—as we gather from Paul's instruction on the use of tongues in 1 Corinthians 14.

Paul's question: "Do all speak in tongues?" (1 Corinthians 12:30)

The implication in this verse is that not everybody speaks in tongues, which seemingly contradicts the above. But the context is important here. Paul is discussing use of the individual gifts of the Spirit in the church setting where, we expect, most or everyone has received the Spirit baptism and spoken in tongues. Some will prophesy, some will minister gifts of healing, some will speak in tongues (in personal worship or in tandem with the gift of interpretation). So, in that sense, and in that context of a church meeting, not all will speak in tongues.

More "evidence":

Remember, our goal in this chapter was to find the evidence, if any, of receiving the baptism in the Holy Spirit. We have discovered clear evidence, expressed in the above table, which summarises Holy Spirit outpourings in Old and New Testaments.

In addition to the table, there are two passages which clearly link the Holy Spirit outpouring to a vocal response, and which add to our case. They are:

- The Joel passage, "And afterward, I will **pour out my Spirit** on all people. Your sons and daughters will **prophesy**..." The Spirit outpouring is directly linked to prophecy (or New Testament tongues).
- The second is Acts 10:45–46: When Peter went to preach to the Gentiles, "The (Jews) who had come with Peter were astonished that the gift of the Holy Spirit had been poured out even on Gentiles. For they heard them speaking in tongues and praising God". The "evidence" that persuaded these sceptical Jews that the despised Gentiles had received the Spirit was speaking in tongues. And, so convincing was that evidence, they were prepared to abandon their rigidly long-held beliefs, and invite the Gentiles into the fold.

NOTE THIS ABOVE ALL

In the Old Testament, the Holy Spirit fell on **just a few, selected** individuals. **Joel's promise** of the Holy Spirit was to **EVERYBODY**. Peter spelled that out in Acts 2:39: "The promise (of the Holy Spirit) is for...**all** who are far off, for **all** whom the Lord our God will call". That means you, me, and any other believer who simply asks.

THE SIXTY-FOUR DOLLAR QUESTION

Does everybody speak in tongues when baptised in the Holy Spirit? (Or, if you haven't spoken in tongues, does that mean you have not been baptised in the Spirit?)

Speaking in tongues is contentious. You can feel it even in these words of Paul, "if everyone speaks in tongues, and inquirers or unbelievers come in, will they not say that you are out of your mind?" (1 Corinthians 14:23).

However, the fact is that speaking in tongues is forever embedded in New Testament pages. God, in his wisdom, is the one who brought this about. He knows best. Speaking in tongues is a wonderful, wonderful gift. Millions testify to its blessing. Some might see it as a stumbling block, but stumbling blocks are not absent in God's dealings with his people.

But, to answer the question, "Does everybody speak in tongues when baptised in the Spirit?" We do not have a *direct scriptural statement*. Paul didn't say (for example), "Pray for the Holy Spirit to come. You will all speak in tongues". No. Remember, we have formulated our doctrine from "THE COMPLETE PICTURE" table above. That table provides these clear facts: when the Holy Spirit fell in the Bible, Old Testament people consistently prophesied, New Testament people consistently spoke in tongues. From those facts we drew our conclusion. The most reasonable conclusion, of course, is that God will do the same today. In our dispensation we speak in tongues.

Different people have verbalised that reality in different ways. Here are some examples.

The Assemblies of God (AG) makes this statement on their website:

> Speaking in tongues was an integral part of Spirit baptism in the Book of Acts. It is the only manifestation associated with Spirit baptism, which is explicitly presented as evidence authenticating the experience, and on that basis should be considered normative.[268]

They have held firmly to that belief since their inception over a hundred years ago. Today, the movement has almost 70 million adherents worldwide. So, we might say, it has served them well.

However, others—particularly among the charismatic movement—have tried to soften that stance, and make it less of a stumbling block. They have taught either that not all will speak in tongues, or that some might exhibit other gifts or manifestations. Still others hold to the AG line, but are more subtle in their wording.

For example, Pentecostal leader David Du Plessis "...often spoke about tongues as a *consequence* or *confirmation* of the Spirit's infilling, rather than the harder-edged *evidence* used in many Pentecostal statements of faith". (Emphasis in original)[269]

Lutheran charismatic pastor and teacher, Larry Christenson, put it this way:

> Does this mean that everyone who receives the Holy Spirit will speak in tongues—that if you have not spoken in tongues you have not really received the Holy Spirit? I do not believe you can make such a case from scripture. However, I do believe that the Book of Acts suggests to us a helpful *pattern*: 1) Receiving the Holy Spirit is a definite, clear-cut, instantaneous experience...2) A simple and God-appointed way for you objectively to manifest the gift of the Holy Spirit is to lift up your voice in faith, and speak out in a new tongue at the prompting of the Holy Spirit.[270]

You see, he didn't say it, but he said it. Wisdom like that can help!

The bottom line: when you pray to receive the Spirit baptism, expect to speak in tongues. If you feel you have had a wonderful experience of the Holy Spirit, but didn't speak in tongues, praise and thank God for what has happened, and keep praying and expecting, knowing he has another very precious, exciting and fulfilling extra blessing awaiting you.

NEXT:

As you can guess, there are a number of objections people raise on this lively subject, and there are more questions that need answers. We need to address those.

*Questions are only offensive to those
who have something to hide.*

GARY HOPKINS

*Difference of opinion is always advantageous
in religion. The several sects perform the
office of a Censor, over each other.*

THOMAS JEFFERSON

*It is wise to direct your anger towards problems, not
people; to focus your energies on answers, not excuses.*

WILLIAM ARTHUR WARD

*I am convinced that sometimes Christians' demands
for exhaustive knowledge are excuses for not
believing in, and acting on, what they know.*

JOHN WIMBER

APPENDIX F
QUESTIONS AND OBJECTIONS

Spirit baptism and speaking in tongues are certainly controversial issues, and many questions call for answers. Too many for a book like this, but I will tackle a few of the more common. Cessationists are prominent critics of Pentecostal and charismatic beliefs, and John MacArthur[271] is probably the best known of them, so I will respond to several of his points in this section.

Does the Pentecostal and charismatic emphasis on the Holy Spirit lead to neglect of Christ?

Jesus said "...when he, the Spirit of truth, comes, he will...glorify me" (John 16:13, 14). Holy Spirit experience ought to produce increased emphasis on Christ. Do Pentecostals and charismatics glorify Christ?

Some say they do not.

John MacArthur says the charismatic movement has "an intense fixation on a caricature of the blessing and gifting of the Holy Spirit [which] has instead taken centre stage".[272] He cites Pentecostal pastor, Jack Hayford, to prove his point. Hayford wrote:

> In the Pentecostal potpourri, only one thing is the same for all: *the passion they have to experience the presence and power of the Holy Spirit*. This is the common denominator. This

emphasis on the Holy Spirit...is what defines the "charismatic century".[273]

Certainly, as Hayford says, the passion to experience the presence and power of the Holy Spirit is the *common denominator* in the potpourri, the characteristic that brings it together. But Pentecostals and charismatics are quick to point out that the Holy Spirit is definitely not *centre stage*. Rather, invigorated by Holy Spirit presence and power, charismatics and Pentecostals unreservedly express heartfelt praise towards their central focus—Jesus Christ. They will tell you that, as they seek and find the Holy Spirit, he points them to Christ, and they respond willingly and fervently.

That passion for Holy Spirit presence and power can be compared to an evangelical's passion for the born-again experience. The born-again experience is not centre stage for an evangelist; it just opens the door so that Christ can take centre stage.

Jack Hayford, mentioned above, was a noted Pentecostal pastor and prolific songwriter, and the words of his most popular song reveal his focus. Here they are:

> Majesty, worship his majesty.
> Unto Jesus, be all glory, power and praise.
> Majesty, kingdom authority,
> Flow from his throne, unto his own, his anthem raise.
> So, exalt, lift up on high, the name of Jesus
> Magnify, come glorify, Christ Jesus the King.
> Majesty, worship his majesty,
> Jesus who died, now glorified, King of all kings.[274]

Millions of Christians, of all kinds, have enthusiastically sung that Christ-focused song for decades.

Of course, in the vast pool of Pentecostals and charismatics, there will be some wayward or misinformed enthusiasts, who might focus excessively on the Holy Spirit, at the expense of Christ. But in my experience, they are certainly not typical of the rest whose heartfelt passion for Christ mirrors the words of that song.

Are modern tongues authentic languages?

On the Day of Pentecost, the 120 disciples all spoke in tongues which were understood by bystanders from many nations. After that, there are two more similar experiences with speaking in tongues in Acts 10:46 and Acts 19:6. Were these tongues understood by bystanders? We are not told, either way. What do we know about them? Here is some insight from Paul from another key passage on tongues.

> Anyone who speaks in a tongue does not speak to people but to God. Indeed, no one understands them; they utter mysteries by the Spirit...Anyone who speaks in a tongue edifies themselves...if I pray in a tongue, my spirit prays but my mind is unfruitful. (1 Corinthians 14:2, 4, 14)

Clearly, these tongues, after Pentecost, are not understood–they are "mysteries". The experience edifies the speaker and, if the utterance is interpreted by the twin gift of interpretation, it edifies the church. So, the words themselves carry meaning, but we do not understand them.

Do modern-day tongues match those of the New Testament?

John MacArthur thinks not. As a cessationist, he believes all New Testament speaking in tongues ended some two thousand years ago. However, his view is contradicted by a modern-day movement of millions of Christians who claim to have spoken in tongues. How does he address this? He writes, "...modern 'tongues' consist wholly of nonsensical babble", describing them as "non-linguistic, irrational gibberish" and "charismatic babble".[275] He cites University of Toronto's linguistics professor, William Samarin, to support his case. (Samarin has researched the subject extensively, visiting charismatic groups in many countries.) MacArthur quotes Samarin as follows:

> There is no mystery about glossolalia. Tape recorded samples are easy to obtain and to analyse. They always turn out to be the same thing: *strings of syllables, made up of sounds taken from among all those that the speaker knows, put together more or less haphazardly but which nevertheless emerge as word-like*

and sentence-like units because of realistic language-like rhythm and melody. (Emphasis in original.) Glossolalia is indeed like language in some ways, but this is only because the speaker (unconsciously) wants it to be like language...All specimens of glossolalia that have ever been studied have produced no features that would even suggest that they reflect some kind of communicative system...[276]

However, another study by linguists was mentioned in John Sherrill's 1964 classic, *They Speak with Other Tongues*. Sherrill, in his long investigation into the "new" phenomenon of tongues, made many recordings of tongues and played them to six linguists: three from Columbia University, two professors from Union Theological Seminary, and one from General Theological Seminary. Two of them specialised in modern languages, three in ancient languages, and one in language structure. Although no language was recognised on the hour long tapes, Sherrill said: "they had frequently identified language *patterns* on the tapes. The 'shape' of real language, the variety of sound combinations, infrequency of repetitions and so forth, is virtually impossible, so they said, to reproduce by deliberate effort". However, they immediately recognised as spurious, two samples of gibberish Sherrill had inserted without telling them.[277]

In addition, in recent times tongues have been recognised as valid languages on many, many occasions. Here are just a few examples from my own personal contacts and study:

- A friend, while ministering in Fiji, told me the local Fijian pastor overheard him praying in tongues, and recognised his language
- At a large charismatic conference in Melbourne, Australia, a Bible college lecturer told me one of his students from a remote village in Africa was astonished to hear the person behind him praying in tongues for his own village, in a little-known dialect of his language
- An Australian missionary visited a remote Papua New Guinea village where English was not known. The chief received the Spirit baptism and burst into tongues—in English. He was saying, "He's not in my head, he's in my heart, and he's changed me!"

- New York Reformed Pastor, Harold Bredesen, dissatisfied with his Christian experience, took a retreat in a mountain cabin. One morning he found himself speaking in tongues. He ran down the mountain still speaking, and a man he met answered him—in Polish. Bredesen was amazed to be told he had been speaking Polish, a language he had never known.[278]

From time to time, while chatting with Christian leaders and pastors, the conversation drifts to this subject. Invariably, I find each can relate a few stories like that. It is interesting to extrapolate. If only one percent of the half a billion Pentecostal and charismatic Christians could tell just one such story, there would be five million of them. And we must remember God's role here. God reveals himself on his own terms, he is not at the beck and call of "research". As I have shown above, there is ample, God-revealed evidence—quite apart from the solid scriptural evidence—to demonstrate that modern tongues are compatible with those of the early church.

One more issue. When the 120 disciples spoke in tongues on the Day of Pentecost, and people understood the meaning, was this a miracle of *speech* or a miracle of *hearing*? In other words, were the speakers miraculously given *recognisable languages*, or were the hearers miraculously given *understanding of unrecognisable* languages. Both are possible. If the hearers are given miraculous understanding, perhaps that has implications in the above discussion. Whatever the case, the fact remains that modern-day stories of recognised tongues are so plentiful and compelling, that they dispel any doubts about authenticity.

Are modern tongues linked to the occult?

Some critics say speaking in tongues occurs in the occult and alternative practices such as hypnotism, and suggest a link to Christians speaking in tongues. MacArthur, for instance, has this to say:

> ...the modern expressions of glossolalia are deceptive and dangerous...there are very good reasons to avoid this

practice. It is, in fact, a common practice in numerous cult groups and false religions—from the voodoo doctors of Africa to the mystic monks of Buddhism to the founders of Mormonism.[279]

To that list of cults and false religions, MacArthur could have added Spiritism. A friend of mine joined a Spiritist church when his mother died, hoping to "hear from her from the other side". During his time with this group, he received the ability to speak in tongues. Eventually, however, he became a Christian and, when he sought the baptism in the Holy Spirit, he spoke in tongues again. However, he told us emphatically, this second experience far, far, surpassed the first. He was overwhelmingly convinced the former was spurious, and the new was authentic.

What lies behind all this?

It is simple. Supernatural experiences from outside the narrow path of Christ are demonic. Satan knows the ways of God—he was with him in the beginning. He mimics those ways, providing counterfeit supernatural experiences to the misguided, to deceive and entrap them, to keep them from the truth, and from salvation found only in Christ. Early examples of such mimicry can be found in the courts of Pharaoh (Exodus 7), where the magicians duplicated the miracles of Moses.

So, yes, it seems there are people outside the Christian faith who speak in some form of tongues. But the source of that ability is very different indeed.

Should we fear a Satanic counterfeit when we seek the baptism in the Spirit? Certainly not. Jesus even promised us protection, as follows:

> Which of you fathers, if his son asks for a fish, will give him a snake instead? Or if he asks for an egg, will give him a scorpion? If you then, who are evil, know how to give good gifts to your children, how much more will your Father in heaven give the Holy Spirit to those who ask him? (Luke 11:11–13)

Our loving, heavenly Father gives good gifts. The Holy Spirit is one of them, and we can trust God to keep us safe in our quest.

What about "silver-tongued evangelists" and "health and wealth" teaching?

John MacArthur writes scathingly of what he calls "the prosperity gospel", promoted by prominent Pentecostal and charismatic televangelists. He quotes John T Allen as follows:

> Perhaps the most controversial element of the Pentecostal outlook is the so called "prosperity gospel", meaning the belief that God will reward those with sufficient faith with both material prosperity and physical health...the Pew Forum data suggests that the prosperity gospel is actually a defining feature of all Pentecostalism; majorities of Pentecostals exceeding 90% in most countries hold to these beliefs."[280]

And, on televangelists:

> "Silver-tongued televangelists boldly promise unending health and wealth to all who have enough faith—and more importantly, to all who send in their money."[281]

Pentecostals and charismatics will agree with some of MacArthur's criticisms, but are also quick to point out that his comments do not accurately reflect the reality. In addition, Pentecostals would say the true biblical picture of God's generous and loving provision is not understood by many mainline churches.

Here are two stories to explain.

A young Hindu girl in Fiji suffered from two inoperable cancerous tumours in her head, causing uncontrollable bleeding from her ears and nose. She was given six months to live. Her family believed a curse had been placed on them (a way of life in that culture) because, every night, reptiles and animals would enter their home. In addition, their crops and animals were poor, and the girl's father and brother could not get work. However, they heard of a pastor who prayed for the sick so, after a long search, they found him. The pastor and his wife (whom I know personally) prayed for the girl, and she completely recovered. The whole family then became Christians, the reptile and animal intrusions stopped, the father and son got jobs, and their animals produced many kids and calves. Curious neighbours noticed that last item, and asked their secret. They were adamant: they fed the goats the same food as everyone else, and attributed their newfound prosperity to the blessing of God.

Another friend, converted to Christianity at 21, made some bad financial decisions and became deeply in debt. He was, he said, the poorest person in the church. However, he developed a profound conviction about God's desire to provide financially from passages such as 2 Corinthians 9:6–10:

> "Whoever sows sparingly will also reap sparingly, and whoever sows generously will also reap generously...And God is able to bless you abundantly, so that in all things at all times, having all that you need, you will abound in every good work...Now he who supplies seed to the sower and bread for food will also supply and increase your store of seed and will enlarge the harvest of your righteousness. You will be enriched in every way so that you can be generous on every occasion..."

He meticulously followed those verses, tithing and giving generously, firmly believing God would prosper him. He especially taught himself the necessity of giving cheerfully from the heart, and anticipating God's blessing, persevering in the face of criticism from some who accused him of hyper-faith. For eight years, he trod this path. Finally, upset by ongoing criticism, and frustrated because he was still in debt, he decided to pray for his critics, one by one, forgiving them, and praying specifically that each would receive from God, twice the financial blessing he sought for himself.

The next day, completely unexpectedly, a stranger walked into his fibreglass business and offered him a contract that would bring him $2,000 a day—building fibreglass bodies for sports cars. From that point, his business flourished. He paid off his debts and prospered. Not only that, but God also began to fulfil a call from years previously, of serving in Sudan, a country he had never even heard of at the time. He has since then been influential in South Sudan, not only in church work, but also in assisting government leaders. He has made 63 International Missions trips, 32 of them to South Sudan. All but five were funded by his prospering business.

Many Pentecostals and charismatics would see such stories and others like them, as fulfilment of God's promises to provide for, and heal, his children. In that sense, they certainly do match John T Allen's observation (above) that "majorities of Pentecostals exceeding 90% in most countries hold to [prosperity] beliefs". But they distance themselves from evangelists who misuse scripture to raise money and spend lavishly on themselves. One prominent Christian magazine, at significant cost to themselves, refuses to accept advertising from such. They see them as fringe groups, not representative of hundreds of millions of everyday Pentecostals and charismatics, who humbly seek healing and provision, according to God's loving promises.

However, it needs to be said, on the other end of the spectrum lies a very different misrepresentation of the faith. It is the belief that asking God for money or material things is selfish and wrong. I recently watched a Christian program during which a farmer was asked if he applied his faith to his farming. He said he did. At harvest time, he said, he prayed against rain or dew, and for a crop that would bring financial reward for his work. Then, looking a little embarrassed, he added, "I know I shouldn't, but I do". The farmer was obviously conflicted. He apparently had an intuitive belief that his heavenly Father provided for his needs, but he had also somewhere absorbed the idea that asking for material things was wrong, which left him feeling guilty. Pentecostals distance themselves from that mindset.

Many non-Pentecostals do not see healing as the will of God. They are reluctant to confront sickness in faith, and believe it will be healed. We need to ask the question, where would the Fijian girl and the businessman be today, if that reticence towards material blessing and healing had not been challenged by Pentecostals and charismatics? And how many other people, like these two, experience ongoing suffering because of this unbiblical view?

Prosperity and healing promises in the Bible are clear and plentiful, but misuse can occur at both ends of the spectrum. Pentecostals and charismatics need to avoid the excesses MacArthur identifies, and others need to address the all-too-common reluctance to see money and healing as a generous provision from a loving heavenly Father.

Is the Pentecostal experience divisive?

The introduction of the charismatic experience into mainline and evangelical churches has sometimes been painful. New charismatics, often bewildered that others don't enthusiastically embrace their new experience, sometimes react unwisely. And their friends can be just as confused about how to reply to over-the-top enthusiasm for a strange new experience. It is not surprising that it so often ends in tears. Dr RT Kendall who, for 25 years pastored Westminster Chapel after the famous Dr Martin Lloyd Jones, said he asked the church to pray for renewal, asking God specifically for the *wisdom to recognise it when it came*. It did come; they had a charismatic renewal and, he said, there was virtually no conflict.[282]

Every new doctrine that has emerged in the church has met with some kind of conflict. Exhibit 1 is the Reformation. Such conflict is usually more a reflection on human nature than the validity of the doctrine. We cannot conclude that divisions over the Pentecostal experience (or any new belief) is evidence that the belief is false.

In fact, for the Pentecostal doctrine, the emergence of the charismatic movement has brought with it a unifying dimension unprecedented in 2000 years of church history. Never before has there been anything like it to unite Christians from virtually all denominations, cultures, educational and theological backgrounds, rich and poor alike.

Did the church fathers believe in cessationism?

Many did.

Typically, they believed that the apostles, as the authorized founders of the church, were provided with spiritual gifts for the establishment of the church. They reasoned that when the scriptures were completed and the apostles died, there was no further need for spiritual gifts. Some, however, while believing that the apostolic and prophetic ministry gifts ceased, did not believe the *spiritual gifts* had ceased. Dr Martin Lloyd Jones was one example. He justified his case with verses like 1 Thessalonians 5:19–21, "Do not quench the Spirit. Do not treat prophecies with contempt but test them all…" So, he was a cessationist with respect to apostolic gifts, but certainly not with respect to spiritual gifts.

Here are quotes from two cessationists, fairly typical of others.

John Chrysostom 347–407 AD. The Archbishop of Constantinople, an early church father, was known for his preaching and prolific writing. He said:

> This whole place (i.e., speaking in tongues) is very obscure: but the obscurity is produced by our ignorance of the facts referred to and by their cessation, being such as then used to occur but now no longer take place.[283]

The great **Augustine** (354-430 AD) also believed the miraculous work of the Holy Spirit had ceased in his time. However, in his later writings he gives clear mention of healing gifts and possibly a reference to speaking in tongues in his time.[284]

George Smeaton (1814–1889) A Scottish professor of theology wrote:

> The supernatural or extraordinary gifts were temporary, and intended to disappear when the church should be founded and the inspired canon of scripture closed; for they were an external proof of an internal inspiration.[285]

Did ALL the church fathers believe in cessationism? No, they didn't. For example, among the early church fathers, **Irenaeus** (130–202 AD) Bishop of Lyons, France, and last known living connection to the apostles, said:

> Similarly, we hear of many members of the church who have prophetic gifts and by the Spirit speak with all kinds of tongues, and bring men's secret thoughts to light for their own good, and expound the mysteries of God.[286]

Justin Martyr about 165 AD, a Christian apologist and teacher, martyred for his faith, wrote: "For the prophetic gifts remain with us even to this time" and, "...now it is possible to see amongst us women and men who possess gifts of the Spirit of God".[287] The "gifts of the Spirit of God" are, of course, listed in 1 Corinthians 12: wisdom, knowledge, faith, healing, miracles, prophecy, discerning of spirits, *speaking in tongues* and interpretation of tongues.

We have also seen **Tertullian** (about 155–240 AD), an early influential Christian apologist and writer. In a letter defending supernatural gifts, he said, "Now all these signs (of spiritual gifts) are forthcoming from my side (i.e., the Montanists he related to) without any difficulty..."[288]

The most significant, though, in my mind, was **John Wesley** (1703–1791 AD), who gave a simple but compelling answer to this question in his sermon *The More Excellent Way*:

> It does not appear that these extraordinary gifts of the Holy Ghost were common in the church for more than two or three centuries. We seldom hear of them after that fatal period when the Emperor Constantine called himself a Christian (about 312 AD), and, from a vain imagination of promoting the Christian cause, thereby heaped riches, and power, and honour, upon the Christians in general; but in particular upon the Christian clergy. From this time, they almost totally ceased; very few instances of the kind were found. The cause of this was not (as has been vulgarly supposed) "because there was no more occasion for them," because all the world was become Christian. This is a miserable mistake; not a twentieth part of it was then nominally Christian. The real cause was, "the love of many," almost of all Christians, so called, was "waxed cold." The Christians had no more of the Spirit of Christ than the other heathens. The Son of Man, when he came to examine his church, could hardly "find faith upon earth." This was the real cause why the extraordinary gifts of the Holy Ghost were no longer to be found in the Christian church—because

the Christians were turned heathens again, and had only a dead form left.[289]

A highly plausible explanation.

Wesley was a man of dynamic faith, prayer and action. He fasted two days a week and expected the same of his leaders. He saw dramatic miracles in his ministry, and knew what caused them: active, living faith. His blunt words are a simple, albeit unpopular, answer to the cessationist view.

The church fathers, for all their godliness, knowledge and wisdom, were flesh and blood— fallible, like all of us. Their writings are not on the same level as scripture, and do not have to define our beliefs today. Much of what they wrote might be correct and helpful, but some can be plain wrong. Chrysostom, Augustine of Hippo and Thomas Aquinas may have been historically correct—the gifts may have been absent from their worlds. But their belief—that tongues had been withdrawn by God—is by no means binding on us.

There is ample evidence today, to convince us that the supernatural gifts of the Spirit remain with us. They have been restored especially in the last century, as part of the long process outlined earlier by Augustus Strong: a slow restoration of basic doctrines, with the Holy Spirit emerging last.

SUMMARISING THESE DEFENCES

Hopefully, the above Appendix chapters have filled in some gaps and answered questions. It is a big subject with many related issues and much to talk about. But you can see that the foundations are not flimsy and, for every objection, there are answers that are not only plausible but compelling. There is every reason for us to be confident that the baptism in the Spirit is a separate experience from salvation, that speaking in tongues can be expected when it happens, and that it provides supernatural, Holy Spirit power to spread the gospel, to perform signs and wonders and miracles, and bring us a richer understanding and appreciation of Jesus and God, the Father.

APPENDIX G

THE APOSTLES' CREED: TOWARDS A TWENTY-FIRST CENTURY VERSION

I try to imagine what the authors of the Apostles' Creed might have written, had its creators witnessed Azusa Street, or any outpouring of the Spirit. How would it read? Here is something to stimulate discussion. I am not a theologian nor an academic, but I do want to highlight the absence of a clear theology and appreciation of the Holy Spirit, and the need for formal recognition of the incredible role he embraced when Jesus passed him the baton, 2,000 years ago.

> I believe in God, the Father Almighty, creator of heaven and earth;
> and in Jesus Christ, his only son, our Lord,
> Who was conceived by the Holy Spirit, born of the virgin Mary, suffered under Pontius Pilate, was crucified, died, and was buried.
> He descended into hell; the third day he rose again from the dead;

He ascended into heaven, and sits at the right hand of God, the Father Almighty; from where he shall come to judge the living and the dead.

I believe in the Holy Spirit, sent to earth by the Father and the Son; to convict the world of sin and lead us into truth; to renew us in salvation, and produce holy fruit in us for the glory of God.

I believe, as a discrete work of grace, that the Holy Spirit provides power to fulfil Christ's great commission, with signs and wonders and miracles in his name, through the baptism in the Holy Spirit, with attesting supernatural languages, together with the nine gifts of the Holy Spirit, distributed according to his will.

I believe in the holy catholic church, the communion of saints, the forgiveness of sins, the resurrection of the body and life everlasting.

APPENDIX H
CHURCH SURVEY— DETAILED INFORMATION

How are results calculated?

Here is a sample calculation for the first question of the first core quality, to show you how I have developed the following tables.

The issue examined in this question is "how important God is in your life?" Respondents were asked to tick one of these two options, "God is more important than most things" OR "God is the most important reality in my life". Results indicated 74% of Pentecostals said God was the most important reality (making them the "top scorer"), compared to 53% for Mainline Protestants (MP), and 65% for Other Protestants (OP). So, Pentecostals were 40% above MPs (74-53/53x100=40%), and 14% above OPs (74-65/65x100=14%). The figures are shown in the table.

Here, now, are the results for the nine categories.

1. ALIVE AND GROWING *FAITH*

CORE QUALITY	TOP SCORER	Score	Above MP by	Above OP by
God most important reality	Pentecostal	74	40%	14%
Devotional life	Pentecostal	79	14%	7%
Much growth in faith	Pentecostal	64	56%	36%

2. VITAL AND NURTURING *WORSHIP*

CORE QUALITY	TOP SCORER	Score	Above MP by	Above OP by
Helpful preaching	Pentecostal	91	11%	10%
Appreciated music	Pentecostal	93	8%	9%
Inspiration	Pentecostal	89	27%	20%
Sense of God's presence	Pentecostal	90	17%	15%
Growth in understanding God	Pentecostal	88	14%	24%
Action challenge	Pentecostal	81	37%	27%

3. STRONG AND GROWING *BELONGING*

CORE QUALITY	TOP SCORER	Score	Above MP by	Above OP by
Usually at church weekly	Baptist, Reformed	76	3%	1%
Strong & growing sense of belonging	Pentecostal	69	38%	30%
Attend small study/prayer groups	C3 Churches (Pent.)*	58	35%	14%
Give 10% or more to local church	Pentecostal	54	170%	54%

*Pentecostals as a whole scored 56 here—equal highest with Reformed, but not the highest result. One of the Pentecostal denominations (C3 Churches) scored a marginally higher result of 58, so it is reasonable to include that here, and identify it as a Pentecostal church. The same happens a couple of other times below.

4. CLEAR AND OWNED *VISION*

CORE QUALITY	TOP SCORER	Score	Above MP by	Above OP by
Strongly committed to vision	Pentecostal	54	54%	38%
Fully confident vision achievable	Pentecostal	76	95%	55%

5. INSPIRING AND EMPOWERING *LEADERSHIP*

CORE QUALITY	TOP SCORER	Score	Above MP by	Above OP by
Gifts, skills greatly encouraged	Pentecostal	40	74%	67%
Leaders take ideas into account	Pentecostal Uniting	43	8%	10%
Would like to be more involved	Pentecostal	31	82%	19%
Leaders inspire us to action	Pentecostal	87	26%	21%
Leaders have a focus on wider community	Pentecostal	90	17%	10%
Agree church has good and clear systems	Pentecostal	87	14%	10%

6. IMAGINATIVE AND FLEXIBLE *INNOVATION*

CORE QUALITY	TOP SCORER	Score	Above MP BY	Above OP BY
Church will try new things	Pentecostal	38	124%*	90%
Leaders encourage innovation	Pentecostal	40	135%	100%
Strongly support new ministry/ mission initiatives	Pentecostal	52	63%	44%

* In this case OP is 20%, so a figure greater than 100% is possible

7. PRACTICAL AND DIVERSE *SERVICE*

CORE QUALITY	TOP SCORER	Score	Above MP by	Above OP by
Church-based service activities	Uniting	41	28%	37%
Community-based service activities	Uniting	38	19%	52%
Informal helping – 3 or more actions in last year	Pentecostal	70	13%	15%

8. WILLING AND EFFECTIVE *FAITH-SHARING*

CORE QUALITY	TOP SCORER	Score	Above MP by	Above OP by
Look for opportunities to share my faith	Pentecostal	29	93%	34%
Have invited people to church in last year	Pentecostal	55	57%	49%
Involved in local church outreach	Int. Network of Churches (Pent)	33	43%	27%

9. INTENTIONAL AND WELCOMING *INCLUSION*

CORE QUALITY	TOP SCORER	Score	Above MP by	Above OP by
Personal follow-up very likely	Pentecostal	28	40%	27%
Always/mostly welcome new arrivals	Int. Network of Churches (Pent)	65	14%	33%
Easy to make friends in this church	Pentecostal	45	15%	36%

SUMMARY

Gathering those results, we can now compare the Pentecostal denomination with the three groups—individual Protestant, mainline Protestant and other Protestant.

INDIVIDUAL Protestant churches: Pentecostals gained the highest score (or equal highest) in **30** of the **33** core quality questions. That is **91%**. (The other three top results were shared by three other denominations.)

MAINLINE Protestant churches as a group: For an approximate measure of this trend, I took the Pentecostal's "above MP by" scores, for all the times they scored highest, and averaged them. The result: Pentecostals scored, on average, **47.5%** higher than mainline Protestants.

OTHER Protestant churches as a group: Using the same method again: Pentecostals scored, on average, **31.5%** higher than other Protestants.

ENDNOTES

CHAPTER 2   GROWTH RATE COMPARISON

1   (Roughly) Burgess and van der Maas 286.
2   Robeck Jr 12–13.

CHAPTER 4   THE HOLY SPIRIT IN MUSIC

3   Glaspey 127.
4   For more details visit www.resource.com.au.
5   National Church Life Survey 15.
6   Kendrick 88–91.

CHAPTER 5   SIGNS, WONDERS AND MIRACLES

7   Macarthur *Strange Fire* 176.
8   Keener *Miracles* 240.
9   For many examples see Keener 360.
10 Hume 30–31, in Keener 107.
11 For a thorough treatment of this subject see Keener.
12 Frodsham 15.
13 ibid 40.
14 Ibid 40.
15 Ibid 43.
16 Ibid 43–44.
17 Ibid 46.
18 Ibid 47.
19 Ibid 47.
20 Ibid 51.
21 Ibid 72–73.

22 Ibid 73.
23 Ibid 67.
24 Ibid 106.
25 Merrill 49.
26 *Bosworth's Life Story: The Life Story of Evangelist F. F. Bosworth, as told by himself in the Alliance Tabernacle, Toronto* 3, cited in Liardon *Healing Evangelists* 22.
27 Perkins, *Joybringer Bosworth*, 129–130, cited in Liardon *Healing Evangelists* 33.
28 Perkins, *Joybringer Bosworth*, 99, 100. Cited in Liardon *Healing Evangelists* 34.
29 https://lifewayresearch.com/2018/02/21/billy-grahams-life-ministry-by-the-numbers/.
30 Bonnke 81.
31 Ibid 81.
32 Ibid 93–95.
33 Ibid 118.
34 Ibid 206.
35 Ibid 145.
36 Ibid 147–149.
37 Ibid 173.
38 Ibid 239–244.
39 Ibid 356.
40 Ibid 249–258.
41 Ibid 482.
42 Ibid 486.
43 Ibid 567.
44 Synan 316.
45 Anacondia 189.
46 Ibid 1.
47 Synan 317.
48 Anacondia 145.
49 Ibid 16.
50 Ibid 178.
51 Ibid 317.
52 *Foreign Field (The Wesleyan Methodist Church)* 22–26, cited in Zarwan.
53 Haliburton 55.
54 Ibid 176–177.
55 Ibid 35.
56 Ibid 36.

57 Ibid 51.
58 Ibid 54.
59 Ibid 81.
60 Ibid 74.
61 Ibid 78.
62 Ibid 102.
63 Ibid 100.
64 Ibid 68–69.
65 *The Gold Coast Leader*, 4 July 1914, cited in Haliburton 80.
66 Ibid 81.
67 W J Platt, *An African Prophet* 34, cited in Haliburton 49.
68 Haliburton 67.
69 Quote from "Harrington, An interview with the 'Black Prophet' " The African Missionary 1917, cited in Haliburton 189–190.
70 Shank.
71 Haliburton 37.
72 For example, David A Shank, *Harris, William Wade (D)*, dacb.org; Professor Elizabeth Isichei, *A Soul of Fire*, christianhistoryinstitute.org; and John Zarwan, *William Wade Harris: The Genesis of an African Religious Movement*, journals.sagepub.com.
73 Oral Roberts, *Expect a Miracle* 90, cited in Liardon Healing Evangelists 174.
74 "Revivalist Magazine" no. 159 (March 1956) 7.
75 Cartwright *The Great Evangelists* 76, cited in Liardon *Healing Evangelists* 61.
76 Liardon *Healing Evangelists* 70.
77 Liardon *Why They Succeeded* 176–177.
78 Lindsay *John G Lake: Apostle to Africa* 53, cited in Liardon *Why They Succeeded* 185.

CHAPTER 7   THE EVIDENCE

79 MacArthur 137.

CHAPTER 8   THE HOLY SPIRIT AND THE RENOWNED REVIVALISTS

80 https://www.georgefox.edu/about/history/namesake.html.
81 Fox's journal, https://www.hallvworthington.com/George_Fox_Selections/fox-miracles.html.

82 Ibid.
83 Ibid.
84 Liardon *God's Generals II* 382.
85 Fox 13.
86 Wesley *Journal of John Wesley* vi.ii.xvi.
87 Southey *Life of Wesley* 123, cited in Liardon *the Revivalists* 59.
88 Telford *Life of John Wesley* 122–123, cited in Liardon *the Revivalists* 61.
89 *Journal of John Wesley Dec 1742*, cited by Foulkes 87.
90 John Wesley *The Works of the Reverend John Wesley, A.M. vol. 3* 274–275, cited in Liardon *the Revivalists* 64.
91 *The Original Memoirs of Charles G. Finney* 66.
92 Ibid 16.
93 Ibid 24.
94 Ibid 43.
95 Finney 2–5.
96 Finney's autobiography, *The Original Memoirs of Charles G. Finney*, relates many such stories.
97 M Laird Simons *Holding the Fort*, cited in Liardon *the Revivalists* 365.
98 R A Torrey *Why God Used D L Moody* Sermon 1923, cited in Liardon *the Revivalists* 365.
99 Sarah A Cooke *The Handmaiden of the Lord, or Wayside Sketches*, cited in Liardon *the Revivalists* 366.
100 Ibid.
101 Moody *Life of Dwight L Moody* 149, cited in Liardon *the Revivalists* 367.
102 R A Torrey *Why God Used D L Moody*, cited in Liardon *the Revivalists* 367.
103 Harper 25–26
104 Booth
105 Catherine Booth, cited in Bramwell-Booth 284.
106 Wallis 83.
107 Ibid 108–109.
108 "The Salvation Army; An All Night Meeting".
109 Chant *Heart of Fire* 109–112.
110 R Goforth 116–117.
111 Ibid 91.
112 Ibid 91.
113 J Goforth 106.

CHAPTER 9 TONGUES AND TWO THOUSAND YEARS: WHAT HAPPENED IN THAT TIME?

114 Eusebius 218–219.
115 Tertullian Chapter 8.
116 John Wesley *The Journal of the Reverend John Wesley Vol 3*, cited in Hyatt 28–29.
117 Keener *Miracles* 864–865.
118 Acta Sanctorum (AASS) January 470, cited in Cooper-Rompato 23.
119 Pachomian Koinonia. *Cistercian Studies*, no. 46, vol. 2. Translated by Arnand Veilleux. Cistercian Publications Inc. 51–52. Cited in charlesasullivan.com. Accessed 23 June 2020.
120 From a sixth century biography about St Ephrem, cited by charlesasullivan.com. Accessed 24 June 2020.
121 Nokephoros *Life of St Andrew the Fool* vol. 2 87, cited in Cooper-Rompato 38–39.
122 AASS June I 815 vol. 24, cited in charlesasullivan.com. Accessed 24 June 2020.
123 From Constantine of Orvieto *Legenda Sancti Dominici*, cited in Cooper-Rompato 34.
124 Lehner *Saint Dominic* 52, cited in Cooper-Rompato 34–35.
125 *Little Flowers of St. Francis* 1390–91, cited in Cooper-Rompato 28.
126 Cooper-Rompato 32.
127 AASS Apr I 495, cited in Cooper-Rompato 26.
128 AASS Oct V 483, cited in Cooper-Rompato 31.
129 Thomas de Cantipre *Life of Lutgard* 267–268, cited in Cooper-Rompato 50.
130 Berengariodi Donadio *Life* (Hagiograpy for Saint Clare), cited in Cooper-Rompato 43.
131 Kempe 119.
132 Ibid 134–135.
133 Cited in Cooper 41.
134 Warren *Monastic Politics* 220, cited in Cooper 42.
135 Cited in Cooper 41.
136 Gottfried of Disibodenberg and Theodoric of Echternach *The Life of the Saintly Hildegard* 26–27, cited in Cooper 68.
137 *Hildegard of Bingen: Scivia* translated by Mother Columba Hart and Jane Bishop (Paulist Press 1990) 9, cited in Baker 157.
138 Thomas of Cantimpre *Life of Christina the Astonishing* 145–146, cited in Cooper 81.

139 Thomas of Cantimpre *Life of Christina the Astonishing* 145–146, cited in Cooper 80.
140 Raymond of Capua (Catherine's spiritual adviser) *Life of Catherine of Sienna* 97, cited in Cooper 63.
141 Cooper 64.
142 Cooper 14.
143 George Fox 13.
144 The reference Charles A Sullivan cites is *Les Prophètes Protestants. Réimpression de l'ouvrage intitulé, Le Théatre Sacré des Cévennes, ou Régit des Diverses Merveilles, edited by A Bost 1847*. I recommend Charles Sullivan's website. He has gathered an extraordinary amount of evidence about tongues through the ages. He draws unorthodox conclusions from them sometimes, but is faithful in providing well documented passages from many obscure sources.
145 Ibid 139.
146 Ibid 142.
147 Ibid 154.
148 I am indebted to Vincent Synan and his excellent book *The Century of the Holy Spirit* for several important aspects in this final section. Direct quotes are acknowledged.
149 John Wesley *The Letters of the Rev John Wesley, edited by John Telford, vol. 5* 223, cited in Baker 106.
150 W E Sangster *The Path to Perfection: an Examination and Restatement of John Wesley's Doctrine of Christian Perfection* 83, cited in Baker 108.
151 Walsh's Journal, 8 March 1750, cited in Foulkes 65.
152 Gary McGee *Initial Evidence: Historical and Biblical Perspective on the Pentecostal Doctrine of Spirit Baptism*, cited in Synan 23.
153 E. Merton Coulter *College Life in the Old South* 194–195, cited in Liardon *the Revivalists* 239.
154 *The Original Memoirs of Charles G Finney* 98.
155 revival-library.org.
156 Brown Chapter 4.
157 "Wesleyan Chronicle" 1 August 1858, 259, cited in Chant *The Spirit of Pentecost* 42.
158 Ibid
159 Michael Harper, *As at the Beginning*, 25, 26
160 Tongues of Fire, July 15, 1898 pg. 107 from an article entitled "Notes from my Journal While En Route for The City of The Great King" by Willard Gleason. Cited on charlesasullivan.com; accessed 27 July 2020

161 Harper 34.
162 Synan 27–28.
163 William Arthur *The Tongue of Fire* 288, 315, 375–376, cited in Synan 25–26.
164 Stanley M Burgess and Eduard M van der Maas 821.
165 spurgeon.org.
166 Reuben A Torrey *The Person and Work of the Holy Spirit* 176–210, cited in Synan 30.
167 Strong 669.

CHAPTER 10 THE AZUSA STREET REVIVAL: CATALYST CHARLES F. PARHAM

168 Parham 2.
169 Ibid 5.
170 Ibid 3.
171 Ibid 23.
172 Ibid 33.
173 Ibid 48.
174 Ibid 48.
175 Ibid 49–50.
176 Ibid 51.
177 Ibid 58.
178 Stephen Merritt was a wealthy New Yorker, known for his benevolence towards overseas missions and the poor, for his studies on the Holy Spirit, for his lengthy prayer meetings, and his association with a famous Liberian prince named Sammy Morris. Sammy's story was unique.

At the age of 14 he was captured by an enemy tribe in Liberia and held to ransom. His father was unable to pay the monthly ransom demanded, so his capturers beat Sammy with poisonous thorns till he was close to death. Their plan was to bury him to his neck, cover his face with honey and leave him to the ants. But one night there was a flash of light, the ropes binding him fell off, and a voice called his name and told him to run. The light guided him through the jungle to a farm where he obtained a job and was converted to Christianity.

He then met an American missionary woman who, prior to leaving America for Africa, and apprehensive about what lay ahead, had been encouraged by Stephen Merritt. The Holy Spirit, he assured her, would empower her for the work. She taught Sammy all she had learned from Merritt about the Holy Spirit.

In 1891 at about 18 years of age, Sammy bravely got on a boat and went to New York to seek out this Merritt and learn more of the Holy Spirit. Landing ashore, the first person he met was an alcoholic who had stayed in one of Merritt's shelters, and was able to lead Sammy to him. Merritt told this story about Sammy:

"I took [Sammy] in a coach with a prancing team of horses ... I said: 'Samuel, I would like to show you something of our city and Central Park.'" While driving along, Sammy asked if he could pray. Merritt describes Sammy's prayer as follows: "He told the Holy Spirit he had come from Africa to talk to me about him, and I talked about everything else, and wanted to show him the church, and the city, and the people, when he was so desirous of hearing and knowing about him; and he asked him if he would not take out of my heart things, and so fill me with himself, that I would never speak or write or preach or talk, only of him. There were three of us in the coach that day. Never have I known such a day. We were filled with the Holy Spirit, and he made him the channel by which I became instructed and then endued as never before." Sammy died in 1893. (From wellsofgrace.com)

179 Robeck Jr 41–42.
180 Parham 58.
181 Watchnight Services are held by many Christian groups late New Year's Eve, to review the past year and pray and prepare for the New Year. It has great significance for the African–American community as many of their ancestors held similar gatherings on New Year's Eve in 1862 in anticipation of news confirming the signing of President Abraham Lincoln's Emancipation Proclamation on 1 January 1863.
182 Parham 52.
183 Ibid 65–68.
184 Ibid 54.
185 Ibid 63.
186 Ibid 54.
187 Ibid 67.
188 "St Louis Globe Democrat" 1 January 1904, cited in Parham 95–96.
189 Parham 96–97.
190 MacArthur 24.
191 Parham 246.

192 Ibid 63–64.
193 Ibid 259.
194 MacArthur 22.
195 Ibid 21.
196 charlesasullivan.com *The Evangelisation of the World: a Missionary Band: a Record of Consecration, and an Appeal. B. Broomhall ed., London: Morgan and Scott. 1889* 53, accessed 27 July 2020.
197 charlesasullivan.com *The Worship and Fellowship of the Church, Weekly Sermon. Wednesday, February 9, 1898, vol. XX. no. 6* 126, accessed 27 July 2020.
198 Garlock 129–134.
199 Phone conversation with Roger Rice, 15 September 2021.
200 Personal email, 10 September 2021.
201 Personal email, 14 September 2021.
202 Zadai 111–115.
203 Hicks 178–179.
204 Ibid 181.

CHAPTER 11   THE AZUSA STREET REVIVAL, WILLIAM SEYMOUR

205 Robeck Jr 35
206 Parham 137.
207 Tinney *In the Tradition of William Seymour 15*, cited in Liardon *Why They Succeeded* 143.
208 Bartleman 32.
209 Robeck Jr 68.
210 Cited in Robeck Jr 9.
211 Synan 4.
212 Bartleman 177.
213 Bartleman 46.
214 pentecostalarchives.org Accessed 29 July 2020.
215 Bartleman 50.
216 Robeck Jr 15.
217 Bartleman 50–51.
218 Ibid 54–55.
219 Ibid 56.
220 Ibid 64.
221 Ibid 56.

222 Ibid 73.
223 Robeck Jr 82.
224 Parham 156.
225 Ibid 168–169.
226 Robeck Jr 128.
227 Bartleman 57.
228 http://nhinet.org/ccs/docs/awaken.htm.
229 Jonathan Edwards *Revival of Religion in Northampton in 1740–1742* 150, cited in Hyatt 110.
230 Robeck Jr 91.
231 Ibid 91.
232 Ibid 92.
233 Ibid 92–93.
234 Ibid 113–114.
235 Merrill 39.
236 "Los Angeles Herald", cited in Robeck Jr 87.
237 Bartleman 79, 129.
238 Stanley M Burgess and Eduard M van der Maas 347.
239 Harper *As at the Beginning* 31.
240 Ibid 32.
241 Ibid 33.
242 Ibid 33.
243 Ibid 37.
244 Ibid 38.
245 About COCHUSA; COCHUSA.org, accessed 9 September 2020.
246 COCHUSA.org.
247 Chant *The Spirit of Pentecost* 3.
248 Ibid 28.
249 *The Torrey-Alexander Souvenir, Special Mission Number of the Southern Cross* (10 September 1902) 77, cited in Chant *The Spirit of Pentecost* 91.
250 Chant *The Spirit of Pentecost* 107.
251 Ibid 348.
252 *Good News* 22:8 August 1931 12, cited in Chant *The Spirit of Pentecost* 348
253 *Good News* 1:6 October 1913 5ff 16:4 April 1925 20, cited in Chant *The Spirit of Pentecost* 112
254 Chant The Spirit of Pentecost 130.
255 Ibid 131.

APPENDIX B   THE NEGLECT, AND WHY IT HAPPENED

256 To be fair, there are about a dozen pages devoted to the Holy Spirit, but *only in the context of the Trinity*, where all three, Father, Son and Holy Spirit, are discussed in their roles as a member of the Trinity. Berkhof is similar.
257 CharlesASullivan.com *Cessation, Miracles and Tongues Part 4.*
258 MacArthur 148.
259 Ibid 149.
260 Strong 669.

APPENDIX C   SALVATION AND SPIRIT BAPTISM–THE DIFFERENCE

261 Kuhn 24.
262 Origen *Origen De Principiis* vol 4 of *The Ante-Nicene Christian Library* 254, cited in Hyatt 19.
263 Cyprian *The Epistles of Cyprian* 387, cited in Hyatt 22.
264 Calvin *Commentary on the Book of Acts, Volume 1* 211, cited in Baker 168.
265 Keener *Gift and Giver* 162.
266 *A sermon on Ephesians 1:13*, www.mljtrust.org.

APPENDIX D   THE FRUIT OF THE SPIRIT

267 Herald 81.

APPENDIX E   IS "TONGUES" THE "EVIDENCE"?

268 https://ag.org/Beliefs/Position-Papers/Baptism-in-the-Holy-Spirit.
269 Merrill 84.
270 "Trinity Magazine" vol. III, no. 1, cited in Merrill 162.

APPENDIX F   QUESTIONS AND OBJECTIONS

271 MacArthur *Strange Fire.*
272 Ibid 41.
273 Jack W Hayford and S David Moore *The Charismatic Century* "Chapter 1" [emphasis in original] cited in MacArthur 41.
274 © 1981 New Spring.

275 MacArthur 133, 136.
276 Samarin *Tongues of Men and of Angels* 127–128, cited in MacArthur 134.
277 Sherrill 131, 132 (More than 2,500,000 copies sold of this book).
278 Merrill 126, 127.
279 MacArthur 137.
280 John T Allen *The Future Church* 382–83, cited in MacArthur 52, 285.
281 MacArthur 9.
282 R T Kendall, an address given to Australian pastors in Melbourne, Australia, about 2005.
283 charlesasullivan.com *Chrysostum, Homily 29 on First Corinthians*, accessed 24 June 2020.
284 Hyatt 44.
285 MacArthur 259.
286 Eusebius 210.
287 Martyr 388, 394.
288 Tertullian, *Against Marcion Book V, Chapter 8*, newadvent.org.
289 John Wesley, *The More Excellent Way*, Sermon 89:2.

BIBLIOGRAPHY

Works Cited

Anacondia, Carlos. *Listen to Me Satan*. Charisma House, 1998, 2008.

Baker, Heidi. *Pentecostal Experience: Towards a Reconstructive Theology of Glossolalia*. 1995. University of London, PhD dissertation.

Bartleman, Frank. *The Azusa Street Revival: An Eyewitness Account*. Lightning Source, Inc., 2008.

Bonnke, Reinhard. *Living a Life of Fire*. Harvester Services Inc., 2009.

Booth, William. "The Pentecostal Baptism of the Holy Ghost". *The East London Evangelist*, 1 April 1869.

Bramwell-Booth, Catherine. *Catherine Booth*. Hodder and Stoughton, 1970.

Brown, Stewart. *Providence and Empire: Religion, Politics and Society in the United Kingdom, 1815-1914*. Routledge, 2008.

Burgess, Stanley M and Eduard M van der Maas. *The New International Dictionary of Pentecostal and Charismatic Movements*. Zondervan, 2002.

Chant, Barry. *Heart of Fire*. Luke Publications, 1973.

---. *The Spirit of Pentecost: The Origins and Development of the Pentecostal Movement in Australia 1870–1939*. Emeth Press, 2011.

Cooper-Rompato, Christine. *The Gift of Tongues: Women's Xenoglossia in the Later Middle Ages*. The Pennsylvania State University Press, 2010.

Eusebius. *The History of the Church*. Translated by G A Williamson, Penguin Classics, 1967.

Finney, Charles. *Power From on High, A Selection of Articles on the Spirit-Filled Life*. Christian Literature Crusade, 2005.

The Original Memoirs of Charles G Finney. Edited by Garth Rosell and Richard Dupuis, Zondervan, 2002.

Foulkes, Ronald. *The Flame Shall not be Quenched*. Methodist Charismatic Fellowship, 1972.

Fox, George. *The Great Mystery of the Great Whore Unfolded*. AMS Press, 1975.

Frodsham, Stanley. *Smith Wigglesworth—Apostle of Faith*. Gospel Publishing House, 1974.

Garlock, Henry B. *Before We Kill and Eat You*. Gospel Light, 2004.

Glaspey, Terry. *75 Masterpieces Every Christian Should Know*. Baker Books, 2015.

Goforth, Jonathan. *By My Spirit*. Bethany House Publishers, 1942.

Goforth, Rosalind. *Jonathan Goforth, Men of Faith Series*. Bethany House Publishers, 1986.

Haliburton, Gordon MacKay. *The Prophet Harris*. Longman Group, 1971.

Harper, Michael. *As at the Beginning*. Hodder and Stoughton, 1966.

Herald, Ivan. *Ultimate Betrayal*. Berea Ministries (Now OzFAME), 2003.

Hicks, Mike. *I Dare You God*. Trailblazer Ministries, 2011.

Hyatt, Eddie L. *2000 Years of Charismatic History*. Charisma House, 2002.

Keener, Craig S. *Gift and Giver*. Baker Academic, 2020.

---. *Miracles: The Credibility of the New Testament Account*. Baker Academic, 2011.

Kempe, Margery. *The Book of Margery Kempe*. Translated by B A Windeatt, Penguin Books, 2004.

Kendrick, Graham. *Worship*. Kingsway Publications, 1984.

Kuhn, Thomas S. "The Structure of Scientific Revolution", cited in *News Weekly*, no. 3099, 18 Aug 2021.

Liardon, Roberts. *God's Generals II*. Whitaker House, 2003.

---. *God's Generals: The Healing Evangelists*. New Kensington Pasadena, Whitaker House, 2011.

---. *God's Generals: The Revivalists*. Whitaker House, 2008.

---. *God's Generals: Why They Succeeded and Why Some Failed*. Whitaker House, 1996.

Macarthur, John. *Strange Fire*. Thomas Nelson, 2013.

Martyr, Justin. *Dialogue with Trypho*, Ante-Nicene Fathers.

Merrill, Dean. *50 Pentecostal and Charismatic Leaders Every Christian Should Know*. Chosen/Baker Books, 2021.

Parham, Sarah E. *The Life of Charles F Parham: Founder of the Apostolic Faith Movement*. HardPress, 2019.

Robeck Jr, Cecil M. *The Azusa Street Mission and Revival*. Thomas Nelson, 2006.

Tertullian. *Against Marcion Book V*, translated by Peter Holmes, edited by Kevin Knight. *New Advent*, https://www.newadvent.org/fathers/03125.htm.

"The Salvation Army; An All Night Meeting", *Newcastle Daily Chronicle*, Wednesday 21 May 1879.

Shank, David A. "William Wadé Harris". https://dacb.org/stories/liberia/harris5-william/

Sherrill, John. *They Speak with Other Tongues*. Chosen/Baker Publishing Group, 2004.

Strong, Augustus Hopkins. *Systematic Theology*. Pickering and Inglis, 1997.

Synan, Vinson. *The Century of the Holy Spirit*. Thomas Nelson, 2001.

Wallis, Humphrey. *The Happy Warrior*. Salvationist Publishing, 1928.

Zadai, Kevin L. *Praying from the Heavenly Realms : Supernatural Secrets to a Lifestyle of Answered Prayer*. Destiny Image, 2018.

Other Sources

ag.org

asiaharvest.org

CharlesASullivan.com, *The Gift of Tongues Project*

georgefox.edu

hallvworthington.com/George_Fox_Selections

John Wesley, *The More Excellent Way*, Sermon

John Zarwan, *William Wade Harris,* journals.sagepub.com, sighted 5 Jan 2021

lifewayresearch.com

mljtrust.org

National Church Life Survey 2016, Initial Impressions, Macquarie Park, NSW, Australia newadvent.org

News Weekly, Balwyn, Vic., Australia

nhinet.org

pentecostalarchives.org.

R.T.Kendall, an address given to Australian pastors in Melbourne Australia, about 2005

Revivalist Magazine No. 159, March 1956

revival-library.org

spurgeon.org

Wesley, *Journal of John Wesley*

BOOKS BY THE SAME AUTHOR

Nine Days in Heaven: A true Story
by Dennis and Nolene Prince

A vivid portrayal of Heaven and Hell. More than 90,000 copies sold.

Just over one hundred and fifty years ago, in Berlin, New York, twenty-five-year-old Marietta Davis suddenly fell into an unconscious state, from which neither family nor physician could arouse her.

When she finally regained consciousness, she described with almost supernatural perception how angels had escorted her spirit to Heaven and Hell. Her story includes delightful insights into the angelic care of infants in heaven, a beautiful encouragement to those who have lost children.

Nine Days in Heaven brings the story of Marietta Davis to a new generation of readers. The flowery nineteenth century language has been updated for the modern reader.

"The most comforting book I have read second to my Bible!" - Reader Review

Available from https://www.amazon.com/dp/B085NGRX7R

Worship is a Bowl of Noodles
OR What would Jesus sing?
By Dennis Prince

After publishing Praise and Worship songs for more than twenty five years, Dennis Prince cautions us that they are, in fact, like **a bowl of noodles**. Yes, they taste great, but there are too many "noodle songs" and hardly any "meat and veggies"— not to mention the occasional "gristle". As a result, the spiritual diets of many churches are lopsided and unhealthy and they struggle with worship that is self-focused and spiritually dry.

The good news is that healthy songs **can be found** by worshippers who are informed, discriminating and pro-active —and the rewards are great. Rigorously but graciously, this long-needed book provides clear biblical principles and strategies that help you to recognise a healthy song, plan a balanced spiritual worship diet, and enjoy rich God-focused worship - a tried and tested catalyst for vibrant Holy Spirit activity.

Not just for worship leaders and songwriters—all worshippers benefit from these principles of worship.

"...teaches us the *criteria* to apply to our songs so that we choose songs that represent good music, lyrics and theology." Robert Webber, Myers Professor of Ministry, Northern Seminary II

"...a <u>must</u> for all discerning Christians...a solid biblical basis for authentic worship." Dr. Terry Cowland, Ph.D.; M.Div.; BA.

Available from www.resource.com.au

I was Wrong – Why the world's most notorious atheist called it quits, and other trouble for the New Atheism
By Dennis Prince

The seeds of this book were planted, ironically, as a response to a Global Atheist Convention in Melbourne, Australia, and expanded into this book. It contains well-documented God interventions in the lives of a kaleidoscope of people, each revealing God in a special and unique way, together with compelling answers to common questions.

Profound insights on atheists and former atheists, scientists, miracles, sexual issues, demonic forces, gaming addiction, heavenly visions, angels, inspired song-writing, Hinduism and Islam and much more.

Available from www.resource.com.au (paperback) and Amazon (Kindle)

Awakening
Who we are, why we're here, where we go, how we know
By Dennis Prince

A book of Christian foundations
72 pages

Each section includes an introductory testimony, simple teaching, relevant bible passages in the text, and discussion questions.

Topics: Who God is and why we exist; Salvation; Knowing God – our relationship with him; Baptism; The Holy Spirit; The new creation; Discipleship; Getting on with others; Prayer, faith and healing; Serving God; God, sex and marriage; The end of the world, Heaven and hell; The bible: how we know it is true.

www.ingramcontent.com/pod-product-compliance
Lightning Source LLC
Chambersburg PA
CBHW020912020526
44107CB00075B/1667